STATE CRIME AND IMMORALITY

The corrupting influence
of the pow

Mark Monaghan and S

First published in Great Britain in 2016 by

Policy Press
University of Bristol
1-9 Old Park Hill
Bristol
BS2 8BB
UK
t: +44 (0)117 954 5940
pp-info@bristol.ac.uk
www.policypress.co.uk

North America office:
Policy Press
c/o The University of Chicago Press
1427 East 60th Street
Chicago, IL 60637, USA
t: +1 773 702 7700
f: +1 773 702 9756
sales@press.uchicago.edu
www.press.uchicago.edu

© Policy Press 2016

British Library Cataloguing in Publication Data
A catalogue record for this book is available from the British Library

Library of Congress Cataloging-in-Publication Data
A catalog record for this book has been requested

ISBN 978 1 44731 675 6 paperback
ISBN 978 1 44731 674 9 hardcover
ISBN 978-1-4473-2341-9 ePub
ISBN 978-1-4473-2342-6 Mobi

The right of Mark Monaghan and Simon Prideaux to be identified as authors of this work has been asserted by them in accordance with the Copyright, Designs and Patents Act 1988.

Cover design by Qube Design, Bristol
Front cover image: Getty
Printed and bound in Great Britain by CMP, Poole
Policy Press uses environmentally responsible print partners

Contents

List of tables

About the authors

Mark Monaghan is a lecturer in sociology, social policy and crime at the University of Leeds, UK. His main area of research considers the scientific and political battles through which policies are made in heavily politicised areas. His most recent publications are in the area of drugs policy.

Simon Prideaux is an associate professor of social policy, sociology, disability studies and crime in the School of Sociology and Social Policy, University of Leeds. His interests take in comparative access policy, welfare discourses, conditionality and political ideologies.

Acknowledgements

This book has been a long time in the making and much has happened since the first lines were penned. We express gratitude to the anonymous reviewers for their helpful comments in helping to clarify some of the arguments we were trying to make and giving extremely useful suggestions on relevant literatures that we had missed. We would also like to thank all students past and present who have completed our module on Organised Crime, Violence and the State – many of the issues discussed in this book were inspired from their ingenuity in seeking out, researching and analysing crimes of the powerful. We hope that this book will prove a valuable resource for the next generation of scholars coming through.

We would also express thanks to our colleagues in the School of Sociology and Social Policy at the University of Leeds. In particular, our gratitude extends to Tom Campbell, Mark Davis, Nick Emmel, Joanne Greenhalgh, Suzanne Hallam, Ana Manzano, Emma Nelson, Kirsteen Paton, Ruth Patrick, Ray Pawson, Emma Wincup and Henry Yeomans, with whom we have discussed ideas and bemoaned the continuously missed deadlines. Outside Leeds, Ian Hamilton, Debbie Hawkins, Charlie Lloyd and James Windle have provided a similar service. We would also like to express our gratitude to everyone at Policy Press, in particular Emily Watt, for initially supporting our early idea, and then Victoria Pittman for seeing the project through when we are sure there were times she wished she had never got involved.

On the domestic front, it has been a time of rapid change. MM would like to express undying gratitude to Sonia for her never-ending patience and continuous support. Much love to her and to our children, Joseph and Rosa, both of whom arrived throughout the duration of writing this book. These two are the reason a significant proportion of the prose was written between the hours of two and four in the morning, so any errors are obviously down to them. In addition, they have provided the perfect excuse for the aforementioned missed deadlines. Finally, SP would like to thank Sammy for her patience and Léon and Hugo for being the grandsons that they are.

ONE

Introduction

In 2012, a permanent sub-committee of the US Senate Committee on Homeland Security and Government Affairs published a 300-page report on the failings of HSBC bank which, according to a BBC report, led to it being used as a conduit 'for drug kingpins and rogue nations' (BBC, 2012). The Committee's investigation and subsequent report led to the bank being fined 'almost $2bn for failing to stop criminals using its systems to launder money'.

Alongside circumventing US laws outlawing trade with Iran, Burma and North Korea, it was the Mexican subsidiary of HSBC (HBMX) that was responsible for laundering money from Mexican drug cartels. Between 2007 and 2008 it was estimated that HBMX shipped $7bn to HSBC's US operation, more than any other HSBC affiliate. This was despite the fact that 'Mexican and US authorities expressed concern that drug traffickers were able to circumvent the anti-money laundering controls at US banks by transporting US dollars to Mexico, and then using HBMX to transfer it to the US' (BBC, 2012).

The BBC report went on to state that the Senate Committee reported that high-profile clients involved in drug trafficking, the bank had had millions of dollars of suspicious bulk traveller's cheques and a resistance to closing accounts that were linked to suspicious activity. The US arm of HSBC (HBUS) nevertheless classed Mexico as a 'low-risk' country and, as a consequence, did not adequately track its transfers and other dealings. In reality, as the Committee noted, 'it had inadequate money laundering controls' in spite of the fact that HBMX was operating in a country 'under siege from drug crime, violence and money laundering' (BBC, 2012).

The case of HSBC is revealing. It is unusual in that it was brought widely to the attention of the public. In other words, it was an example where the criminal activities of the powerful become newsworthy.

Revisiting the dark figure of crime

A key lesson from the criminological literature – and one that is widely acknowledged – is that the media have a significant role in creating crime and for current purposes they have systematically misrepresented the nature of criminality. Reinarman (1997, p101) commented that the 'mass media has engaged in ... the routinization of caricature – rhetorically recrafting worst cases into typical cases and the episodic into the epidemic'. Writing over 40 years ago, Jock Young stipulated that as the media are preoccupied over what they perceive to be 'newsworthy', they are capable of distorting the true nature of crime in society (Young, 1974). For many years, the issue of corporate crime was considered mundane and not consistent with the professional imperatives of journalism (Chibnall, 2004), which need crimes to be sensational and graphic if they are to reach the pages of the printing press. According to Young: 'The media does not reflect the real world but, instead, newspapers select events which are *atypical*, present them in a *stereotypical* fashion and contrast them against a backcloth of normality which is *overtypical*' (Young, 1974, emphasis added).

Reiner (2007, p382-3) observed that crimes reported in the *Daily Mirror* and *The Times* increased from 8% to 21% between 1945 and 1991 (with present political focus on crime and disorder probably higher still). The type of crime reported has changed. Ditton and Duffy (1983) and Smith (1984) found that newspapers distort the official picture of crimes reported *to* and recorded *by* the police. For example, violent and sex-related crimes received a distorted amount of reporting. Ditton and Duffy (1983, p164) found these two types of crime account for 2.4% of all reported incidents committed in the Strathclyde region of Scotland in 1981, yet in most widely circulated newspapers for this region they constituted 45.8% of crime reportage. The local news tells a similar story. Smith (1984, p290) illustrated how, in Birmingham, personal attacks (that is robbery or assault) equals 6% of reported crime but appeared in 52.7% of the space designated to crime stories. Similar findings were reported from a multitude of other studies whereby the picture of crime obtained from the media in many ways 'inverts' that derived from official crime statistics. This is because, as a general rule, the more a crime takes place, the less frequently it is reported (Katz, 1987). It is in this context, we suggest, that state and other allied forms of crime are under-reported.

The case of HSBC is further revealing, as it demonstrates the intermingling of corporate, organised and state criminality. These crime types are often dealt with in isolation in the criminological literature, but they frequently coalesce, as the HSBC case reveals. We refer to these crimes as 'non-conventional' on the grounds that they have been relatively neglected in the criminological canon until recently (De Keseredy, 2011), thus constituting something of a 'dark figure'. As far back as the early 19th century, attempts have been made to monitor the epidemiology of crime in society. Arguably, the first instance of this was in 1827, when the first national crime statistics were published in France. Newburn (2007, p51) suggested that the Belgian astronomer Adolphe Quetelet was one of the first scholars to take a serious interest in criminal statistics. Although he began his career as an astronomer with an interest in 'celestial mechanics' on moving to Paris from Belgium, Quetelet became concerned with the difficulties of developing adequate statistics on social phenomenon. As this was the case, he was one of the first scholars to take an interest in what has since become known as the 'dark figure' of crime. These are the unknown crimes that take place, but are not recorded and therefore do not find their way into the official statistics.

An interest in the dark figure of crime has since been taken up by other scholars. Sutherland (1949) drew attention to crimes in offices and workplaces, crimes of the educated, well respected and of high status. These, he stressed, were widespread but undetected and thus not recorded. Frequently they had more damaging effects than delinquency. Sutherland criticised official systems and academics for concentrating on lower-class offenders and crimes. This is still the case today, leading Coleman and Moynihan (1996) to suggest that the picture of crime that we get from the official statistics is just the 'tip of the iceberg' and that the majority of crime is hidden, invisible and unrecorded. Indeed, it has become common wisdom that the production of crime statistics is a social process and, as such, these statistics are social constructions (Cicourel, 1964). By this it is meant that definitions of crimes reflect broader social processes of religious, cultural and political frameworks that reinforce the social values of society. Crime statistics are, therefore, socially defined and constructed in the same way as the laws that create them. The statistics that are created within this context are not wholly representative of what they purport to measure.

This sets the scene for the current project, which focuses on one area of criminality generally thought to be largely responsible for a significant proportion of the dark figure: non-street-based criminality. The operative word in the previous sentence is 'thought'. In reality, it is unknown as to whether the total amount of recorded crime is the tip of the iceberg because, by definition, the remainder is unknown. It lurks below the surface. It is impossible to tell whether this crime is qualitatively similar to that already known and just of a larger quantity, or whether it is qualitatively different. In the context of state crime and criminality, one explanation for this is that these crimes are notoriously difficult to monitor and measure, while the agencies responsible for monitoring and measurement are often the perpetrators. It is, therefore, no coincidence that, as Tombs and Whyte (2002) have noticed, there is a disproportional focus on crimes of those of lower social status, to which recent events testify.

In the UK in the second decade of the 21st century, we have witnessed the most widespread urban unrest in the last 30 years. In the aftermath of the London disturbances, for instance, Mayor Boris Johnson proclaimed that economic and sociological explanations were unnecessary as the rioting was nothing more than wanton criminality. Some days later he retreated from such a stance. Nevertheless, a closer examination of these events – occurring in the summer of 2010 – revealed that simmering beneath the surface was a growing resentment of a system in which the rich were, and still are, getting richer and the poor, by contrast, getting poorer; increasingly facing imprisonment or strictly monitored through community-based supervision orders; experiencing their benefits being the focus of cuts and, in some cases, being shot at by the authorities. In short, as Wacquant (2001, 2009) pointed out, in many western societies the poor are disproportionately at the receiving end of punitive action.

There are many reasons for the control of the poor, who can see themselves as being under attack. This is, of course, nothing new and can be traced as far back as the Elizabethan poor laws, which created the now ingrained distinction between the 'deserving' and 'undeserving' poor. The welfare reforms implemented by the UK coalition government (2010-15) carry many of the hallmarks of the Elizabethan laws, subsequent Poor Laws and the underclass debate that emerged during the 1970s (which was enhanced by *The Sunday Times* paying for and inviting Charles Murray to lecture on the dangers of such a growing 'class' in the UK). Reducing perceived excessive welfare payments has become a – if not *the* – priority of government under what Deacon and Patrick (2011) termed the 'new welfare settlement'. This also enjoys reasonably widespread public support, albeit support based on shaky foundations. Back in 2012, Polly Toynbee noted that the British Social Attitudes Survey revealed how the Conservative-led coalition government had general support for reducing the welfare spending and, to some extent, revising the policies (in name if not in nature) of the previous Labour government (Toynbee, 2012). Although Toynbee's predictions of a backlash against the Conservatives did not happen, it is the case that support can be shown to quickly drain as the harsh reality of public spending cuts become progressively more apparent. We need only witness the growing support for the anti-austerity policies of the Scottish National Party (SNP) in the 2015 UK General Election as testament to this.

The logic of austerity-led welfare cuts is simple: it is one of divide and rule. It is to make a distinction between those who work hard but need a helping hand and the 'idle' and 'feckless', who apparently could find work in paid employment but refuse to do so. As Toynbee (2012) observed, the coalition had been successful through their endeavours to stir 'up those on quite low incomes against those on very low incomes'. Despite this focus on the 'feckless' and regardless of the truth behind such accusations, it does deflect attention away from the decisions, motivations and consequences of political actions both at home and abroad. It is important to highlight this deflection, as it neglects the contention of this book that part of the explanation for the aforementioned riots was a growing resentment at the actions of these power elites and, in particular, of nation states as a whole.

With this in mind, and to some extent echoing C. Wright Mills' understanding of the 'power elite' (Mills, 1956, p117), this book turns such attention on its head and places an emphasis on the activities of powerful members in a variety of states who have traditionally been shielded from the worst effects of the growth in crime prevention measures over the last 30 years or so. For Mills:

> The very rich do not reign alone on top of visible and simple hierarchies. But that they have been supplemented by agents and by hierarchies in the corporate structure of the economy and of the state does not mean that they have been displaced. Economically and socially, the very rich have not declined. After the crash and after the New Deal, the very rich have to operate with skilled legal technicians (both in and out of governments) whose services are essential in the fields of taxes and government regulations, corporate reorganization and merger, war contracts and public relations. They have also adopted every conceivable type of protective coloration for the essentially irresponsible nature of their power, creating the image of the small-town boy who made good, the 'industrial statesman', the great inventor who 'provides jobs', but who, withal, remains just an average guy. (Mills, 1956, p117)

Herein lies the crux of our argument. We, like Mills, are not necessarily concerned with the super-rich – others have covered this ground (Atkinson, 2013; Dorling, 2014; Piketty, 2014; Milner Jr, 2015; Savage, 2015). We do, however, seek to document the operations of powerful, skilled technicians in society, whose actions are often overtly criminal, but not always. Mills encourages us to intensify the focus on those who use their power for illicit gain. We begin to do this by concentrating on the activities of state actors and agencies. Although we are primarily concerned with criminality, lessons from the criminological literature on crimes of the powerful (for example Sutherland, 1949) show that interrelated interpretations of deviance, immorality and irresponsibility and the incessant pursuit of profit as an inherent motivation for criminal state activity or dubious political practices will also enter into the discussions. Of course, when the focus shifts away from criminality towards deviance, the discussion becomes more subjective. With this in mind, in subsequent chapters, where applicable, we draw on the social harm literature to illustrate our cases. What unites our discussion is that the nefarious activities of powerful state actors are set against a backdrop of the decline of 'welfarism' (made explicit by the more punitive stance still being taken against the so-called 'feckless') in the post-modern crime complex (Garland, 2000, 2001) and under conditions of permanent austerity (Pierson, 2002). In other words, we have taken a closer look at the activities of the rich and powerful at precisely the same time that they have taken aim at the poor and dispossessed. In doing so, we suggest that a reframed understanding of Garland's crime complex is necessary.

Rethinking 'the crime complex'

Around 20 years ago, Garland (1994, 1996) outlined how criminology, as a discipline, has been characterised by a governmental project to chart the patterns of crime and monitor the practices of police and prisons. The politics of law and order is serious and big business. Since the last quarter of the 20th century, it has resided at – or close to – the summit of significant political issues. As this is so, the issue also enjoys a high profile in the media, taking up a high proportion of column inches or megabytes. Garland (2001) referred to this as 'the crime complex'; a concept closely linked to the 'high crime society' (Garland, 2000). A key aspect of the high crime society is that the fear of crime has become a prominent theme in criminal justice in and of itself under the conditions of what Furedi (2002) coined as the 'culture of fear'.

Whereas prior to the 1970s fear of crime was 'regarded as a localized, situational anxiety, afflicting the worst-off individuals and neighbourhoods', it has since then 'come to be regarded as a major social problem and a characteristic of contemporary culture' (Garland, 2001, p10). This is so, even if people have little experience of victimisation. As a consequence, policies specifically aimed at reducing the fear of crime have become *a la mode*. Garland also pointed out how:

> the emergence of fear of crime as a prominent theme is confirmed by public opinion research that finds that there is a settled assumption on the part of a large majority of the public in the US and the UK that crime rates are getting worse, whatever the patterns, and that there is little public confidence in the ability of the criminal justice system to do anything about this. (Garland, 2001, p10)

Of course, since Garland's seminal work was published, many states seem to be in the midst of a 'crime drop' as measures show a continual decline in crime rates over recent years (for example Farrell, 2013). This drop does not seem to be matched by a reduction of fear. Indeed, the growing concern over the fear of crime is difficult to deny (Garland, 1996, 2000) and is tied into various other themes that dominate discussion in contemporary society. These include the pursuit for security, the fear of insecurity, a belief in punitive sanctions as a deterrent for criminal activity, protecting the public and acclimatising to risk (Cochrane and Talbot, 2008; Mythen, 2014). It is necessary to say, however, that the types of crime that arouse fear are of a specific variety. According to Wacquant (2001), various political parties across the 'Western' hemisphere have continued to raise concern over street-based, urban violence and policies have developed off the back of this. In a later publication, Wacquant (2009) went on to suggest that such crime prevention strategies have little to do with the crime rate, but have everything to do with the fear of public disorder. An increase of public disorder is thought to be a distinct possibility as the gap between the rich and the poor in most western states has continued to rise over generations and this has coincided with increased control of the latter by the former. Nowhere is this more apparent than in drug policy. As Stevens (2011, p115-6) showed, the main thrust of US drug policy still bore down most heavily on the socially and racially marginalised residents of the deindustrialised American city.

For now, it is fair to comment that the period in question can be seen as an era of 'populist punitiveness' (Bottoms, 1995), 'totemic toughness' (Stevens, 2011) and 'populist posturing' (Tonry, 2010). Even so, it should also be borne in mind that this was frequently non-discursive rhetoric and the reality is that, despite increasing acceptance that punitiveness shapes current criminal justice policy, this concept has not been fully elaborated (for example Farrall and Hay, 2010). In turn, however, this must be tempered by the fact that the notion that 'prison works' gained currency and the prison population began to swell in the UK and, indeed in much of Western Europe, particularly under John Major's premiership with Michael Howard in the Home Office (but with support from the then Labour opposition, that continued with their election in 1997). For Feeley and Simon (2003, p439), the swelling prison population was tied to developments relating to what they termed the 'new penology'. Primarily, they argued, the rising numbers of those incarcerated is linked to the labelling of risky populations and is part of a growing acceptance that the prison is no longer a 'special institution capable of making a difference in the individuals who pass through it'. By contrast, it is part of a concatenation of intertwined correctional and custodial networks, which govern to control the behaviour of those identified as a risk to society, including suspected terrorists, drug users, traffickers, paedophiles and knife- or gun-using youths. Elite crimes, state crimes and, for the purposes of this book, other kinds of organised crime are absent from such rhetoric, and part of the task we have set ourselves in this book is to consider why this is the case.

To complete this task, the book examines the often reprehensible activities of a number of 'so-called' role models of UK and international society. A central focus is to consider the notion of an ideal state and to examine those associations and activities of both notorious and respected states that can be deemed to have immoral, if not criminal, connotations. Associated individual subjects (albeit powerful individuals) will also be discussed and as the book unfolds it will describe how the activities of the powerful can have an immoral and corrupting influence on the state, corporations and organisations alike (Friedrichs, 1998; Green and Ward, 2004). The book will not argue that all states, corporations and their leaders are naturally prone to criminal activities, but it will point out that some states commit crimes in allegiance with corporations, commit crimes against other corporations, and conduct business with criminal organisations, whereas some criminal elements operate under the guise of respectable business (Chambliss, 1989; Barak, 1991; Doig, 2011). Furthermore, these powerful individuals, corporations and organisations can – and often do – exert a political influence: Murdoch's support for the invasion of Iraq, which many believed to be illegal, was a case in point.

In this respect, the book also develops the argument that the state can act as a terrorist by invading another state on the pretext of the 'war on terror' or the 'war on drugs', which tend to get conflated as these terms are used to justify many invasive actions taken by the UK, the US and their 'security' organisations (Makarenko, 2004; Björnehed, 2005; Felbab-Brown, 2010). The book will also demonstrate how a state can terrorise its own people (semi-overtly as with the disappearance of many Argentinians to eliminate any Peronist threat after the military coup of 1976). A more insidious example will be that of Orgreave in 1984, where Margaret Thatcher – under the pretext of dealing with 'the enemy within' – condoned organised violence against picketing miners (Goodman, 1985; Reed and Adamson, 1985). It is equally the case, though, that 'terror' is too pernicious a term to describe the activities of state agencies in controlling their populations. Where one stands on such debates is often a political question. The case of paramilitary collusion in Northern Ireland by both the British and Irish governments will be used to highlight just some of the complexities entailed in unravelling the concept of state crime and immorality.

Researching 'non-conventional criminality'

Before moving on to consider the structure of this book, it is necessary to state that the information contained in the following pages is at best an informed estimate of the true nature of state criminality. In discussing the irksome nature of corporate crime, Braithwaite (1989, p124) made the point that 'most criminologists are less informed about crime in the suites than they are about crime in the streets'. He used Wilson and Herrnstein's (1985) theory about low IQ and impulsiveness as being the cause of criminality as an exemplar here, stating that if this was a useful explanation of all criminality, it is 'wilfully blind' to the fact that one would expect most corporate criminals to be 'intelligent and scheming rather than stupid and impulsive'. Difficulties in researching non-conventional crimes are multifarious. While not wishing to downplay the differences between researching different kinds of crime and the methodological approaches required, there are areas of overlap in the challenges presented.

Nelken (2007, p734-5) postulated that one key problem in getting comprehensive data on corporate crime stems from the fact that research is very much concentrated in particular areas, mainly in the US. He suggests that the reason for this may link to what Mills (1956) perceived to be the small-town values of American social reformers and the turbulent relationship between American citizens and big business, which is tied up with issues of the relationship between capitalism (the success of big business) and liberalism (the freedom of the individual and the efficacy of the market).

Another key drawback to effective research in the area is that those who are in a position to carry out such a task frequently do not operate with significant research budgets. In a discussion over the accuracy of the Kefauver Committee's work into organised crime in the United States (to which we shall subsequently return), Bell (1953) asked:

> Why did the Senate Crime Committee plump so hard for its theory of the Mafia and a national crime syndicate? In part, they may have been misled by their own hearsay. The Senate Committee was not in the position to do original research, and its staff, both legal and investigative, was incredibly small. Senator Kefauver had begun the investigation with the attitude that with so much smoke there must be a raging fire. But smoke can also mean a smoke screen. Mob activities is a field in which busy gossip and exaggeration flourish even more readily than in a radical political sect. (Bell, 1953, p144)

Tombs and Whyte (2002, 2010) pointed out that another main difficulty in researching corporate crime relates to the implications of the advancement of neo-liberalism in the main institutions in society, which has served to silence many voices. This point was illustrated subsequently in a discussion of New Labour's record on health and safety regulation, which they maintained was degraded throughout New Labour's time in office. Tombs and Whyte also pointed out how the university is no different and is probably atypical of the maintenance of the neo-liberal hegemony, as research agendas 'have increasingly been defined in terms of that which is immediately relevant for neo-liberal ideologues and their bureaucratic handmaidens' (Tombs and Whyte, 2002, p217). Frequently, business schools employ staff who are sponsored by local businesses and they also tender for research grants from the business community. One outcome of such a relationship is a decline of critical research.

This point is explained by Doig (2011) who, in the context of a discussion of state crimes, alerted the reader to the difficulties in compiling evidence where the perpetrator can hide behind a cloak of anonymity in the form of 'the state'. As Doig elaborated – albeit mimicking Donald Rumsfeld's roundabout statement on the fragile basis for forward planning in times of conflict – state crimes are the 'unknown unknowns' of the crime world. These are things that we generally do not know that we do not know. More generously, and as Nelken (2007) has outlined, more and more is being revealed about crimes of the powerful so that we may even say that state crime has achieved the status of a 'known unknown' (a thing we know that we don't know). Nonetheless, what is required is a full-blown conversion to a 'known known' (a thing we know that we know). To rephrase this, Doig (2011) commented that the nature of the evidence of state crime is not always in the public domain and if it is:

> [T]he problem for many state crime authors is that those sources tend to be limited to official papers or records and the limited geographic and subject matter focus of the material produced by activist NGOs such as Amnesty International, Human Rights Watch and Global Witness. Indeed, many authors have to draw upon official reports and inquiries, set up as often as not by the states themselves as a consequence of public or other extra-state pressure. (Doig, 2011, p55)

Problems relating to the use of official reports and inquiries as a benchmark for evidence are brought into focus in the case study of Northern Ireland, more specifically in the aftermath of Bloody Sunday. The Saville Inquiry was set up by the New Labour government in 1998 to look into the events of Sunday, 30 January 1972, widely referred to as 'Bloody Sunday'. Doig (2011) pointed out that a new enquiry into Bloody Sunday was set up to examine why a peaceful human rights march by the predominantly Catholic, nationalist community in Derry was fired upon by the 1st Battalion, the Parachute Regiment killing 13 and mortally wounding one more. These shootings have been surrounded by conspiracy and controversy ever since, not least because it was an example of 'western liberal democratic state opening fire on its own citizens exercising their right to peaceful protest against the policies of the region's government' (Doig, 2011, p3). The main areas of controversy surround whether or not the soldiers were fired on first or whether they opened fire unilaterally and without provocation.

An official inquiry undertaken at the time – the Widgery Inquiry – was unequivocal in its designation of blame. It concluded, among other things, that:

> There would have been no deaths in Londonderry on 30 January if those who organised the illegal march had not thereby created a highly dangerous situation in which a clash between demonstrators and the security forces was almost inevitable ... Soldiers who identified armed gunmen fired

upon them in accordance with the standing orders in the Yellow Card. Each soldier was his own judge of whether he had identified a gunman. Their training made them aggressive and quick in decision and some showed more restraint in opening fire than others. At one end of the scale some soldiers showed a high degree of responsibility; at the other, notably in Glenfada Park, firing bordered on the reckless. These distinctions reflect differences in the character and temperament of the soldiers concerned … None of the deceased or wounded is proved to have been shot whilst handling a firearm or bomb. Some are wholly acquitted of complicity in such action; but there is a strong suspicion that some others had been firing weapons or handling bombs in the course of the afternoon and that yet others had been closely supporting them … There was no general breakdown in discipline. For the most part the soldiers acted as they did because they thought their orders required it. No order and no training can ensure that a soldier will always act wisely, as well as bravely and with initiative. The individual soldier ought not to have to bear the burden of deciding whether to open fire in confusion such as prevailed on 30 January. In the conditions prevailing in Northern Ireland, however, this is often inescapable. (Widgery, 1972)

These conclusions covered the whole gamut of why the true version of events remains the source of much dispute. On the one hand, Widgery offered a mild rebuke to the actions of certain soldiers, accusing them of recklessness, but on the other hand this is justified as being part and parcel of law enforcement in Northern Ireland at the time. Additionally, Widgery tried to explain that it was the actions of the protestors themselves who were partly responsible for the outcomes.

As Doig (2011) illustrated, the findings of the Widgery Inquiry have been called into question. A different version of events, and one that is unsurprisingly critical of Widgery, was produced by the Irish government in 1997. This stated:

It can be concluded that the Widgery Report was fundamentally flawed. It was incomplete in terms of its description of events on the day and in terms of how those events were apparently shaped by the prior intentions and decisions of the authorities. It was a startlingly partisan version of events ... contrary to the weight of evidence and even its own findings, it exculpated individual soldiers who used lethal force and thereby exonerated those who were responsible for their deployment and actions. (Department of the Taoiseach, 1997, cited in Doig, 2011, p5)

The key belief of the Irish government report was to exonerate the victims themselves from any wrong. The most recent inquiry into the events of Bloody Sunday (Saville, 2010), while providing no evidence of state crime, concluded that when British Soldiers moved into the Bogside (the area of Derry in which the incident took place):

> ... the explanation for such firing by Support Company soldiers ... was in most cases probably the mistaken belief among them that republican paramilitaries were responding in force to their arrival in the Bogside. This belief was initiated by the first shots fired by Lieutenant N and reinforced by the further shots that followed soon after. In this belief soldiers reacted by losing their self-control and firing themselves, forgetting or ignoring their instructions and training and failing to satisfy themselves that they had identified targets posing a threat of causing death or serious injury. In the case of those soldiers who fired in either the knowledge or belief that no-one in the areas into which they fired was posing a threat of causing death or serious injury, or not caring whether or not anyone there was posing such a threat, it is at least possible that they did so in the indefensible belief that all the civilians they fired at were probably either members of the Provisional or Official IRA or were supporters of one or other of these paramilitary organisations; and so deserved to be shot notwithstanding that they were not armed or posing any threat of causing death or serious injury. Our overall conclusion is that there was a serious and widespread loss of fire discipline among the soldiers of Support Company ... The firing by soldiers of 1 PARA on Bloody Sunday caused the deaths of 13 people and injury to a similar number, none of whom was posing a threat of causing death or serious injury. What happened on Bloody Sunday strengthened the Provisional IRA, increased nationalist resentment and hostility towards the Army and exacerbated the violent conflict of the years that followed. Bloody Sunday was a

tragedy for the bereaved and the wounded, and a catastrophe for the people of Northern Ireland. (Saville, 2010, Vol. I, Ch. 5, paras 5.4–5.5)

Before the publication of the findings, Rolston and Scraton (2005, p561) noted that 'in commissioning Saville, the British State conceded and acknowledged a key campaign demand: the victims of Bloody Sunday were unarmed civilians'. The campaign referred to here was the campaign for a new inquiry into the events in Derry in January 1972. After publication, in an address to the House of Commons, the Prime Minister, David Cameron, stated:

> I know that some people wonder whether, nearly 40 years on from an event, a prime minister needs to issue an apology. For someone of my generation, Bloody Sunday and the early 1970s are something we feel we have learnt about rather than lived through. But what happened should never, ever have happened. The families of those who died should not have had to live with the pain and the hurt of that day and with a lifetime of loss. Some members of our armed forces acted wrongly. The government is ultimately responsible for the conduct of the armed forces and for that, on behalf of the government, indeed, on behalf of our country, I am deeply sorry. (BBC, 2010)

From looking at the conclusions of the Saville report and the text of the Prime Minister's apology, it appears that the British state seemed to have been exonerated from committing state crimes in this most high-profile incidence of the Troubles, but the difference in detail and conclusions from the two main inquiries is of paramount significance to us and others.

Drawing on ground-breaking work conducted over 30 years ago by US scholars Reiss and Biderman (1980), Slapper and Tombs (2002) highlighted the difficulties faced by researchers wishing to get some indication of the true extent of corporate crime in society. This is very much an artefact of the way that the data were compiled. Taking the example of fraud, although this is by no means an isolated example, to get an idea of the extent to which this activity occurs requires:

> examination, dissection and re-categorisation of data from a whole range of bodies, including the Police, the SFO [Serious Fraud Office], the European Commission, the

British Rail Consortium, the Association of British Insurers,
the Association of Payment Clearing Systems, the Credit
Industry Fraud Avoidance Scheme, the Audit Commission,
the Charity Commission, the Inland Revenue and HM
Treasury. (Slapper and Tombs, 2002, p106-7)

Slapper and Tombs went on to stipulate how it is now conventional
in criminology to use alternative forms of measurement, such as
victimisation surveys, to ascertain a more accurate picture of the
levels of crime in society. In essence, victimisation surveys are seen
to be essential in revealing the dark figure of crime. In England and
Wales, these have generally entailed recourse to the British Crime
Survey (BCS). The BCS started out as an independent survey of crime
victimisation. It proved to be such a useful resource for policy makers
and the public that it is now carried out with the sponsorship of the
Home Office. In general terms it asks about people's experiences of
crime to their property and person in the previous year. The initial
target sample for the research has continued to rise, reaching 40,000
in the year 2000 and it has since risen to 51,000, which is the present
figure. Up to 2001 there had been eight waves of the survey. Since
2001, the survey has been conducted annually from April to March,
but the findings are not published until at least a year after (Maguire,
2007; Hoyle and Zedner, 2007).

The BCS provides more than just a count of crime. Since its
inception, it has provided a wealth of information on criminal
victimisation for over 30 years. In terms of design and methodology,
respondents are asked a range of questions about crime experiences
in previous years. These are then followed up by further questions
relating to their responses, covering issues about whether they chose
to report their experience of crime to the police. Because the method
requires face-to-face interviews, the researchers are more able to
delve into background data about crimes and victims, covering issues
about perceptions of whether crimes are racially motivated or not
and the efficiency of key institutions in the criminal justice system,
such as policing, prosecutions and victim support (Newburn, 2007).
Furthermore, it can also deal with 'sensitive topics', such as domestic
violence, stalking and sexual harassment. Crimes such as domestic
violence have been thought to constitute a key aspect of the total
amount of 'hidden' crime in society as victims may be too afraid to
report such incidences. Victims may not even be aware that a crime
has been committed in the case of emotional or psychological bullying
(Hoyle and Zedner, 2007).

Although victimisation surveys offer some potential in revealing the 'dark figure' of crime, they too are beset with problems and have been the subject of much criticism. It is not the time for a thorough synopsis here – suffice to say that corporate crime represents a challenge for victimisation surveys for many of the same reasons as the official statistics. These stem primarily from the fact that many victims are unaware they have been a victim of corporate crime, or in cases such as fraud when the victim is a corporation, they will want to avoid the negative publicity that would stem from admitting that they have been vulnerable or compromised (Nelken, 2007). In addition, the problem is heightened by the fact that the BCS makes no attempt to ask questions about this, and uncovering corporate crime has been quite a way down the list of political priorities as governments have preferred to sponsor survey research looking at businesses and corporations as the victims – rather than as the perpetrators – of crime (for example Mirrlees-Black and Ross, 1995).

This discussion mirrors debates occurring in the 'organised crime' literature. Here, thinkers such as Woodiwiss (2005) have suggested that the bulk of such crime is committed by business people as part of their occupational roles. Levi (2007, p779) pointed out, however, that this 'ignores the often unwanted parasitical and predatory crimes committed *against* business by crime groups, in which business people get locked into a system of paying to both obtain contracts and to avoid harm from regulators and enforcement personnel'. This is often referred to as 'extortion'.

In recent years the Home Office has become increasingly aware of the need for this information to be improved' and in 2010 it commissioned researchers from the polling organisation IPSOS Mori (Smith and Harvey, 2010) to look at the feasibility of producing a new survey to measure commercial victimisation. Despite this, there has generally been very little survey research forthcoming dealing with corporations or states as the perpetrators of crime. What data there are, although piecemeal, reveal some interesting findings. Primary among these is that victims *are* frequently aware of their victimisation at the hands of corporations. According to Slapper and Tombs (2002), the Second Islington Crime Survey (victim surveys developed by thinkers from the left realist criminological tradition), showed that when respondents were asked about corporate crime, they were aware of their victimisation. From October 2015, new questions on the nature and extent of fraud and other cyber crime victimisation have been trialled. The Office for National Statistics Website noted that the scale of computer misuse offences, banking and credit card fraud could yield an additional 3.6 to 3.8 million further offences in the Crime Survey for England and Wales (ONS, 2015). At the moment, these represent best estimates as the questions have not gone 'live', but the findings of the trial do have implications for the supposed crime drop thesis. For instance, when questioned about their experience of purchasing goods and services over the previous 12 months, approximately 11% stated that they had been given misleading information, 21% believed they had been deliberately overcharged and 24 percent paid for what turned out to be defective goods or services. These figures are significant on their own, but when a point of comparison is introduced, further subtleties are revealed. For instance, the same survey indicated that 4% of respondents had had their car stolen, 7% had been burgled and 7% had been the victim of a theft or attempted theft from their person (Slapper and Tombs, 2002, p107). On the basis of this, the authors concluded that incidences of commercial crimes are high in both relative and absolute terms.

The absence of data on non-conventional crimes is linked to the fact that much of this kind of criminality is difficult to detect. This may be because there are multiple victims or there are no apparent victims. Further, policing non-conventional criminality is much more difficult. According to Friedrichs (1996), this difficulty in detection is a consequence of non-conventional criminality being much harder to decipher from standard behaviour. The example of deception in the marketplace is often given here. Additionally, the perpetrators of such actions are not as immediately (physically) identifiable, as they are able to avoid the stigma associated with many kinds of more conventional offending.

One neglected issue, but one that has recently been brought into sharp relief, concerns the dangers in researching non-conventional criminality as typified in the case of the Boston College Tapes. The Boston College tapes represented an interesting case study in the difficulties behind the research of state crime. The tapes were a collaboration between the journalist Ed Moloney and the Boston College, and offer an insight into the nature of the troubles in Northern Ireland from the perspective of those who were at the 'deep end'. Initially, the tapes involved interviews with prominent paramilitary members from both the Loyalist and Republican communities. It was not intended that the information contained in these interviews would be released until after the death of those participating. However, a relatively recent court case in the United States, detailing whether the Federal Court could subpoena the information in the tapes, called this into question. Early in 2014, the sensitive nature of the material was brought to light, when the Sinn Fein president Gerry Adams was arrested on the grounds that information contained in the Boston College tapes was sufficiently damning. The episode was significant, in that it highlights the ethical difficulties entailed in researching issues around state criminality. This case in particular introduced key concerns around the issue of informed consent, as those taking part in the research did so on the grounds that the information they gave would not be released until after their death. This has not happened: again highlighting the tumultuous nature of researching state criminality.

An overview of this book

Chapter Two focuses on definitions of the state and, more importantly, what constitutes an ideal state and what does not. It introduces the institutions, organisations and major protagonists involved in the maintenance of social order and, indeed, social control. In so doing, the notion of democracy and beyond that the alliances that politicians make with business organisations, media moguls and the relationship and use of the armed forces and policing arrangements will briefly be introduced, as will some comment on globalising processes (such as neo-liberalism) that have simultaneously undermined the notion of the state yet provided the impetus for claims to sovereignty in other areas (Green and Ward, 2004; Hesmondhalgh, 2006; Michalowski, 2010; Doig, 2011). Attention is drawn to the 'free market', neo-liberal economy, which has the potential to satiate individuals through reward/remuneration for successful effort and participation. Moreover, Chapter Two highlights the New Right belief that these market configurations are democratic and impartial in nature: hence the conviction that they cannot be condemned for being 'just' or, more importantly, 'unjust'. In a similar vein, political citizenship, the neutral 'umpire' role of government and the democratic process beyond the market is introduced, to demonstrate how the state ideal is premised upon acquiescence, alliance and, to a lesser extent, fear. In this way, it was argued by the New Right thinkers (for example Hayek, 1944, 1988) that legitimation is achieved as the roles and duties of state institutions are mainly directed at the maintenance and perpetuation of social cohesion through socialisation and guidance, the reproduction of habit (what works, past and present), the provision of electoral avenues for the public 'voice' to be heard and the management/supervision of the principles surrounding law and order issues. The latter part of Chapter Two takes a more negative stance, contesting the belief in the existence of an ideal state. Conflict, disagreement, alienation, fear and oppression are introduced to demonstrate the potential – and actual – pitfalls and consequences of an unbalanced, dysfunctional state typical of the modern epoch. Questions of whether or not the market is 'just' or democracy is truly representative of the public voice are engaged with, under the aegis of a discussion of the corrupting influence of neo-liberalism. Towards the end of Chapter Two, we take some tentative steps towards producing a working definition of state crime and immorality. In doing so, we consider a range of explanations across the realist/constructivist spectrum from state crime as breaches of international law, human rights violations, organisational deviance and social harm encapsulated by the growing debates around 'social injury' and 'social harm' as discussed by Hillyard et al (2004), Michalowski (2010) and Doig (2011).

Chapter Two provides the context and basis of understanding for the ensuing chapters as they examine specific state crimes and case studies. Chapters Three to Eight pick up on themes relating to neo-liberalism and hidden criminality and the frequent 'moments of rupture' (Whyte, 2014) that emerge between the state, corporations, organised criminal groups and other powerful actors. Although we focus on high-profile examples, this is not to downplay the fact that, as Whyte acknowledged, much criminality is located in the deep structural relations between states and corporations and, indeed, various other powerful constituencies of society. Running through our discussion, then, is a debate which implies that the turn to neo-liberalism towards the latter part of the 20th century has become a facilitator of state deviance, crime and immorality.

With this in mind, *Chapter Three* also clears some ground, by picking up on the theme of terminological confusion and overlap stemming from the different appreciations of state crime discussed in Chapter Two. Essentially, we deal in some detail with the issue of corporate criminality and we highlight how official recording procedures of crime rates downplay the extent of corporate criminality. We introduce the concept of organised criminality to show how definitions labelled as such can also apply to much state criminality, but also consider how much of this activity is consistent with Reuter's (1983) disorganised crime thesis. Here we take something of a precautionary stance, calling into question the overarching perception that there exists a dominant symbiosis of organised crime and nationwide crime syndicates or family/kinship systems. We return to the issue of state collusion and acquiescence in the corrupt practices of various groupings in society, before providing an overview of what might fall under the ambit of state crime and immorality. Ultimately, Chapter Three is concerned with considering how the terminological overlap that exists between different crime types serves as a means of obfuscating knowledge about the extent of state criminality.

Chapter Four continues with the themes introduced in Chapter Three, by addressing the issues of the international drugs trade. In so doing, Chapter Four opens up the possibility that while states may be the perpetrators of a non-trivial degree of criminality, they can also be the victims of political crimes. Ruggiero (1999) referred to this as 'state crime from above' (that perpetrated by the state) and 'state crime from below' (that perpetrated against the state). The first part of Chapter Four traces the origins of international drug control and looks at examples of where a 'blind eye' has been turned by law enforcement agencies when it has been perceived that there is a greater good or more pressing need. Drawing on evidence from broad case studies of US foreign policy (in particular the activities of the US government and its agencies in Central America in the 1980s), government collusion at worst or government toleration at best (from the perspective of prominent politicians and government officials) is highlighted. In essence, we consider the role of the state in the international narcotics trade and how responses to this frequently transgress national and international law as the Iran/Contra scandal demonstrated. Moving on, we discuss how, since 9/11, there has in policy circles been a conflation of the 'war on drugs' with the 'war on terror' – often referred to as 'combatting narco-terror' (Makarenko, 2004; Dishman, 2005; Felbab-Brown, 2010). We consider how the former has been fought sporadically to accommodate the goals of the latter, often to the detriment of both, arguably creating a situation where extreme, exceptional measures are needed, particularly in the fighting of terror.

While acknowledging the complexity of the relationship, *Chapter Five* looks at the role of the media in shielding the state from unwanted intrusion. We revisit the concept of immorality. Of course, not all corporate and state activity is as obviously criminal as the aforementioned activities of those involved in the international narcotics trade. Indeed, when it comes to the media – and especially media moguls like Rupert Murdoch – it could be argued that they are speaking on behalf of the government and/or the people, thus obfuscating the real, more insidious, purpose of their supportive actions. Since 1968, when Rupert Murdoch bought the now-defunct *News of the World* and later *The Sun* newspapers, Murdoch's influence on politicians and the electorate began to grow. Other titles soon followed, to secure his influence even further. Indeed, his support helped to secure the election of Margaret Thatcher on the right, demonise the so-called 'underclass' with an overtly neo-liberal agenda and, later, contribute to the election of Tony Blair on the left (Shawcross, 1993; Crainer, 2002; Watson and Hickman, 2012). When, however, New Labour was in decline in 2010, Murdoch switched his allegiance back to the Conservatives. In the eyes of Patrick Wintour (the Political Editor of *The Guardian*), what the Murdoch press tended to do was 'realise who is going to win the next election, or who is liable to win the next election, and ... [then] back them'. This was graphically demonstrated when – amid the 2009 Labour Party conference – the Murdoch press made it public that they had dropped Gordon Brown. Using the headline of 'Labour's Lost It', *The Sun* stated that it was going to back David Cameron instead. Indeed, Murdoch was the first newspaper proprietor to be granted an audience with David Cameron, the new prime minister, in May 2010. Cameron also had meetings with Murdoch's son, James, and Rebekah Brooks, who quit as head of Murdoch's UK newspaper arm over the phone-hacking scandal. These examples are only the tip of an iceberg. They are just a few of the examples of the way in which Rupert Murdoch came to be known as the 'kingmaker' in British politics (Arsenault and Castells, 2008). Nevertheless, Chapter Five does not confine itself to how widespread and just how powerful the Murdoch 'empire' became within the British political arena; it also charts similar activities to gain influence in the US and beyond. It highlights how the Murdoch 'empire' made significant political US campaign contributions to various high-profile politicians, Republicans and Democrats. Likewise, Murdoch's use of HarperCollins to offer book contracts to key and strategically placed political figures, most of whom signed lucrative deals despite the knowledge that (on Murdoch's part at least) the extent of the advances offered could not be recouped through book sales alone (McKnight and Hobbs, 2011). Such deals may be legal, but Chapter Five investigates what Murdoch demanded in return and whether these demands were criminal, deviant or immoral. More to the point, Murdoch and his media 'empire's' influence over the invasion of Iraq – which in itself can be seen both as an affront to UK and US democracy – can be seen as an example of bipartite state terrorism.

Chapter Six contains a discussion of state violence and goes on to consider the complexity surrounding international law in the decision to go to war in Iraq. It is acknowledged that violence is a widespread resort utilised by people and governments around the world to achieve political ends (Ross, 2012). Numerous groups and, indeed, individuals believe that existing political systems will refuse to recognise and respond to their political ambitions and demands.

Violence – in the form of terrorism, for example – can thus be justified and deemed necessary by many groups and individuals in their pursuit of differing political agendas (Ruggiero, 1999). In a similar vein, the chapter points out that many governments around the world also resort to the use of violence. On the one hand, governments may use violence to intimidate their own population into acquiescence (Schwartzmantel, 2011). On the other, governments may also use force to defend their country from outside invasion or other threats such as terrorist bombings (Ruggiero, 1999; Gupta, 2008). Accordingly, Chapter Six describes a number of different forms that political violence can take and explains why committing violence can be deemed necessary by the perpetrators (possibly as a last resort) or why violence can be viewed as the preferred option (for some) to take.

Chapter Seven depicts a case study of state crime/terrorism in the UK and Ireland by considering the issue of collusion between various paramilitary groups in Northern Ireland and the British and Irish Police (Garda). In effect, Chapter Seven turns to the issue of states using proxies to carry out their crimes. It will be argued that actions undertaken by the Royal Ulster Constabulary could be deemed to be examples of state crime/terrorism from within as they occurred on UK territory. On this basis, and despite the claim that Northern Ireland is part of a united Ireland, the actions of the Garda can be interpreted as state crime/terrorism from without. Whichever side of the argument one wants to take, there can be little dispute that actions taken from both sides constitute state criminality, as such collusion with paramilitary groups was undertaken by organisations of the state whether it be of the UK or Eire (Taylor, 1998, 2000, 2002). To fully draw out the nuances of such distinctions and to present the case that collusion represents both criminal and terroristic activity, Chapter Seven covers some of the background to the 'troubles' in Northern Ireland and introduces key terminology and symbolism fuelling the dispute. In addition, the main part of Chapter Seven discusses the issue of collusion in terms of how agencies of law enforcement are suspected of facilitating murder in the province over a number of years (Mulcahy, 2006).

Chapter Eight looks at Argentina's 'Dirty War', which commenced in 1976, and the UK miners' strike (1984-85). Both were undertaken in the defence of neo-liberal policies, yet they were events undertaken by two different types of regimes: one a right-wing dictatorship, while the other was a right-wing democratically elected government. Initially, and with the benefit of hindsight, Argentina's 'Dirty War' is introduced as an obvious yet relatively hidden example of a state terrorising its own people through abduction and execution. Chapter Eight charts how – following

Isobel Peron's use of excessive force and power to combat right-wing opposition – a military coup headed by Videla took control of Argentina in 1976 (Marchak with Marchak, 1999). Neo-liberal economic policies became the order of the day, while the opposition to such policies were branded 'subversives', and violence was used as a means to repress and control (Cox et al, 2008). Few were left immune from these attacks as the 'subversives' were never truly defined. Moreover, Chapter Eight also demonstrates how the Junta had learnt from the violent, public atrocities in Chile (during Pinochet's dictatorship) and attempted to keep hidden their attempts to eradicate any possible Peronist threat. State-ordered disappearances were viewed as the best means to both eliminate the 'enemy' and to remain undetected. In the absence of corpses or public arrest records, the government was able to deny all wrongdoing despite the estimated disappearance of over tens of thousands of people (Wright, 2007). By contrast, Chapter Eight also shows how, in the pursuit of a monetarist, free-market agenda, Margaret Thatcher utilised British police to break the resistance of one of the country's most powerful unions, the National Union of Mineworkers (NUM) (MacGregor with Tyler, 1986; McCabe et al, 1988). In order to show the gravity of the actions taken by the Thatcherite government, the chapter focuses on events surrounding the NUM picket of Orgreave coking plant, near Sheffield, in 1984. At least 5,000 miners gathered to try and stop British Steel's coke convoys, but they were met by police from 10 different counties. During fierce clashes, 81 people were arrested, while 41 police officers and 28 strikers were injured. Arthur Scargill, the NUM president, declared: 'We've had riot shields, we've had riot gear, we've had police on horseback charging into our people, we've had people hit with truncheons and people kicked to the ground' (cited in Metcalf et al, 2014, p89). In response to these accusations, Chapter Eight details the aims and reasoning used by the Conservative government of the time to justify the tactics and measures deployed. Indeed, the chapter takes a step further, by constructing a convincing argument that the Thatcher government used such violent, premeditated tactics to terrorise a section of its own community in pursuit of a specific ideological agenda whatever the cost. In other words, such actions constituted state terrorism. Both examples in Chapter Eight demonstrate the extent to which a state will terrorise its own people and the extent to which they will either legitimate or hide their actions in an attempt to pursue their own dogmas and ideologies (even if they are purportedly pursuing the same agenda).

Finally, we round up our discussion with some concluding comments in *Chapter Nine*.

TWO

Defining the state and its institutions, allies and protagonists

In order to allow a fuller focus on state crime throughout the book, Chapter Two initially defines what is meant by the state and, more importantly, what constitutes an ideal state that will act as a foil to a criminal or immoral state. Taking a leaf out of Ruggiero's (1999) book, this chapter outlines the concept of an ideal state as a single, functioning whole, where resistance is managed, where social upheaval, separatist activity, revolution and 'coups d'état' are unthinkable, and where such a state appears to ensure uniformity in the name of legitimacy.

Of course, this pursuit of legitimacy depends on many factors. As a consequence, the chapter introduces the institutions, organisations and major protagonists involved in the maintenance of social order and, indeed, social control. We seek to balance this, however, by considering the introduction of a system of checks and balances through the extension of political citizenship as broadly as possible. Moving on, we turn to the issue of the socioeconomic structures of the modern state and the opportunities afforded by neo-liberal arrangements, with the full recognition that not all states are organised in such a way. Drawing on the work of Habermas, we then go on to demonstrate how the maintenance of order and the establishment of legitimacy require a delicate balancing act. As a result, we discuss the notion of democracy and, beyond that, the alliances that politicians make with business organisations, media moguls and the relationship and use of the armed forces, along with the policing arrangements deployed to achieve these ends.

By outlining an ideal state, it is then possible for the second part of the chapter to detail the ways that states do not, in many ways, constitute the given ideal (in terms of the dangers associated with the neo-liberal thinking and the maintenance of legitimacy and state power). We then take some tentative steps towards defining state crime and immorality, looking at how they can be conceived on a scale of realism to constructivism through their application as breaches of international rules and regulations, breaches of human rights legislation, as state organised deviance or as social harms.

Taken as a whole, this chapter thus initiates a discussion of the problem of trying to locate and define state crime and immoral acts. Indeed, such definitions are problematic precisely because in western democracies we have become accustomed to the state being the key agency for law making, law enforcement and defining what constitutes criminal behaviour as the ideal state thesis suggests. Nevertheless, states also engage in unlawful acts (Croall, 1998) but, importantly, they have the power to legitimise such actions and often do so by their failure to pursue often nefarious activities.

This chapter provides the platform for Chapter Three, which further considers the terminological overlap that hinders definitions of state criminality.

The ideal state: an introduction

According to Alvarez (2001), the state is often described as a set of relations linked to government and, therefore, is purely seen as an institutional nexus of governmental decrees and administration within a given society. In this respect, Held (1995) identified six specific characteristics intrinsically connected with the emergence of the state:

> (1) the growing coincidence of territorial boundaries with a uniform system of rule; (2) the creation of new mechanisms of law-making and enforcement; (3) the centralization of administrative power; (4) the alteration and extension of fiscal management; (5) the formalization of relations among states and through the development of diplomacy and diplomatic institutions; and (6) the introduction of a standing army. (Held, 1995, p36)

It has long been recognised that a decisive feature of the state is its monopoly on the means of 'legitimate' violence within any given territory (Weber, 1948). For Elias (2000), this was a defining tenet of what he referred to as the 'civilising process'.

Although some of the features described by Alvarez (2001) have come under threat from other forces such as globalisation, it can be argued that these pressures have not led to a radical departure from state formation or state development of previous epochs. To illustrate this, Doig (2011) drew upon the work of Strange (1996) to show how the role of the state can be exemplified on a scale ranging from low to high in terms of importance. To begin with, ownership of the means of violence sits at the bottom and is of low importance. Of higher importance is the need for the state to ensure that it is prominent in world markets through effective competition. Responsibility for building the economic infrastructure (ports, roads, and so on) and control over foreign trade (especially imports and responsibility for taxation) were next on the list. Moving further up, providing a safety net (welfare state) for the most vulnerable in the market economy and correcting market tendencies for boom and bust used to be seen as significant and had been since the 1930s until the decline of 'welfarist' principles from the late 1970s onwards (see also the section on neo–liberalism later in this chapter). Finally for Doig (2011), and indeed Strange (1996), the most significant roles of the state in reverse order were: choosing the appropriate form of capitalist development; maintaining the value of the currency; and the right to sacrifice the lives of individual citizens in the defence of national territory from foreign invasion.

Expanding on these observations, McAuley (2003) noted that it is necessary to consider the nature of the state in two main ways: as the apparatus of the rule of government within a particular geographical area; and as the social system that is subject to a particular set of rules or domination. Hall and Ilkenberry's (1989) previous study added to this list with their observation that the state also has the monopoly of rule-making. Within this framework, as Hall (1984) pointed out, there are a number of subthemes related to the modern state. These include the notions that: a) power is shared and is fully secular; b) the rights to participate in government are legally or constitutionally defined; c) that representation is wide; and d) that the boundaries of national sovereignty are clearly defined (cited in McAuley, 2003, p20). The state, however, is not a single self-serving entity. Indeed, the modern, most pervasive state is seen in liberal eyes as neutral arbiter, 'umpire' or 'referee', in which elected politicians stand at the hub of operations (Heywood, 2004, p79).

From all of this, it can be deduced that – despite different formulations and depending on one's own standpoint – the state plays a direct role in our daily existence. Yet what we know about the state is only learnt in the abstract. McAuley (2003) demonstrated, for example, how it is very different from other institutions in society such as 'the family', of which most people have direct experience. Lister (2010, p18) commented that the abstract nature of the state: 'lies in the fact that it is distinct from the government of the day and from the individuals who staff it, even though it is politicians who carry out the state's functions and who represent the "human" face of the state at both national and local level'. Paraphrasing the work of Pierson (1996), Lister (2010, p18) also suggested that while there is difficulty in defining the state, we recognise it in action, 'when it requires us to send our children to school at a certain age, goes to war in our name, bans or polices an anti-war demonstration, sends us a tax demand or provides us with benefits or pensions when we are unable to work'.

Michalowski (2010, p24) offers us a summary of the discussion so far with the contention that the state can thus be seen as a combination of dynamic processes which encompass 'capital accumulation, political governance and ideological construction' in a fluid, interpenetrating combination developed geographically – intentionally or unintentionally over time – to construct a sociopolitical order. And, because of this fluidity, it becomes extremely difficult to draw boundaries between the state, the economy and culture within such a configuration (see Poulantzas, 1968; Foucault, 1977; Jessop, 1990). This, of course, helps in the understanding of why states differ from each other, yet (as will become apparent as the book unfolds) all of this complexity adds to the difficulties surrounding any attempt to theorise about state crime.

Undoubtedly a key component of the state, as pointed out by Lister and others, is its ability to enforce certain behavioural expectations of its citizenry. This is not a linear process. Indeed, one aspect relating to the creation and maintenance of legitimacy is the granting of political citizenship to the subjects of the state. By implication, the extension of the electoral franchise to as many of the citizens as is generally deemed appropriate has a major part to play in legitimising state actions through the democratic process. That is, of course, granting the right to vote to those who are not legally incapacitated. According to Sear (2005), when discussing the UK legal context, electoral incapacity relates to:

- anyone under 18 years old on polling day
- Members of the House of Lords, including life peers, Church of England archbishops and bishops and hereditary peers who have retained their seat in the House of Lords (who can, however, vote at elections to local authorities, devolved legislatures and the European Parliament)
- European Union citizens (who can, however, vote at local government, devolved legislature and European parliamentary elections)
- citizens of any country apart from the Irish Republic and Commonwealth countries
- convicted persons detained in pursuance of their sentences (though remand prisoners, unconvicted prisoners and civil prisoners in

default of fine or breach of recognisances can vote if they are on the electoral register), including offenders detained in mental hospitals
- anyone found guilty within the previous five years of corrupt or illegal practices in connection with an election
- under common law, people with mental disabilities if, on polling day, they are incapable of making a reasoned judgement. (adapted from Sear, 2005)

Putting these exclusions to one side, full citizenship allows the citizen to partake in the democratic process which, in turn, theoretically assists the general population to hold the government or state to account for its actions, to obtain access to the prevailing social contract and to provide the means to define the conduct of proceedings (Clark and Dear, 1984; Saward, 1992). Furthermore, democracy facilitates state or governmental power to become a recognisable and acceptable form of governance as consensus provides a pathway towards achieving the 'common good' and, as such, promotes an attempt to meet the demands made in the name of 'public interest' (Schaar, 1981).

Without such theorising and examination of the respective state-building processes (and the provision of at least a working definition of an ideal state and its various components), a more holistic understanding of state criminality is rendered somewhat incomplete and potentially confusing, if not diversionary (in terms of the focus on blame), rather than informative and illuminating.

Neo-liberalism as a dynamic source of social cohesion

In keeping with the aforementioned need to take a more rounded look at what constitutes a state, even if it is not the ultimate ideal state, it is imperative first to undertake a discussion of the socioeconomic structures of the state (as it is understood in the modern era). Increasingly, Western democratic states are embracing the principles of neo-liberalism as the only way in which a stable, cohesive society can operate, satisfy and motivate 'responsible' hard-working members of its citizenry. Neo-liberal theory (united under the aegis of the New Right in the late 1970s and consolidated with the Thatcher and Reagan administrations in the UK and the US respectively in the 1980s) dictated that individuals need clear inducements to behave appropriately. Risk, uncertainty and the prospect of failure are necessary for human and social functioning, because uncertainty and fear provide individuals with dynamic incentives as insecurity and failure demand discipline and motivation. Contained within this logic, is the belief that freedom – or rather negative freedom – is the most coveted of all values. Freedom in this context is defined as an absence of coercion – or negative freedom – which entails the freedom to act (being *free* to do something) and is not about being *able* to do something or being *enabled* to do something. In support of this train of thought, the New Right also denies any possibility of a valid concept of social justice in the respect that the outcomes of 'natural' socioeconomic processes (that is the 'free' market) cannot be defined as 'just' or 'unjust', because they are 'unintended' and not deliberate. By contrast, only deliberated procedures set in place by interventionist governments can be seen to be 'just' or 'unjust' (George and Wilding, 1994).

By way of explanation, Hayek (1944) – a major protagonist of the New Right from the 1940s until his death in 1992 – critiqued the growth in welfare provision in Western democracies. In essence, he argued that the arbitrary decision-making of the welfare state represented the first step down the road to serfdom. Consequently, he and the New Right argued that welfare is objectionable on the following grounds:

- The expansion of government erodes both individual freedom and individual responsibility as government exerts requirements upon individuals. When government intervenes to determine needs and wants through welfare, there is an erosion of the need to be responsible for oneself and family. Reliance and the loss of autonomy are, as a consequence, encouraged.
- The vision of an ideal society is threatening, as it is deemed impossible for collective goals and social purposes to suit and cater for all. To enforce income redistribution, for instance, would be an affront to individual liberty and, as such, would be immoral due to a lack of universal agreement.
- The egalitarianism associated with the welfare state and the associated redistribution of resources is seen as coercive, in that it involves a violation of the property rights of those individuals from whom income is taken.
- The paternalism and authoritarianism that the New Right associates with the welfare state threatens freedom, by failing to offer people choice – a lack of alternatives.
- The welfare state is monopolistic – it allows powerful bureaucracies and influential, powerful groups to dominate and dictate what can (and should) be provided (i.e. provides producer power over the consumer).

Taken together, these five objections are seen by the New Right to be damaging to both the political development and the economic progression of the state. On the political front, damage is caused by the government – and by implication the state – being undermined by the continuing demands for the government to take a lead in eradicating poverty and to provide equality of education, to name but two examples. This increasing enlargement of the role of the government and state apparatus is, in the eyes of the New Right, doomed to inevitable failure, resulting in a loss of standing for the government. Moreover, the growth in powerful interest groups and bureaucracies results in more pressure on government to attend to their need and not the needs of the state as a whole. As a consequence, perceived state wrongdoings are brought to the fore to promote desired rights of the powerful few. At the same time, expansion of government policies results in more reliance on key producer groups to deliver, as government resources become stretched. All of these objections, it is argued, reduce government legitimacy (George and Wilding, 1994).

To reiterate, economic damage occurs through welfare eroding competition with the decline of market rewards for the energetic and punishment of failure for the idle. Welfare softens the effects of failure and thus reduces the desire, drive or need to be efficient and cost-effective. Moreover, welfare payments, along with the activities of trade unions, are deemed by the New Right to determine artificial wage levels, as the employer is forced to pay a higher rate as an incentive to the employee to give up benefits (Mishra, 1990). To make matters worse from the New Right perspective, government provision lessens the desire to save (for retirement, and so on), as it involves high taxation. High taxation, in turn, reduces individual reward, which negatively impacts upon individual effort. Overall, the argument continues, welfare sends the wrong message, as it undermines the economy by reducing work to an option rather than a necessity (George and Wilding, 1994).

The solution is to reduce welfare by cutting public expenditure (Lund, 2002), increase privatisation, lower taxation and implement a truly free market economy not hampered by collectives (trade unions, and so on), bureaucracies and monopolies (Mishra, 1984, 1990; Clarke et al, 1987). Where welfare survives, it should be provided through the market and at a level of subsistence. The market is seen by the New Right to be the best mechanism for discovering and coordinating dispersed knowledge and preferences. The market – through demand – detects what people want and, in so doing, avoids arbitrary decisions being made by so- called experts. Questions of who needs what and when are, therefore, avoided. Through competition the market also demands efficiency (in theory at least) and delivers a wider range of choice (Butler, 1995). As Hayek (1988, p85) put it, 'the self-ordering process will secure for any random member of such a group better choice over a wide range of opportunities available to all than any rival system could offer'. Crucially, markets are not dependent on benevolent providers. On the contrary, markets compel providers (through the need to survive and be successful in a market environment) to be sensitive to the needs of potential users. In turn, this compulsion reduces the power of providers with the removal of discretionary and uncontrollable power accrued by bureaucrats, professionals and the officials of monopolistic public systems.

On the other side of the coin, market competition benefits the consumer in that prices are kept down and quality is maintained, if not improved, as expensive, poor-quality providers see demand fall (Butler, 1995). In essence, though, market provision suits the realities of human nature (as the New Right perceives it), in that it ultimately places faith in the individual. In terms of human nature, market provision promotes individual responsibility by satiating the essential self- and family-centred outlook of people by circumventing a dependency on fallible notions of altruism and communal obligation. In the words of leading New Right thinker and politician Sir Keith Joseph (1976), this market circumvention occurs as a consequence of his belief that 'the blind, unplanned, uncoordinated wisdom of the market is ... overwhelmingly superior to the well-researched, rational, systematic, well-meaning cooperative, science based, forward looking, respectable plans of government' (cited in Roulstone and Prideaux, 2012, p97).

Put another way, the market reinforces the essence of human nature by being more democratic. It is more democratic on the basis that it attacks the autonomy and lack of accountability of welfare bureaucracies, by placing emphasis on the recipients of services and goods. From the New Right perspective, markets facilitate an environment where everyone counts and the consumer rules (George and Wilding, 1994). This, in turn, pampers to the New Right belief that individuals – unlike systems and institutions – can overcome almost any problem or difficulty. Indeed, markets are seen to push individuals to rely on their own resources, thus shifting responsibility where it should rest. Overall, personal and familial responsibility is ultimately beneficial for individuals and society as a whole, as it promotes less (and ideally no) reliance on state provision.

The final piece in the New Right jigsaw is that state provision is further reduced by the 'trickle down' effect. In essence, the 'trickle down' effect ensures social cohesion. As with functionalist interpretations of society – especially those from Talcott Parsons (Parsons, 1967) – the economy is seen to provide individuals with a sense of direction, responsibility and motivation. Society in this context can be seen as a multi-level, hierarchical pyramid, whereby individuals compete to find their natural level within the hierarchy and to be rewarded or remunerated appropriately. With lower taxation, and lower spending on benefits, it is believed that the most prosperous (entrepreneurs, if you like) will be free to accrue a fortune, from which they will reinvest in the economy by creating new businesses or expanding existing ones (Alcock, 1996). In turn, this will create more employment and will provide opportunities for other individuals to enter the paid labour market, be responsible and become financially independent of state welfare as they cater for the needs of both themselves and their immediate family. The net effect is that unemployment will decrease, the economy will prosper and participation in the paid labour market will inculcate a sense of self-worth – hence the belief that such machinations provide the social glue to promote a cohesive and orderly society, in which each and everyone has a role to play.

In sum, individuals are seen to be naturally lazy and will go to significant lengths to avoid pain. People will not exert themselves for a wider good and will not apply themselves if rewards are marginal. Nor, as this discussion of neo-liberal ideology has made clear, will they continue if the cost of failure is softened, reduced or eliminated by welfare benefits (Murray, 1984, 1996a, 1996b, 2001). Indeed, the reality from this perspective is that people are self-centred and will only exert themselves for personal gain or to avoid painful punishment. On the whole, the New Right assumes that motivation is purely individualistic and denounces the idea of an overarching social good. More specifically, the New Right assumes that individual action primarily rotates around a reward/punishment axis as a source for motivation and action (see George and Wilding, 1994; Hayek, 1944; Friedman, 1962; Lund, 2002; Page, 2007). This vision of the capitalist system envisages that neo-liberalism has, as such, a fourfold effect on the maintenance of an ideal state:

- economic prosperity is maintained from the dynamic of market competition
- the pain/punishment axis encourages and cajoles the majority of citizens into behaving responsibly
- democracy is enhanced by the lack of government intervention/ (negative) freedom paradigm

- social cohesion is maintained through prosperity and responsible behaviour.

This diagnosis of society's problems as involving an overreliance on inefficient, bureaucratic welfare states letting naturally lazy individuals avoid pain is dealt with by a concomitant treatment outlined in the fourfold maintenance of the ideal state listed here. It is highly dependent on a balance between rewards and deterrents being met. Otherwise, criminal behaviour could manifest itself if the rewards of the socioeconomic system are seen to be too great and the deterrents (infliction of pain) are seen to be minimal: hence the need for legitimacy and law and order.

The delicate balance of state legitimation and the maintenance of order

Of course, not every state can be seen as neo-liberal or as democratic. Yet there tends to be one universal defining characteristic when it comes to criminal behaviour by or on behalf of the state. In this respect, it is important to recognise Green and Ward's (2004, p3) observation that all states, whether they be liberal or autocratic, claim the 'legitimate right to perform acts that if anyone else did them would constitute violence and extortion'.

This is made more poignant when one includes Hall and Ilkenberry's (1989) previous observation that the state and its institutions of law and order are the main agents for making laws and therefore maintaining order. Authority, legislation and regulation are, as a consequence, three prominent factors in the legitimation of a state's actions. In its purest form, then, state or indeed political legitimacy is a characteristic of the relationship between government and the governed 'or of the processes or structures of government' (Barker, 2012, p21). In effect, legitimacy is both a reflection of a political function and the consolidation of political relationships, whereby such legitimacy can be seen as 'derived from acquiescences or alliances which have their basis in interest, habit … [or] fear' (Barker, 2012, p23).

Despite the last allusion to coercion, acquiescence and alliance are the main sources of cohesion and legitimacy in an ideal state, whereas 'interest' not only relates to rewards gained from a successful neo-liberal economy but also to the benefits of political citizenship and a thriving community. In addition, 'interest' helps to consolidate the sovereignty of the state in that the wants and demands of the state citizenry are met within the context of a neo-liberal society. Habit, of course, refers to what has gone before. If successful for the continued existence of the state, governmental structures and citizens, then these thriving examples of social cohesion should be continued and perpetuated through socialisation over time. Ultimately, such a process becomes embedded within the individual and acceptance of social structures, and expectations become habitual for the responsible citizen.

By way of summary of the discussion so far, it can be argued that the state, or more specifically the ideal state, is defined by its capacity to achieve a consensual cum tacit form of legitimacy through communicative action. Such ideas have been central to a body of work associated with Habermas (1971, 1976, 1979, 1987, 1990, 1996). Using a two-faceted, interactive and interrelated model of modern industrial/ capitalist society, Habermas reasoned that on one side of the model is the 'lifeworld' (which comprises both the 'private' and 'public' spheres'), while on the other there is the 'subsystem' of the economy and state. Integral to Habermas's historical argument was his firm conviction that legitimation is achieved through the specific ways in which these two facets interrelate during the modernising process. Indeed, he argued that with the continued development of capitalism's industrial base, modern societies are increasingly being characterised by the ever-growing role that the economy and state have to play in the 'lifeworld'. As a result, the 'private' sphere is significantly influenced by economic wage-labour relations and by exchange and demand processes for goods and services. Conversely, the 'public' sphere is subject to taxation and administration, whereas politics increasingly demands an 'input of mass loyalty that is as diffuse as possible' (Habermas, 1976, p46).

Accordingly, the state (with its growing neo-liberal interest) faces a contradiction that requires it, on the one hand, to selectively raise and administer the requisite finances to cover the costs of its responsibilities to the citizenry. Crucially, this task has to be performed in such a way that effectively avoids the 'crisis ridden disturbance of growth' (Habermas, 1976, p61). On the other hand, however, the raising and distribution of taxes has to be prioritised and undertaken rationally, so that conflicting interests can be reconciled as and when the need arises. Failure in the former task results in a concomitant breakdown of administrative rationality, whereas failure in the latter constitutes the beginnings of a legitimation crisis (Craib, 1984). Maintaining and achieving the delicate balance between the two spheres of society is, therefore, the priority for the state in its pursuit of legitimacy.

State maintenance, institutional power and governmental alliances

Naturally, the state cannot simply legitimise itself, as it is not a single thinking entity capable of independent action, nor is it confined to action, compromises and allegiances purely within the state. As touched upon earlier, the ideal state is maintained and held to account by a freely elected government that facilitates the basis for popular consent. Legitimacy is thus founded on the 'willing and rational obedience of the governed; government is rightful only so long as it responds to popular pressure' (Heywood, 2004, p143) and the prevailing norms of society.

In this latter aspect, the education system serves to socialise individuals and perpetuate this willing obedience. Likewise the institution of the family helps, in theory if not in practice, to inculcate acceptance of the existing social system and state legitimacy. A sense of community, or rather communitarianism (Etzioni, 1995, 1997, 1998), can also perpetuate the socialisation process, by ensuring that a balance – through moral (per)suasion – is maintained 'between social forces and the person, between community and autonomy, between the common good and individual liberty, between individual rights and social responsibilities' (Etzioni, 1998, x).

Outside the socialisation and democratic processes, the police and the criminal justice system are tasked with the roles of maintaining these social norms and social coherence through the enforcement and prosecution of those who do not conform to the prevailing rules, laws and regulations implemented by the government on behalf of the state. In the face of internal and external threats, however, the army can impose a more draconian response to both internal and external turmoil. The media too play a decisive role. On one level they are set the task of informing the public about 'public issues' (Mills, 1959), but on the other they have competing priorities and responsibilities to shareholders. It is in this context that their role becomes of paramount importance and centres on the opaque issue of shaping public opinion. We return to the role of the media in Chapter Five, but all of these institutions, in an ideal state can be described as essential characteristics of an effective and cohesive state serving its citizenry.

Summarising the state, its allies, institutions and protagonists

Up to now we have somewhat benignly yet positively examined a number of the major features of an ideal state. Attention has been drawn to the 'free market', neo-liberal economy, which has the potential to satiate individuals through reward/remuneration for successful effort and participation. Moreover, this chapter has highlighted the New Right belief that these market configurations are democratic and impartial in nature: hence the conviction that they cannot be condemned for being 'just' or, more importantly, 'unjust'.

In a similar vein, political citizenship, the neutral 'umpire' role of government and the democratic process beyond the market were introduced to demonstrate how the state ideal is premised upon acquiescence, alliance and, to a lesser extent, fear. In this way, it was argued, legitimation is achieved as the roles and duties of state institutions are mainly directed at the maintenance and perpetuation of social cohesion through socialisation and guidance, the reproduction of habit (what works, past and present), the provision of electoral avenues for the public 'voice' to be heard and the management/supervision of the principles surrounding law and order issues.

The next section, however, takes a more negative stance. This part of the chapter not only reflects our beliefs, but also reflects upon the possibilities of an ideal state existing in its purest – or even close to its purest – form. Conflict, disagreement, alienation, fear and oppression are introduced, to demonstrate the potential – and actual – pitfalls and consequences of an unbalanced, dysfunctional state typical of the modern epoch. Questions of whether or not the market is 'just' or democracy is truly representative of the public voice are engaged with. Institutional roles, in the benign sense, are also questioned. So too are the reactions to external threats to this internal status quo.

The (im)possibility of the ideal state

The notion of an ideal state is, of course, rather simplistic and, as such, fraught with problems. Indeed, Williams (2010, p741) asserts that '[t]hroughout history states have committed crimes which dwarf those of "conventional" offenders or even organised criminal groups; their actions have often been costly, exceptionally violent and destructive of both property and people.' Yet they often go unpunished. One question we wish to address throughout the book is why? One part of the answer may be that the idea of government tends to deflect attention towards the 'leaders' of that social framework which, in turn, obfuscates the role of deviant organisations within the state apparatus. Moreover, this governmental and administrative analysis regards government as organisationally distinct from economic institutions and civil society (Michalowski, 2010, p14).

As a consequence of this separation, focus – from both an academic and public perspective – tends to shift towards how free market societies are supposed to function in the eyes of government, as opposed to looking at the after-effects (positive or negative) of how they actually function in practice. It is precisely that lack of functionality that can cause problems for a state in terms of legitimacy and the wellbeing of the state's citizens. As Klein (2007) powerfully demonstrated in her analysis of the spread of neo-liberal, free market principles across the globe: 'The economic crusade managed to cling to a veneer of respectability and lawfulness as it progressed. Now that veneer was being very publicly stripped away to reveal a system of gross wealth inequalities, often opened up with the aid of grotesque criminality.'

Neo-liberalism as a corrupting and dangerous influence

As we intimated in the earlier part of this chapter, the initial separation of government, the economy and administrative apparatus is a somewhat myopic description of an ideal state, to say the least. Nowhere is this better expressed than in the 'revolving door' between government and business. Seen to be a relatively new phenomenon, it was indeed a concern for Mills as far back as the 1950s:

> [T]he growth of the great corporation and the increased intervention of government into the economic realm have selected and formed and privileged economic men who are less hagglers and bargainers on any market than professional executives and adroit economic politicians. For today the successful economic man ... must influence or control those positions in the state in which decisions of consequence to his corporate activities are made. This trend ... is of course, facilitated by war, which thus creates the need to continue corporate activities with political as well as the economic means. War is of course the health of the corporate economy; during war the political economy tends to become more unified, and moreover, political legitimations of the most unquestionable sort – national security itself – are gained for corporate activities. (Mills, 1956, p167)

In many ways, Mills pre-empted what others have gone on to demonstrate: that states have frequently been 'captured' by elites for their own ends. This idea has been picked up by various thinkers. In his exposition of 'The Establishment', Jones (2014, p70) remarked on how the boundary between politics and business has become so porous that it is no longer possible or appropriate to consider them as separate entities. Drawing on work conducted on behalf of the independent research organisation Democratic Audit (Wilks-Heeg et al, 2012), Jones went on to demonstrate how over ninety per cent of the top fifty publicly traded firms had a British parliamentarian in a senior capacity as either a shareholder or director.

In his discussion of the Big Four accountancy firms, Sikka (2015) revealed that the former chairman of KPMG International, Sir Michael Rake, became an adviser to David Cameron, while the Conservative Party MP Nick Gibb, an erstwhile employee of KPMG, has held ministerial appointments in government. Meanwhile at PriceWaterhouseCoopers (PWC), former employee Mark Hoban took up a position in the Department for Work and Pensions after holding a Treasury position with responsibility for reforming the UK tax laws. Furthermore, Justine Greening, another former PWC employee, has held senior positions in both the Treasury and the Department for Transport. These are just a small number of handpicked examples. As Sikka (2015) also noted, the door revolves the other way as well, that is former senior figures in the last Labour government have taken up positions in the private sector: namely Lord Warner of Brockley, who gained employment as a strategic adviser to Deloitte's public sector team, and Lord Mandelson, who on his resignation from government in 1998 was subsequently hired by Ernst & Young.

Wilks-Heeg (2015) extended this analysis into the policy realm, discussing how the revolving door can or at least be implicated in policy failure as a result of being 'captured' by those with potential conflicts of interest. Referring to the light-touch regulation of the financial sector, he disparaged over-private corporations being:

> ... able to exert a dominating influence over government decision-making. The extent of corporate power implied by 'policy capture' ... requires corporate interests to go beyond the opportunities to 'revolve in' to government directly. Of equal importance are the indirect means of capturing policy through corporate support for a variety of lobby groups, research institutes and think tanks, and via an associated capacity to shape media reporting. (Wilks-Heeg, 2015, unpaginated)

The process of policy capture via revolving doors and insipid regulation is, for Wilks-Heeg, perhaps best illustrated by considering the role of the now defunct UK Financial Services Authority, which 'conflated public interest with the interests of the financial sector'. The FSA came into being in 2000 as an independent overseer of the financial sector, funded by the financial sector. Wilks-Heeg (2015) demonstrated how it can now be considered as a 'paradigmatic example of the failure of self-regulation' on the grounds that it was implicated in the financial crash of 2008-09. In part, its failures stemmed from the 'extensive interplay' between the banks and its board. So acute were these issues that from 2004 to 2009 the Chief Executive of HBOS, James Crosby, was a board member of the FSA, meaning that the head of a regulated institution (HBOS) was overseeing the regulator (OECD, 2009).

The issue for scholars of state criminality is that such developments do not necessarily entail crime per se. They are, however, part of the morality of neo-liberalism. Weigratz (2015) suggests that quite often the kinds of capitalist ventures discussed are seen to be void of morality, but this is not strictly true. Instead, a new morality has accompanied neo-liberalism tied to its cultural project. Bolstered by a sympathetic right-wing media in the UK (see Chapter Five), the greedy and the corrupt are actually aspiring to and conforming with, rather than breaking with, the dominant social values of achievement and wealth. As a consequence:

> New-liberalism not only advances certain values (those that generally serve individual interests), it does so at the expense of other values (those that generally serve collective interests), such as the concern for the welfare of others. In short, neo-liberalism is a 'cultural programme' that promotes pro-self interest values and norms. Taking this argument a step further allows us to see that the issue might not be erosion or decline of morals (or norms generally) as such, but the transformation of (especially socially dominant) morals: that is, the shift from pro-social moral norms to pro-self interest moral norms. (Weigratz, 2015, unpaginated)

We would generally accept this analysis. However, it is this morality that we would refer to as immoral. Here we nail our flag to the mast. We are approaching our analysis from the perspective of social policy and the principles of welfare and care for others. From this stance, we are left with little option but to conclude that the activities of states and powerful members of society who act to reproduce and only serve the self-interest of privileged groups at the expense of others is immoral behaviour, to say the least.

The discussion of the cultural programme of neo-liberalism and the way this can facilitate particular kinds of policy capture do, however, serve to remind us that the way in which states operate, and the way that they are viewed, has to be looked at through a much wider lens before any discussion of state crime and subterfuge can be fully explored and, hopefully, exposed. That is not to say that governmental, economic and administrative institutions do not constitute key elements within a state but, instead, they are only a part of a skeleton upon which more flesh and bone needs to be added. In this respect, Tilly (1985, p171) equates states to protection rackets in that they 'are coalitions of coercive and self-seeking entrepreneurs ... [with] a durable interest in promoting the accumulation of capital' (cited in Green and Ward, 2004, p2). As we shall see, the hegemony of neo-liberalism is a powerful driving force behind the state committing – or at least colluding with perpetrators of – serious acts of crime.

This line of reasoning was further developed by Box with his examination of the categories used in criminal law. Initially, he described how the focus of criminal law categories (such as murder, rape, robbery, assault and burglary, and so on) represented ideological constructs which are illusory and tend to deflect attention away from crimes of the powerful. Box stated that:

> For every 100 persons convicted of these serious crimes, 85 are male. Amongst this convicted male population, those aged less than 30 years, and particularly those aged between 15 and 21 years are over-represented. Similarly, the educational non-achievers are over-represented – at the other end of the educational achievement ladder there appear to be hardly any criminals ... The unemployed are currently only [sic] 14 per cent of the available labour force, but they constitute approximately 40 per cent of those convicted. (Box, 2001, p246)

Similar facts and figures can be produced today, thus reinforcing the argument that criminal law categories serve the interests of capital in general (and neo-liberalism in particular) through the social control of the powerless who do not, in many instances, have the skills and wealth to defend themselves or to resist the ruling hegemony. Žižek (2008) presented a comparable argument when proclaiming the existence of two types of violence. On the one hand, there is *subjective violence* which is enacted by social agents, evil individuals and oppressive apparatuses; on the other, *objective violence* emanates from capitalism itself and the neo-liberal pursuit of profit.

On one level, the unequal application of drugs legislation in the US and the UK serves as an example. Recent figures from the campaigning organisation Release (Eastwood et al, 2014) highlighted the ethnic disparities in stop-and-search figures which lead to significant discrepancies in arrest rates for drug offences. In 2009-10, for example, the overall search rate for drugs across the entire population was 10 searchers per 1,000 people. For those from white ethnic groups it was 7 per 1,000 in contrast to 45 per 1,000 for those identifying as black. Stevens (2011, p99), meanwhile, commented on the case of the wealthy white couple, Hans and Eva Rausing. In 2008, they were reportedly caught in possession of over £2,000 worth of cocaine and some heroin. But they had powerful friends and the financial wherewithal to engage the Crown Prosecution Service in lengthy correspondence. Stevens concluded that the Rausings were given individually tailored conditional cautions, yet less powerful and wealthy individuals 'would not have benefitted from similar treatment'.

For Box, then, this focus on 'conventional' crimes, which undoubtedly exists, may be 'a trick to deflect our attention away from other, even more serious crimes and victimising behaviours, which objectively cause the vast bulk of avoidable death, injury and deprivation' (Box, 2001, p246). As a result, this pervasion of capitalist ideology within criminal law categories excludes, for example, the 'extra tax citizens … have to pay because … Defence Department officials have been bribed to order more expensive weaponry systems or missiles in excess of those "needed"' (Box, 2001, p251-2).

Going beyond this interpretation, an argument can also be made about how capitalism/neo-liberalism is inherently criminal. Integral to this step forward is the ideological pursuit of profit that acts a social dynamic. As the early part of this chapter made clear, this dynamic is believed to provide and promote social cohesion, competition and greater efficiency. However, increased competition, the threat of redundancy or bankruptcy alongside the potential for higher levels of unemployment and the rising gap between the rich and poor tend to militate against any potential benefits that a neo-liberal system may have on offer.

A crisis of legitimacy and state power

As we saw earlier, the establishment and maintenance of state legitimacy rely on the state safeguarding the balance between the 'lifeworld' and the subsystem of the economy and the state. According to Habermas, a crisis occurs when the state and the economy encroach too far into the 'lifeworld'. As a result, the 'private' sphere is significantly influenced by economic wage-labour relations and by exchange and demand processes for goods and services. Conversely, the 'public' sphere is subject to taxation and administration, whereas politics increasingly demands an 'input of mass loyalty that is as diffuse as possible' (Habermas, 1976, p46).

For Habermas, such a situation became problematic during the 1970s with the increased willingness of many European states to introduce economic controls to help implement more comprehensive systems of welfare. Arguably, this was a foretaste of the problems that have ensued today. In effect, states in the early 1970s were demonstrating their ability to exercise a purposive rationality designed to regulate the economy and help counter the extreme vicissitudes of the 'free' market. Crucially, this state rationality, or instrumental reasoning, represented the beginnings of a reciprocal interaction with the individuals of the 'lifeworld'. Successful application, therefore, depended on the correct interpretation and utilisation of the actions, motivations and needs of these individuals (Habermas, 1976, 1979, 1996). Yet this dependency and increased concern for aspects of the 'lifeworld' contributed to the politicisation of economic relations: especially when such relations were set alongside the implicit loss of the self-legitimising function of the 'free' market economy that accompanied any need for state intervention. Consequently, inequalities in wealth distribution no longer appeared to be the 'functioning of a nature-like' market mechanism (Scott, 1995, p70). Rather, inequality and poverty had become part of the political agenda where 'the state ... altered the determinants of the realisation process itself ... [and where] the administrative system gains a limited planning capacity, which can be used, within the framework of a formally democratic procurement of legitimation, for purposes of reactive crisis avoidance' (Habermas, 1976, p61).

Nonetheless, this was still problematic in the eyes of Habermas, since the state, with its 'collective capitalist interest' (1976, p61) in maintaining the system, had not only to compete with the opposing aims of separate capitalist collaborations, but also with the general values and interests of the populace at large. Even though the cyclical nature of economic crisis of that period had been distributed over time and defused of its social consequences (through its replacement with a combination of inflation and an enduring crisis in public finance), its permanence still depended on:

> ... whether capital expended so as to be only indirectly productive does attain an increase in the productivity of labor, and on whether the distribution of the growth in productivity in line with functional requirements of the system is sufficient to guarantee mass loyalty and, simultaneously, keep the accumulation process moving. (Habermas, 1976, p61)

Accordingly, the state faced a contradiction that required it, on the one hand, to selectively raise and administer the requisite finances to cover the costs of its new self-imposed responsibilities in such a way that effectively avoids the 'crisis ridden disturbance of growth' (Habermas, 1976, p61). On the other hand, the raising and distribution of taxes has to be prioritised and undertaken rationally, so that conflicting interests can be reconciled as and when the need arises. Failure in the former task results in a concomitant breakdown of administrative rationality, whereas failure in the latter constitutes the beginnings of a legitimation crisis (Craib, 1984).

In this respect, Habermas implicitly recognised that legitimacy reflects the 'worthiness' of a political order to be recognised and respected by its citizenry. Moreover:

> [the] *claim to legitimacy* is related to the social-integrative preservation of a normatively determined social identity. *Legitimations* serve to make good this claim, that is, to show how and why existing (or recommended) institutions are fit to employ political power in such a way that the values constitutive for the identity of the society will be realized. (Habermas, 1979, p182-3)

Yet the aforementioned rationality and legitimacy problems of state administration are further compounded by an increased participation of capitalists and sectional interests in the decision-making process, as we have seen and will further demonstrate. Indeed, the contribution of these special interest groups within the administrative system of the state allows for a displacement of 'the competition between individual social interests into the state apparatus' (Habermas, 1976, p62). The state's ability to make independent decisions is jeopardised as a consequence. Furthermore, the related socialisation of production, which still congregates around private interest, creates another paradox. Under these circumstances, the state has to act as a collective capitalist, promoting the imperative of state expansion and planning. At the same time, the state also has to prevent this expansion from threatening the very essence of capitalism itself. The dilemma is encapsulated by the fact that increased planning of the economy entails the abolition of the freedom to invest and, as a result, reduces the competitive 'drive' or 'dynamic' of capitalism. In response: 'the state apparatus vacillates between expected intervention and forced renunciation of intervention, between becoming independent of its clients in a way that threatens the system and subordinating itself to their particular interests' (Habermas, 1976, p62-3).

Unavoidably, this 'entrapment' within contradictory relations and demands results in repeated rationality problems, from which additional preconditions for a legitimation crisis arise.

All in all, the 'expansion of state activity produces the side effect of a disproportionate increase in the need for legitimation' (Habermas, 1976, p71). With the increasing number of tasks that the state is expected to undertake, the state begins to lose its ability to normatively justify the effectiveness of its policies (Habermas, 1996). This is problematic on two levels. Not only does the expansion of state activity hinder the state's ability to secure mass loyalty, but this increase in planning and expansion also entails the state assuming greater responsibility for the hitherto private affairs of the cultural sphere. Education, for example, competes with familial upbringing with the imposition of a national curriculum. Likewise, welfare provision removes familial provision for the poor. In effect, areas previously reserved for the private sphere are 'colonised' by the political. As the administrative system increasingly affects the cultural sphere, previously unquestioned characteristics of the economy and state action are undermined. Traditional attitudes are threatened, rendered uncertain and suffer a loss of power (Wiggershaus, 1986). Blind allegiance to, or at least acceptance of, events or policies no longer represents the norm for individual behaviour. At every level, continued Habermas:

> administrative planning produces unintended unsettling and
> publicizing effects. These effects weaken the justification
> potential of traditions that have been flushed out of their
> nature-like course of development. The stirring up of
> cultural affairs that are taken for granted thus furthers the

politicization of areas of life previously assigned to the private sphere. (Habermas, 1976: 72)

To make matters worse from Habermas's perspective, this is the starting point for a vicious spiral of decay. Increased efforts by the population to participate in governmental planning worryingly reflect a larger interaction, where the more that administrative planning has an effect on the cultural world, the more tenuous traditional values become. To counter the trend, thresholds of acceptability have to undergo a continual process of realignment. But to successfully implement further innovative planning, there develops a greater need for the administration to seek the involvement of those affected. Otherwise, there is a crisis of legitimacy, which can lead to internal public demonstrations, riots and protest.

The same can be held to be true of today. With the decline in 'welfarism' and the resurgence of neo-liberal principles, the 1980s and, more recently, with the riots of 2011 in the UK, a number of disturbing events have occurred. Reactions on behalf of the state have not always been as benign as the earlier part of this chapter might suggest; nor have the case studies in this book been confined to the UK. In relation to state crime, for example, the use of police and army against the National Union of Mineworkers' picket of the Orgreave coking plant near Sheffield in 1984, and the military coup to take control of Argentina in 1976 headed by Videla (see Chapter Eight) reflect not only governmental drives to assert legitimacy but also the lengths and measures that a state will go to in the ideological pursuit of a neo-liberal agenda. Naturally, states can be threatened by other agendas (such as terrorism motivated by religious and/or political ambitions), and these too can result in a crisis in legitimacy that culminates in the taking or condoning of drastic actions on behalf of the state (see Chapter Seven on Northern Ireland in particular, and see also later in this chapter).

The concept of the revolving door is tied to the crisis in legitimacy. States have traditionally been very slow in bringing their own agents to account. Public inquiries have often been ineffective and powerless and have asked the wrong questions. The example of Northern Ireland is a case in point. A number of official inquiries have been held into the actions of various state agencies in Northern Ireland since partition. In turn, there have been different schools of thought looking at the efficacy of these inquiries. Rolston and Scraton (2005), for example, drew on the work of Ralph Miliband (1969) to demonstrate how official inquiries in Ireland lack legitimacy. Initially intended to restore faith in democratic institutions and agencies concerned with ensuring the impartiality of the rule of law, in reality, inquiries into the machinations of such agencies have only served to give the appearance of this to international audiences, while lacking credibility to many on the island of Ireland, but particularly to nationalists from the north (Rolston and Scraton, 2005, p558).

Partly this is a product of their make-up. Inquiries are often chaired by high-profile public figures who frequently share a 'coincidence of interests' with those under scrutiny. In an earlier paper, Scraton (2004, p49) pointed out how they are staffed by the civil service, who have a particular *modus operandi* that is not attuned to questioning the status quo, but to reinforcing it. These are perhaps the most benign features of inquiries in Northern Ireland and a somewhat more malign influence has underpinned other attempts to bring the agents of the state to accountability. Nowhere is this more apparent than with the Stalker investigation into the killing of six republicans by the police in County Armagh between November and December 1982.

Lawther (2010, p464) showed how, according to his own memoirs, John Stalker (the erstwhile Deputy Chief Constable of Manchester) suggested that the RUC engaged in systematic obfuscation led by the then Chief Constable, Sir Jack Hermon, alongside other senior officers. Nonetheless, Rolston and Scraton (2005, p558) argued that Stalker's inquiry was one of only a small number of incidences when a principled investigation was carried out in Northern Ireland. They suggested that Stalker 'found fault with the RUC's investigation of the murder' with particular criticisms reserved for the Special Branch. On commencing interviews with Hermon and senior colleagues, Stalker was removed from the investigation 'and faced disciplinary charges in Manchester that were eventually dismissed'. The example serves to highlight and reinforce the point that controlling, policing and prosecuting state criminality is beset with danger.

Defining state crime, governmental crime and political crime

For reasons discussed, state crime cannot easily be defined due to the overriding fact that the state, as a social actor, is a leading force in the social construction of crime. Therefore the state defines what constitutes a crime and what does not. The state can legitimise its actions, which in turn is problematic, to say the least. As Matthews and Kauzlarich (2007, p47) put it, '[when] states violate their own laws, clearly state crimes are being committed ... [However, the] question of state crime, for criminologists working within a legalistic framework, is not whether it is a real phenomenon, but rather which legal definition(s) to use.'

To complicate issues further, Williams (2010) remonstrated on how many states operate on federal principles which are sometimes in conflict and sometimes not in accord with local interests, despite the state being a constituted central power, theoretically recognised by its people (Green and Ward, 2004). In other cases – particularly under the conditions of neo-liberalism where many of the traditional functions of the state (that is specific kinds of public service delivery) have been farmed out to private and third sector organisations – there are a whole host of subgroups and other agencies. These act for the state but are separate from it, thus complicating the problems of definition even more.

Nevertheless, McAuley (2003, p20), in his overview of the diversity of writings on the state, suggested that despite all the divergence, one area of notable convergence is the view that since the 19th century, the state had become the most important political actor in most developed countries. Indeed, as we witnessed in the previous chapter of this book, at its highpoint in the early to mid-20th century, under the conditions of 'welfarism', the state promised to 'intervene directly to provide care and support for its citizens from cradle to grave' (McAuley, 203, p 20). Yet, as will become clear later in this chapter, towards the end of the 20th century and into present times there has been a distinct hollowing out of the functions of the state, in part due to the primacy of neo-liberal political philosophies in much of the Western hemisphere.

As a consequence of the ongoing fundamental changes to the role and nature of the neo-liberal state, it is also necessary to include a discussion that inevitably requires some engagement with new modes of governance. Stoker (1998), for instance, has identified how governance is an intrinsically complex concept, with numerous possible meanings and applications. Broadly speaking, it can be said to refer to changes in the activity and composition of the government. In other words, governance 'refers to a set of institutions and actors that are drawn from but also beyond government' (Stoker, 1998, p18). Under the conditions of governance, coalitions of key stakeholders are embroiled in attempts to shape policy agendas. Certainly, the governance of any advanced capitalist society now entails coordination between various layers of agents and structures of control. This means that there are numerous levels of decision-making that take place and these have to be consistently and coherently managed (Pierre and Stoker, 2000).

In the UK, this was most closely associated with the Thatcher era, which for Gamble (1988) entailed a free economy alongside a strong state. In other words, this combined economic liberalism with social conservatism. As Lister (2010, p42) observed, in most cases the two strands reinforced each other, although there were times of conflict. A key example was Conservative education policy in the 1980s – in particular, the introduction of a national curriculum that sought to universalise teaching practice at the same time as a quasi-market was being proposed across the sector. Lister (2010, p42) went on to note that for the most part, economic liberalism was the dominant strand, creating a 'very positive attitude towards the market and a very negative attitude towards the state', especially as a source of welfare. Consequently, the state had become much less interventionist and much more regulatory, increasingly managing its citizens at arm's length – through the development of various semi-autonomous agencies – rather than directly impacting on their daily lives.

A seeming paradox of this situation, however, was that the hollowing out of the state came to be combined with a concentration in power at the epicentre of the executive. In other words, the 1980s witnessed a transition from Cabinet government to Prime Ministerial government. For some thinkers (Held, 1989; Burnham and Pyper, 2008), this amounted less to a hollowing out of the state, but to a reassertion of the traditional symbols of the state; a strong core executive being one of these and providing the buttress to the flexing of muscles on the global stage and recovering national self-confidence that had taken a hit in the previous decade, when Britain had applied to the IMF for emergency loans and financial aid.

Crucially for current purposes, the simultaneous concentration of power in the centre alongside its dispersal elsewhere creates new possibilities for state criminality. This raises a number of implications for determining state crime. As the list of actors becomes diffuse, it becomes more difficult to ascertain whether criminality is for state or personal gain. Such debates, as we shall see, mirror those in the corporate/white-collar crime literature. The state crime example developed by Green and Ward (2004) and cited by Williams (2010) is that of a soldier who, for personal gratification, rapes one of the enemy. This act may also further the interests of the state, for example through ethnic cleansing or degradation of the enemy. If the state does not impose a sanction on the perpetrator in this scenario, by definition of failing to act, it is, therefore, committing a state crime.

State crime as the breach of national and international rules and regulations

There is, then, a growing amount of commentary on the nature of state crime, each with an associated attempt at producing a working definition. From a sweep of the relevant literature, it is clear that definitions of state crime range from the narrow to the all-encompassing and span the constructivist–realist scale. The picture is further confused as a consequence of definitional overlap with other forms of crime under discussion in this volume. Thus some authors use the terms 'state crime' and 'political crime' interchangeably, whereas others prefer to speak of governmental crime, 'state-sponsored corporate crime', state-political crime or state-organised crime. Ross (2003, p4) offered an initial explanation of the terminology, when suggesting that 'in general, an actor has committed a political crime if he or she has a political or ideological intention or motivation to cause harm … state political crime consists of an action perpetrated by the government to illegally minimise or eliminate threats to its rule'.

In his attempt to unpack the terminology, Friedrichs (2000) stipulated:

> *Governmental crime* is the broad, all-encompassing term for a range of illegal and demonstrably harmful activities carried out from within, or in association with, governmental status. The conventional term *political crime* has been used to embrace crimes committed by those within the government and by those acting against the state, and is probably more readily associated with the latter type of activity. The term *state crime*, which has been quite widely quoted in more recent times, refers only to one major class of crimes that can be committed by those acting within a government. (Friedrichs, 2000, p74)

The accounts by both Ross and Friedrichs are, according to Doig (2011), in turn borrowed from the seminal work by Chambliss (1989) on this matter. In his 1988 Presidential Address to the American Society of Criminology, Chambliss emphasised that:

> The most important type of criminality organized by the state consists of acts defined by law as criminal and committed by state officials in the pursuit of their job as representatives of the state. Examples include a state's

complicity in piracy, smuggling, assassinations, and criminal conspiracies, acting as an accessory before and after the fact, and violating laws that limit their activities ... [S]tate-organized crime does not include criminal acts that benefit only individual officeholders, such as the acceptance of bribes or the illegal use of violence by the police against individuals, unless such acts violate existing criminal law and are official policy. (Chambliss, 1989, p 184)

For Barak (1991, p275) political crimes related to 'acts committed by and/or on behalf of the state and its dominant ruling elites are political crimes essentially because they have been rationalised or justified in order to preserve and maintain the status quo'. Barak's definition of political crime bears more than a close resemblance to the way we have chosen to operationalise state crime (see Chapter Three). We will leave a discussion of how we are defining political crime until Chapter Three.

A further layer of complexity is supplied by Kauzlarich et al (2001) in their discussion of the victims of state crime, or 'governmental crime', as they term it. Their attempts to ascertain the true extent of state criminality have considered the issue from the point of view of the victims rather than the perpetrators. They suggested that victims of state crime generally fall into two categories: 'domestic state crime occurs when a government acts to undermine the social, economic, or political rights of its own citizens'; and 'international state crime occurs when a government violates the economic, political, or social rights of citizens in other countries' (Kauzlarich et al, 2001, p177). They added a further layer of analysis to this, by suggesting that crimes that violate international law or treaties including human rights can be seen to be qualitatively separate from actions that violate domestic criminal or regulatory codes. The resultant typology is depicted in Table 2.1, replete with a number of their own examples.

State crime, or to be more specific political crime, can also be divided into two major categories: crimes committed by government; and crimes committed against government. In relation to the former, such acts consist of: genocide, torture, assassination and related acts of violence, surveillance, infiltration and disruption, legal repression, political corruption with the intent to make personal economic gain or the abuse of political power and influence and, finally, illegal invasion. On the other hand, crimes against a government relate to mass political violence (that is rebellion, rioting, terrorism, political assassination and civil disobedience), espionage and treason. All these

Table 2.1: Types of international governmental crime

Domestic-International Governmental Crime (DICG)	International-International Governmental Crime (IIGC)
Occurs within the geographic jurisdiction of a State; entails actions in contravention of international law or human rights standards	Occurs outside the geographic jurisdiction of a State; entails actions in contravention of international law or human rights standards
Examples:	**Examples:**
Institutional Racism DOE Human Radiation Experiments	Economic Terrorism
Domestic-Domestic Governmental Crime (DDGC)	**International-Domestic Governmental Crime (IDGC)**
Occurs within the geographic jurisdiction of a State; entails actions in contravention of criminal, regulatory, or procedural laws or codes	Occurs outside the geographic jurisdiction of a State; entails actions in contravention of criminal, regulatory, or procedural laws or codes
Examples:	**Examples:**
COINTELPRO[1] DOE Environmental Degradation[2]	Iran-Contra

Notes: [1] COINTELPRO is an acronym for the FBI's Counter Intelligence Programme whereby organisations deemed to provide a threat to national security or to be subversive were placed under surveillance, infiltrated or discredited. These activities were often an infringement of the rights of American citizens as defined by the Constitution.

[2] DOE Environmental Degradation refers to the US Department of Energy nuclear weapons tests carried out in the Western part of the US, which have been linked to tens of thousands of cases of thyroid cancer diagnoses in the regions affected (Kauzlarich, 2001, p180).

Source: Kauzlarich et al, 2001

issues – along with those documenting the difficulties in researching the topic – significantly impact on estimations of how pervasive the problem is.

Determining when an international law has been breached is not an easy task. In Chapter Six we show how there is a significant amount of interpretation in the application of international law, as the case for the war in Iraq shows. Furthermore, international laws stemming from United Nations conventions are only binding when they are ratified by particular countries. Consequently, they are not a universal panacea, as not all countries ratify every Convention. In addition, most conventions leave room for manoeuvre. One needs only to consider the 1961 Single Convention on Narcotic Drugs, which aimed to standardise the control of narcotics across nations so that certain drugs could be used only for scientific, medical and, in some cases, industrial purposes. This was achieved by arranging drugs into schedules and applying appropriate controls based on their harm and toxicity. Any Article in contravention of the Convention was a punishable offence, with a custodial term for serious breaches (Fortson, 2005).

Although this is the case, member states have developed specific drug strategies to tackle the problem within their borders. These are developed by using up-to-date epidemiological information on drug prevalence and they also have in-built evaluation and monitoring apparatus to gauge their achievements and effectiveness. Yet differences in substantive policy remain. Nowhere is this more apparent than the divergent philosophies marking the Portuguese preference for an approach decriminalising all drug possession in a bid to tackle the public health effects of drugs (Hughes and Stevens, 2010) and the Swedish inclination towards drug prevention and a zero-tolerance approach to drug possession (Chatwin, 2003).

State crime as human rights violations

Using violations of rights as a benchmark of human criminality provides a further opportunity in the operationalisation of state crime. This also proves problematic on the grounds that these are also not uniformly universal standards. For some states, the concept of human rights may be interpreted differently than the international norm as was/is the case with interpretations of international conventions. That said, Williams (2010, p744) argued that it is necessary for the definition of state crime to appeal to more than one recognised authority and to extend the remit beyond the contravention of international criminal law, as we have discussed. It is also important that this is an internationally recognised but 'independent theoretical base' and not one that reproduces the interests of a powerful minority.

Appealing to rights can bring certain activities under the bailiwick of state crime that would be difficult to prove in a criminal court. The rights issue is tied into the avoidance of social harm (see later in this chapter). By focusing on 'protecting the physical person, human dignity and social-psychological well-being from the excesses of the state and its organs of power' (Williams, 2010, p 744), a more fluid concept of state crime can be revealed. This can help with prosecutions when certain policies or practices adopted by the state, but which are not in and of themselves illegal, are carried out. Williams (2010, p745) cited the example of the Great Depression of the 1930s and/or the Chinese Famine of 1959-60, when policies were developed and continued despite the detrimental impact they were having on citizens. For human rights advocates, these would be viewed as types of crime, whereas for international law they would be merely 'inadequate, inequitable' and 'exploitative' courses of action. The point does remain, however, that for these reasons listed here (among others) state crime is difficult to detect and so understanding its prevalence is a difficult challenge.

The social construction of state crime and organised deviance

Doig (2011) has produced a useful framework in which to explore the minutiae of state crime, whereby he compares two (not entirely discrete) formats. For Doig, state crime can be analysed by looking at state crime as state-corporate crime or state crime as organisational deviance. The former views state crime as being endemic to certain organisations and mirrors the Marxist interpretations of corporate crime, which highlight the intrinsic nature of capitalist enterprises. It operates with a narrow concept of the 'state', but broad concept of crime, and sees the state driven to criminality in a bid to further or protect its corporate interests. This perspective is more specifically focused on the interconnections between the state and commerce that facilitates criminal behaviours. For Doig (2011, p80-1) there are three dimensions to state-corporate crime:

- 'it argues for a broad interpretation of crime' where the types of offences range across various responsibilities, activities and obligations of the state
- it makes a distinction between 'an intention for the crime to take place, and allowing it to take place
- it provides the explanation for the motive.

Arguably, Doig's three dimensions have their origins in Sutherland's work on white collar crime and are closely aligned with Friedrichs' (2003) notion of governmental crime (see also Chapter Three).

From this perspective, the corporate sector is the driving influence of criminal activity and it is other agencies of the state that acquiesce with, or are active facilitators of, such activity. According to Ross (2003, p148), state-corporate crimes are committed by individuals who abuse their state authority or who fail to exercise it when working with people and organisations in the private sector and when their actions result in social harms. There is overlap here with the literature on the regulation of health and safety matters, which is targeted primarily at the behaviour of corporate or other elites and so is enforced sporadically, even toothlessly, via regulatory law as opposed to criminal law (for example Tombs and Whyte, 2007). Indeed, we have seen how, through the revolving door, this is made feasible. It is, however, worth bearing in mind Nelken's (2007) warning about how not all capitalist enterprise is inherently criminogenic, not least because it struggles to explain the increasing checks and balances placed into the capitalist system in the form of improvements in safety and the quality of goods. Bad publicity in either domain is best avoided and it is this that provides Nelken's departure to organisational deviance.

Literature on organisational deviance tends to be divided into two categories. As with Doig's (2011) aforementioned three dimensions, one of these foci also follows the lead of Sutherland by considering the activities of low-status employees of large organisations who use their insider status to make the most of criminal opportunities presented to them. This often relates to low-level offending, such as raiding the supplies of the company, but can involve more serious offences, such as defrauding the company or its customers (Benson and Simpson, 2009). The other focus is on well-placed (often high-ranking) employees, such as managers or executives within specific organisations (Doig, 2011). These may be individuals who are acting to further the interests of the organisation or may be using the organisation as a shield to further their own interests. For Punch (1996), one explanation for the perpetration of organisational deviance is that this is often the means by which an employee can show commitment to a company ethos. Thus to progress up the organisational ladder, employees often engage in 'group think'. Doig (2011, p88) explains this as a 'reinforcing dynamic that gives managers the rationale for what they are doing and comfort that they are doing what others are doing and what will bring approval of peers and superiors'.

Although organisational deviance tends to refer to the criminogenic nature of organisations, or 'white-collar crime' in earlier parlance, Doig (2011) maintains that it can offer transferable lessons when trying to account for state-related crime. For him, group think was clearly visible in the decision by the Bush administration to invade Iraq in the aftermath of the 9/11 terrorist attacks. The rationale for an attack, therefore, took on an impetus of its own, despite the now realised shaky intelligence foundations on which war was premised, that is the supposed link between Saddam Hussein's Iraqi regime and al Qaeda, to name but one contested aspect (see Chapter Six).

Doig (2011) went on to draw on the ideas of Croall (2001), to elucidate upon how the leap from white-collar crime to state crime is a small one, due to the fact that occupational offences by those in private institutions often share the same features as those in public agencies:

[B]ecause they take place in the private sphere of the workplace they are relatively *invisible* and can be concealed more easily; because they are committed during the course of an occupation, they involve the abuse of the *trust* inherent in an occupational role; offences are possible by the use of some form of *technical* or *'insider'* knowledge; this makes many offences *complex*, and the extent duration and details of offending are difficult to determine; offences may be sins of 'omission' or 'commission', with a long 'paper trail' and cover-ups often being involved; many are highly *organised* and involve several participants with differing levels of responsibility; in many cases, determining who is responsible is difficult because of the *diffusion of responsibility* in organisations; offences also involve different patterns of victimisation, and many offences are characterised as victimless. (Croall, 2001, p8-9)

Where state crime is concerned, there is often a single, recognisable victim, whose victimisation is severe. High-profile torture cases are a case in point. One further point worthy of note – and one that supports the organisational deviance perspective – is that many variants of state crime are long-running episodes of criminality. As a result, explanations of state or organised crimes which equate the activities with a 'few bad apples' have shortcomings, in that one would expect the criminality to cease once those individuals move on (Kauzlarich et al, 2001). Yet longevity seems to be a feature of much elite criminality.

Social harm: additional expressions of state criminality and deviance?

By introducing notions of social harm, an even wider accountability can be imposed on governments, especially those of the neo-liberal persuasion (Doig, 2011). As previously pointed out, the neo-liberal ethos has often perpetuated the rich/poor, powerful/powerless divides. When this is tied to notions of responsibility, irresponsibility and the propensity to cut welfare benefits, a fairly convincing case that the government is neglecting its duty to maintain the welfare of all its citizenry – and not just the privileged few – can be made. More broadly, however, a government can be accused of inflicting social harm on the poorer sections of its own citizenry and – as the later chapters of this book will demonstrate – citizens of other states.

In essence, the government, or to be more precise, the state can be accused of committing social harm when they have violated 'universally defined human rights (such as food, shelter, self-determination)' (Doig, 2011, p47). In this respect, state harms could be said to include actions where – whether they be committed directly, in collusion or passively accepted – there is no existing legal definition of criminality or, indeed, any corresponding definition of crime (Matthews and Kauzlarich, 2007). As Hillyard and Tombs (2007) succinctly put it:

> Many events and incidents which cause serious harm are either not covered by criminal law or, if they could be or are encompassed within this ambit, are either ignored or handled without resort to it: corporate crime and state crime are obvious, heterogeneous categories of offence that remain largely marginal to dominant legal, policy enforcement, and indeed academic agendas, while at the same time creating widespread harm, not least amongst already relatively disadvantaged and powerless peoples. (Hillyard and Tombs, 2007, p12)

From this it follows that the explicit actions of a state which inflict harm, or even a neglect to end suffering of needy communities, can be said to be criminal when measured against a spectrum of social harm. Actions not directly defined by criminal law would, therefore, be open to sanctions based on the degree to which social harm is inflicted. When taken in conjunction with international and domestic human rights, there emerges a sharper focus on political *responsibility* as opposed to political *necessity*. As such, responsibility becomes a key consideration when examining state crime and what constitutes state crime. In turn, state power, influence and control now have to be viewed from the perspective of the state's obligations to uphold human respect and social security. Through this perspective, a state can thus be held justifiably accountable if security and respect are not politically achieved.

As this book will make clear in the later chapters, this focus encompasses many crimes that have avoided criminal definitions. Examples include:

- the circumvention of media regulation by powerful media conglomerates
- the destruction of Iraq and the denial of wealth-creating opportunities for its citizens

- the devastation and heartache inflicted upon broken families during and well after the 'dirty war' in Argentina
- the denial of community life with pit closures in the UK and the undermining of trade union rights.

Social harm can also take an ecological dimension. Oil spillages – again a feature of the Iraq conflict – are one prime example. Radiation from the mass use of weaponry can also be considered, especially when both are viewed in conjunction with the withering effects that oil and radiation can have on land and communities reliant on the land and its potential revenues. The use of toxic chemicals as part of crop eradication schemes in the war on drugs can also come under the social harm microscope.

Summary

This chapter has theorised at length what might constitute the ideal state, before demonstrating the ways in which states rarely (if ever) live up to the ideal. It has documented the multifarious challenges of trying to locate and define state crime and immoral acts. In part, developments of governance under neo-liberalism have made this difficult, by simultaneously concentrating power in a tighter centre, while in other ways increasing the number of actors who are performing what were once considered functions of the state.

Furthermore, drawing on the work of various thinkers, we have shown how neo-liberalism through the revolving door of the public and private sector has facilitated opportunities for corrupt practices and has also led to the distinct possibility of a legitimation crisis. From this, we have attempted to develop and explain some of the ways in which state crime has been conceived, which range from the breaching of national and international laws, to human rights violations, organised deviance and social harms.

This chapter builds a platform upon which the rest of the book develops. Anti-democratic measures, such as the invasions of other nation states (see Chapter Six on state terrorism from without), the idea that the media can both reinforce and influence the state (see Chapter Five, which relates to personal benefits for both politicians and media moguls), the notion that the state can collude with non-governmental, criminal enterprises for their own ends (see Chapter Seven) and the problems overzealous policing of a state's own populace (see Chapter Eight and the discussion about ideological enforcement) are all touched upon. Similarly, unhealthy cooperation with – and susceptibility to –

corrupt organisations and their practices (see Chapter Three) is also introduced. Primarily, though, these discussions allow the book to build a more nuanced and comprehensive discussion of state crime and state immorality/deviance.

THREE

The state, corporations and organised crime

Chapter Two discussed in detail the nature of states and how they rarely live up to the ideal. It did so by engaging with Williams' (2010, p741) assertion that it is states more than individual actors or any other grouping that commit crimes of a magnitude far in excess of anything else. The chapter documented the multifarious challenges of trying to locate and define state crime and immoral acts. Indeed, such definitions are problematic precisely because (in Western democracies at least) we have become accustomed to the state as being the key agency for law-making, for law enforcement and for defining what constitutes criminal behaviour.

Chapter Three picks up on this theme, but suggests that one of the main difficulties in delineating state criminality from other forms of crime is that many forms of criminality involve the collusion of state and other non-state, but nonetheless powerful, actors. With this in mind, the present chapter starts with a discussion of the difficulties in applying a label to what we termed in the introduction 'non-conventional criminality'. We use this as a generic term to describe non-street-based offences. State crime would be one example but, as we shall see, there are others.

The difficulties in labelling certain offences can be traced back to the seminal work of Edwin Sutherland (1949) on white-collar crime. Although Sutherland never meant the category to be definitive, it is clear that it has led to a degree of conceptual ambiguity. It is the task of this chapter to start to cut a swathe through this dense thicket. In doing so, we are somewhat selective in the crimes we discuss, but have chosen to concentrate on those that sit at the boundaries of state crime, sometimes overlapping.

Here we focus on organised criminality and corporate criminality. With the former, we discuss the nature of organised criminality. We note at this point that the state can be seen to be complicit in organised crime in two main ways: first in the construction of the concept and its associated features, which provide a platform for the proliferation of state intimidation against certain groups; second, through complicity and collusion in illegal acts. We consider the pervasive nature of corporate criminality and state acquiescence contra to its documentation in the official accounts of crime prevalence crimes against corporations. We then look at the relationship between these issues and state crime in a discussion of collusion, condolence and acquiescence in such matters under the aegis of an analysis of corruption in contemporary Britain. We round off the chapter with a discussion of terminological uncertainty and seek to point a way ahead.

Problematic definitions and terminological overlap

Edwin Sutherland is a central figure in the history of criminology. Regarding Sutherland's contribution to the disciplinary canon, Herbert Mannheim once stated: 'There is no Nobel Prize as yet for criminologists, and probably there never will be one, but if it had been available, Sutherland would have been one of the most deserving candidates for his work on WCC [white-collar crime]' (Mannheim, 1965, p470).

In his major works, Sutherland (1949, 1983) drew attention to what has become known as the 'dark figure of crime'. These are crimes that are frequent in nature but rarely make it into any official measures of criminality. They are crimes and misdemeanours that occur in offices and workplaces. They are crimes of the educated, the well respected and those of high status, or what he termed 'white collar' crimes. For Sutherland these had more damaging effects than recorded delinquency. In effect, Sutherland criticised official systems and academics for concentrating on lower-class offenders and crimes. We have witnessed how, since the 1980s, there has been much heated debate on the nature of crime in society and how a vast 'crime complex' has emerged in response to rapidly rising crime rates throughout the latter part of the 20th century. But these developments have taken place without paying heed to the warnings delivered by Sutherland in the preceding decades.

Ever since Sutherland published his seminal work on white-collar crime in 1949, debates about what we have termed 'non-conventional criminality' have been prominent in criminology. Nelken (2007) traced these issues back to ambiguities surrounding Sutherland's conceptualisation of white-collar crime. Alluding to Mannheim's suggestion that, Sutherland should be awarded a Nobel prize, Nelken (2007, p738) commented that if Sutherland did merit such a prestigious award, it was not 'for the clarity or serviceableness of his definition' (of white-collar crime). Friedrichs (1996) pointed out that 'economic crime', 'commercial crime', 'business crime', 'consumer crime', 'respectable crime', 'crime at the top', 'suite crime', 'elite crime and deviance', 'official crime and deviance', 'political crime', 'governmental crime', 'state (or state-organised) crime', 'corporate crime', 'occupational crime', 'employee crime', 'avocational crime', 'techno-crime', 'computer crime' and 'folk crime' are all terms that are closely linked to the concept of white-collar crime.

There is little doubt, then, that 'white-collar crime' is an elusive term, but in Sutherland's own words, it was never 'intended to be definitive':

> My thesis, stated positively, is that persons of the upper socioeconomic class engage in much criminal behaviour; that this criminal behaviour differs from the criminal behaviour of the lower socioeconomic class principally in the administrative procedures which are used in dealing with the offenders; and that variations in administrative procedures are not significant from the point of view of causation of crime ... These violations of law by persons in the upper socioeconomic class are, for convenience, called 'white-collar crimes'. (Sutherland, 1949, p9)

For Sutherland, the concept served as an awareness-raising exercise that the critical gaze of criminology had not been looking in entirely the right places and was producing skewed data as a consequence. Sutherland's broad idea was that crime perpetration permeates all strata of society and cannot be solely explained with reference to individual pathologies or as a product of poverty and inequality. Thus, although crime statistics showed that much crime was committed by offenders from lower socioeconomic groups, this was very much an artefact of the way that the statistics were compiled and by the operation of the criminal justice system more generally, which was systematically administered by those from the upper socioeconomic classes and worked to protect their interests. In short, as Sutherland demonstrated, those of the upper socioeconomic groups were able to use various forms of capital at their disposal to escape, or avoid being embroiled in, the criminal justice system, a luxury not afforded to those at the bottom of the social pile.

Although widely celebrated, Sutherland's account was also the subject of criticism almost immediately. For Tappan, the term was no more than fashionable dogma and as a concept is almost impossible to operationalise, therefore making it of limited research value:

> Who should be considered the white-collar criminal? Is it the merchant who, out of greed, business acumen, or

competitive motivations, breaches a trust with his consumer by 'puffing his wares' beyond their merits, by pricing them beyond their value, or by ordinary advertising? Is it he who breaks trust with his employers in order to keep wages down, refusing to permit labor organization or to bargain collectively, and who is found guilty by a labor relations board of an unfair labor practice? May it be the white-collar worker who breaches trust with his employers by inefficient performance at work, by sympathetic strike or secondary boycott? Or is it the merchandiser who violates ethics by under-cutting the prices of his fellow merchants? (Tappan, 1947, p99)

Tappan went on to state that not all these acts are actually violations of criminal law and it is this issue that has perplexed scholars ever since. Indeed, this issue can also be extended to much state activity which, although not always criminal, is certainly of dubious morality – a point also noted by Durkheim in his questioning of the morality surrounding crime and its appropriate categorisation:

> Even when a criminal act is certainly harmful to society, it is not true that the amount of harm that it does is regularly related to the intensity of the repression which it calls forth. In the penal law of the most civilized people, murder is universally regarded as the greatest of crimes. However, an economic crisis, a stock-market crash, even a failure, can disorganize the social body more severely than an isolated homicide. No doubt murder is always an evil, but there is no proof that it is the greatest of evils. What is one man less to society? What does one lost cell matter to the organism? We say that the future general security would be menaced if the act remained unpunished; but if we compare the significance of the danger, real as it is, and that of the punishment, the disproportion is striking. Moreover, the examples we have just cited show that an act can be disastrous to society without incurring the least repression. This definition of crime is, then, completely inadequate. (Durkheim, 1893 [1964], p73)

Organised criminality

It is clear from the preceding discussion that there are a number of grey areas in the definition of corporate crime. A further aspect of this confusion is the way in which the term 'corporate crime' is used interchangeably with the term 'organisational crime'. 'Organisational crime', in turn, differs from 'organised crime' – the latter is usually related to the activities of organisations such as the Mafia and other 'gangsters'. This is not to say that links between corporate or organisational and organised crime are superfluous. Ruggiero (1996) has pointed to the various ways in which organised crime increasingly runs along the same principles as legitimate business. That is, 'it involves the same flexible consumer-oriented behaviour that characterizes all successful business behaviour' (Nelken, 2007, p738).

There is much misinformation surrounding the concept of organised crime, stemming from the often xenophobic historical accounts of its nature. We deal with these issues later in this chapter, as well as looking at attempts to produce a working definition, before moving on to consider the interplay between the state and organised criminality. It is important to reiterate that the state can be seen to be complicit in organised crime in two main ways: first, in the construction of the concept of organised crime and its associated features, which provide a platform for the proliferation of state intimidation against certain groups; second, through complicity and collusion in illegal acts.

Defining organised crime

There have been various attempts by statutory and non-statutory bodies to refine definitions of organised crime in order to try and establish some control over the problem. These included the: UK Threat Assessment to Organised Crime (UKTA) (2009-10); US Racketeer Influenced and Corrupt Organizations (RICO) Act 1970; European Union Joint Action (1998); and UN Transnational Organised Crime Convention (2000). According to Levi (2007), there is a fundamental tension in the development of all these, relating to whether the legislation should be broad enough so that the net is cast wide or whether it should be tightly drawn so that potentially key individuals and organisations are targeted. Levi (2007) revealed that broad legislation has been the preferred option. This makes it easier in many ways for law enforcement agencies to secure convictions, yet these convictions are less likely to snare the high-profile targets. The by-product of this is that it can make the problem of organised crime seem unwieldy and unsolvable and a catch-all term for quite disparate forms of criminality.

In trying to overcome some of the limitations pointed out by Levi, Wright (2011, p 9) turned to the European Commission (2001), which (in a joint statement with Europol) stipulated that organised crime must contain at least six of the following and all of the factors in italics:

> *Collaboration of more than two people*; Each with their own appointed tasks; *For a prolonged period of time*; Using some form of discipline and control; *Suspected of the commission of serious criminal offences*; Operating at an international level; Using violence or other means suitable for intimidation; Using commercial or businesslike structures; Engaged in money laundering; Exerting influence on politics, the media, public administration, judicial authorities or the economy; *Determined by the pursuit of profit and/or power*. (European Commission, 2001)

Article 2 of the UN Convention against Transnational Organised Crime, meanwhile, attempted to unpick some of the key terminology used in definitions of organised crime. Under these criteria:

> a) 'Organized criminal' group shall mean a structured group of three or more persons, existing for a period of time and acting in concert with the aim of committing on one or more serious crimes or offences established in accordance with this Convention, in order to obtain, directly or indirectly, a financial or other material benefit;
> b) 'Serious crime' shall mean conduct constituting an offence punishable by a maximum deprivation of liberty of at least four years or more serious penalty;
> c) 'Structured group' shall mean a group that is not randomly formed for the immediate commission of an offence and that does not need to have formally defined roles for its members, continuity of its membership or a developed structure. (United Nations, 2000)

Drawing on the policy statements of various national and international departmental and political bodies, including the Council of Europe, Europol, the Organised Crime Task Force and the Serious Organised Crime Agency (SOCA), Levi (2007) described organised crime as involving criminal actors and their activities:

> Nowadays, these for-profit activities would be taken to include drugs-trafficking; trafficking in people; extortion; kidnapping for profit; illegal toxic waste dumping (environmental crime); sophisticated credit card fraud; fraud against the European Union; smuggling to evade excise tax on alcohol and tobacco; intellectual property theft (video and audio piracy and product-counterfeiting); VAT evasion (including Missing Trader Intra-Community frauds) [and] corruption to achieve these offences. (Levi, 2007, p777)

The legislation on organised crime has developed alongside academic accounts of the phenomenon. Whereas illegal gambling was taken to be the epitome of organised criminality, it is clear from these representations that activities falling under the label are broader in scope. The origins of the groupings that are 'not randomly formed' (United Nations, 2000) and have continuity of membership are revealing. They are frequently considered to hail from outside the state or territory in which their criminal activity takes place. There is a footprint of xenophobia that has typified much of the discussion of organised crime, particularly in the US.

Albanese (2004, p9) noticed that 'separating fictional images of organised crime from the real thing has not been easy'. As an ideal type, organised crime is often taken to relate to the *modus operandi* of criminal syndicates such as the Mafia, Camorra, Triads and Yakuza and countless other organisations emerging from specific nation states. This, however, is based on a number of unsubstantiated assumptions such as the rigid hierarchy within kinship groups as the main form of organisation. Indeed, Levi (2007) suggested that:

> ... few academics have been convinced by the Valachi Boss – Underboss Soldier model – as a portrait of organised crime in America: although ... Jacobs et al (1994) and Jacobs and Gouldin (1999) put up a spirited defence that LCN (La Cosa Nostra) organized crime families do exist in cities like New York (as confirmed by wiretap evidence as well as informants), there is little confirmed evidence of such gang *domination* of criminal activity, even in north-east USA. (Levi, 2007, p778)

If not accepted wisdom, it is certainly established folklore that in the early to mid-20th century, organised crime was dominated by nationwide crime syndicates or family/kinship systems. This, according to Woodiwiss and Hobbs (2009), involved some collusion between government and popular culture in its depiction. With regard to the former, it was the work of the Kefauver Committee that consolidated the link, as its *Third Interim Report* asserted that America's organised crime problems 'were of Sicilian origin and that a nationwide crime syndicate known as the Mafia dominated gambling and other forms of organized crime in America' (cited in Woodiwiss and Hobbs, 2009, p111). This was supported by Bell's (1953) account close to the time, in which he stated that the Kefauver Committee concluded:

> There is a nationwide crime syndicate known as the Mafia ... Its leaders are usually found in control of the most lucrative rackets in their cities. There are indications of a centralized direction and control of these rackets ... The Mafia is the cement that helps to bind the Costello-Adonis-Lansky syndicate of New York and the Accardo-Guzik-Fischetti syndicate of Chicago. (Bell, 1953, p143)

Woodiwiss and Hobbs (2009) went on to show how such assertions were undermined from the outset on the grounds that the known illegal syndicates were from a range of nationalities and ethnic groups. That certain forms of organised criminal activity were taking place was not in doubt, but pigeonholing this as the work of one particular organisation was misleading. It is interesting to note that one key critic of such explanations was J. Edgar Hoover, the erstwhile director of the FBI. Hoover had always taken significant lengths to downplay the magnitude of organised crime in the US, seeing this as not a federal matter, but one that should be the responsibility of the individual states. Much gossip and rumour has surrounded this stance, with some claiming that Hoover's refusal to target organised criminality was down to the fact that he was being blackmailed by the mafia over his alleged homosexuality (Summers, 2012).

Yet despite Hoover's interventions, the Kefauver Committee was the recognised authority, whose findings became a vital resource for media commentators, thus consolidating it as the principal source of expertise on organised crime. Woodiwiss and Hobbs (2009, p111) argued that when discussing the true extent of the problem of organised crime in US society in the 1950s, there was little systematic research carried out on which to buttress the committee's recommendations. Drawing on Singer's (1971) investigations of the Kefauver committee and his notion of the 'vitality of mythical numbers', Woodiwiss and Hobbs neatly illustrated the paucity of evidence, showing how Singer found out that the committee had settled on a figure of $20 billion for the total worth of the gambling trade to the Mafia in America. For Singer, this figure was essentially drawn from thin air, encompassing approximately the median average of two other guesses by the California Crime Commission, who had said $12 billion, and Virgil Peterson of Chicago, who said $30 billion.

Such were the limitations of the evidence base on organised crime that partial truths obtained the status of cold, hard facts. Bell (1953) noted:

> Although it never showed up in the gross national product, gambling in the last decade was one of the largest industries in the United States. The Kefauver Committee estimated it as a twenty-billion-dollar business. This figure has been picked up and widely quoted, but in truth no one knows what the gambling 'turnover' and 'take' actually is, nor how much is bet legally (pari-mutuel, etc.) and how much illegally. In fact, the figure cited by the committee was arbitrary and arrived at quite sloppily. (Bell, 1953, p136)

That the Sicilian Mafia were 'known' to control the lucrative gambling trade in the US was a product of collusion between writers of crime fiction and non-fiction. With the benefit of hindsight, however, the latter has come very much to resemble a different manifestation of the former. Off the back of the Kefauver report, as Woodiwiss and Hobbs ascertain, popular crime writers now had a 'formula' for writing about organised crime:

> The trick was to describe briefly how a secret criminal brotherhood developed in feudal Sicily was transplanted to urban America at the end of the nineteenth century, and took over organised crime in the whole country. As 'proof', all that editors and publishers required were unrelated anecdotes about Italian–American gangsters, mostly from New York, with the narrative livened up with words like 'godfather' ... (Woodiwiss and Hobbs, 2009, p111)

In this way, the connection was further constructed, and it further established the Sicilians as an alien 'other', whose norms and values were in direct contrast to those of puritan America. By the end of the 1950s, there was almost a popular consensus on the validity of the theory that organised crime in America was the product of one single alien syndicate. That the kin of this syndicate happened to be on the opposing side to the Americans in the Second World War was also significant. In effect, the Mafia were taking on the hallmarks of a 'suitable enemy' (Christie, 1986).

The stereotype of organised criminality seems to be a hierarchical mafia-like organisation, engaging in various types of criminal activity. The final piece of the jigsaw was put in place when academic support of the thesis was published (see Cressey, 1969). Woodiwiss and Hobbs (2009, p112) commented on how Cressey suggested that the Mafia – or 'La Cosa Nostra' as he, following J. Edgar Hoover, referred to them – controlled a significant, even majority proportion of organised crime in the US. This, then, formed the basis of Richard Nixon's support for the US Congress implementation of the Organized Crime Control Act 1970, which 'increased federal jurisdiction over criminal activity to unprecedented levels' (Woodiwiss and Hobbs, 2009, p112). Among other things, this enabled law enforcement agencies to employ a number of techniques with increasing impunity. This included the widespread use of wiretaps and other close listening devices, and cultivating informants in a bid to ensure convictions. Allied to this were longer sentences and powers of asset seizure. Such tactics have been adopted in other areas and to even greater extremes, as we shall witness in subsequent chapters, raising the possibility that responses to organised criminality of various hues have in turn become criminal.

From the 1980s onwards, an increasing body of research has cast doubt on the ideal-type explanation for three, overlapping reasons:

- First, the extent to which the Mafia consisted of a national syndicate has been questioned. Woodiwiss and Hobbs (2009, p112) stated that the involvement of the mafia in organised crime is not in doubt. What is unclear is how this was manifest. It is likely that stories of blood oaths and inter-state alliances colluding to fix prices of goods and services were overestimated. The authors demonstrate this, by drawing on the work of Jacobs, 'a law professor in the Cressey tradition', who suggested that it is best to think of the *modus operandi* of the mafia as a 'melange of locally based crime families, each of which has exclusive jurisdiction in its territory' (Jacobs, 1999, p9, cited in Woodiwiss and Hobbs, 2009, p112).
- Second, Albanese (2004) drew attention to the range of technological advances (particularly in global communication networks and in transport), which resulted in organised crime becoming more transnational. This was, and is, epitomised by the international trade in narcotics and other forms of trafficking. As the research base on

organised crime developed over the course of the 1980s and 1990s, it became increasingly obvious that the perpetrators of organised crime encapsulated a much more diverse range of actors than just those of Sicilian descent (Albanese, 2004). The Mafia-thesis had thus become challenged as the dominant explanation of organised crime, not least because of the emergence of various other crime cartels with their origins in Latin America and elsewhere, and with the global movement of populations since the fall of the Berlin Wall and the collapse of the former Soviet Union. This did not radically alter the alien conspiracy, in that it was still maintained, particularly in political rhetoric. Organised crime was still, somehow, un-American and it was considered that it was forces 'outside mainstream American culture' that threatened 'otherwise morally sound American institutions' (Woodiwiss and Hobbs, 2009, p113).

- Third, from the 1980s onwards, and based on a number of empirical studies, a more varied picture emerged, which questioned the extent to which the criminality in question was, in fact, organised. Research findings have demonstrated that 'fragmented organisation structures' with 'a lack of centralised control and formal lines of communication' are more typical of the structures involved in non-conventional criminality than the close-knit, often family-based, kinship structures (Wright, 2011, p15). Reuter's (1983) study of illegal markets in New York showed how organised crime was sporadic and fragmented, and that the notion that drug markets were somehow mafia controlled was also the stuff of legend. This was not to suggest that Mafia organisations were not prominent, only that they were part of a kaleidoscope of an underworld characterised by networks of affiliations, whose complexity defies any form of neat description. By analysing police files as well as conducting interviews with 'insider' informants, Reuter demonstrated how the industries typically associated with organised criminality, such as 'bookmaking' and 'loan sharking', ran on the principles of economic laws rather than in the absence of a rule of law. In other words, Reuter found little evidence of intimidation and violence in the operation of the markets and an absence of mafia domination. On the contrary, the industries were characterised by high levels of competition, as the market facilitated easy entry for those wishing to start up.

Yet it was the alien syndicate explanation that remained remarkably persistent. Bearing remarkable resemblance to the construction of the 'drug problem' as a foreign menace, the history of organised crime in the US has also traded in xenophobia and misinformation. The parallels between the cases are striking and it is worth, therefore, pausing to consider the former in some detail. For Albanese (2004, p11), early explanations of organised crime in the US fell into the 'ethnicity trap', whereby 'organised crime is explained in terms of the ethnicity of its members, rather than by the organised criminal conduct itself'.

The origins of this are probably down to the trial and reporting of Joe Valachi, the first known mafia member turned informer, but also from the profile of the gangster era, where figures such as Al Capone and Charles Luciano enjoyed significant notoriety. Yet xenophobic and racist attitudes towards criminal activity have been prominent in US history, illustrated in the beliefs of Harry Anslinger and the way he shaped domestic – and then global – drug policy in the middle of the 20th century (Hari, 2015). The authority enjoyed by Harry Anslinger – the epitome of what Becker (1963) termed a 'moral entrepreneur' and described by Kinder (1981) as a 'bureaucratic cold war warrior' – as head of the Federal Bureau of Narcotics was unquestioned. Kinder illustrated how Anslinger's racism was an everyday part of his drug prohibition strategy. Blackman (2004) noted how Anslinger, with a budget of over a million dollars (a staggering figure considering this coincided with the onset of the Great Depression) and commanding in excess of 300 agents, set about gathering negative evidence on the use of marijuana, based on racist stereotypes of drugs.

The use of xenophobic rhetoric to show how drug use was anti-American helped Anslinger to portray marijuana use as un-American, arguing that the drug was used firstly by 'Ancient Egyptians, Persians and the military order of the Assassins', the purpose of which was 'to turn young men into swine and under the influence of hashish engage in violent and bloody deeds' (Blackman, 2004, p16). Anslinger backed up his assertions with carefully selected evidence suggesting that it was proven that marijuana use led to 'rape, insanity, the murder of children, young people, parents and police officers'. The frequent inclusion of these stories in the popular press meant that they became 'everyday' accounts of drug use (Becker, 1963). Anslinger's personal favourite was the story of Victor Licata, a 21-year-old Mexican living in Florida, who murdered his family with an axe after, according to Anslinger, smoking marijuana. McWilliams (1991, p367) commented that:

> Anslinger's testimony was factual, but it was not complete. He did not mention that eleven days after the murder a psychiatric examination report appeared in the *Tampa Times* confirming that Licata was criminally insane and subject to 'hallucinations accompanied by homicidal impulses'.

> Authorities also concluded that that his insanity was 'most likely inherited and was not marijuana induced' ... (cited in Blackman, 2004, p16)

One key outcome of Anslinger's crusade was the witch-hunt of known users of marijuana. These often included high-profile, black jazz musicians, most notoriously Billie Holliday, whose music frequently made reference to the more positive aspects of the drug's effects (Shapiro, 1999; Hari, 2015).

The authority enjoyed by Anslinger meant that he was a US representative on UN drug control bodies from 1930 to 1970. Such was Anslinger's political sway that he was able to influence policy on a global scale via the passing of the 1961 United Nations Single Convention on Narcotic Drugs. The 1961 legislation had marijuana placed in the category of the most dangerous drugs. This was primarily achieved by 'withholding statistics and manipulating records to establish the US government's position that marijuana caused insanity' (Blackman, 2004, p17). A similar claim is made by King (1972, p71), who argued that Anslinger 'opposed all public discussion aimed at enlightening Americans about the drug problem' or exploring alternatives to his overbearing policies, on the grounds that anything akin to education or open-mindedness would aggravate the situation and stir the potential curiosity of potential new victims. Those who questioned his bureau were denounced as 'self-style experts', 'bleeding hearts', 'axe-grinders' and 'meddling do-gooders'. Throughout the 1960s, the 'gateway' theory being championed by Anslinger – that marijuana caused further experiments with the illicit, and could even lead to murder – became widely discredited as marijuana consumption became more widespread with no discernible rise in the murder rate. The notion that marijuana use was distinctly anti-American had by now become engrained in the consciousness of many Americans, who found comfort in the fact that such a threat to their society was 'alien' in origin.

In his review of the North American literature, Albanese (2004) demonstrated how the literature remains divided on the issue of definitions, with certain authors focusing on the structure (and membership) of organisations and what binds them together (the organisation) and others concentrating on illegal activities (the crime). Reuter's 'disorganised crime' thesis has undoubtedly influenced more recent perceptions of this issue. For Reuter, the benchmark for an 'organisation' is that pursued by legitimate, industrial operations. In other words, one might expect illicit organisations acting in an organised manner to aim for the most efficacious means of controlling markets – the establishment of cartels buttressed by violence. As Wright (2011) explained, Reuter was influenced by the work of Scherer (1970) in this respect, and while he did find evidence of violence in much criminality in New York at the time, this was not for the end of maintaining business supremacy. For Wright (2011), Reuter is overprescriptive in his notion of what constituted an organisation. Wright maintained that although cartels were not established, this does not, by definition, negate 'organisation' and that organisations can be perceived in different ways.

Drawing on the work of Scott (1992), Wright showed how organisations can be organised along the lines of (a) rational systems, (b) natural systems and (c) open systems. Rational systems are those with highly formalised structures. These are akin to Reuter's understandings of organisations. According to Wright (2011, p17), they have 'formal systems of rules that set out the authority and competence of all members at all levels'. What is more, they do this to maximise their potential to meet specific targets. Natural systems, meanwhile, 'are characterised by complexity in goals and the means of achieving them' (Wright, 2011, p 17). They are often composed of informal structures and relationships between their members. It is a shared ethos, vision and/or set of values that binds these collectives together; profit-seeking is not always the *modus operandi*. Alternatively, open systems are 'characterised by a high-level of interdependence between themselves and the environment within which they operate' (Wright, 2011, p17-8). Furthermore, they are characterised by contingency, which means that a plurality of relationship models may exist at any one time. The absence of a rigid structure means that such organisations are able to adapt to times of flux, especially when the period of change is rapid. It is quite possible that many crime groups are organised on the principles of an 'open system' and able to capitalise on new opportunities brought about by changes in technology as in the various kinds of cyber-crime in society. Opportunities for moving goods and services more efficiently around the globe, as globalising processes have presented such possibilities, may also be capitalised on (as the discussion of drug trafficking in Chapter Four demonstrates).

Wright further maintained that Reuter did find an amount of coordinated, 'managerial activity' that was persistent over time. In this way, the groupings were consistent with the descriptions of organised crime employed by the UN and by Europol. Although the true picture is blurry, more recently something of a consensus has emerged. Even though criminal activity is frequently violent and unlikely to be modelled specifically on the inherently rational structures of legitimate enterprise, there is still much about it that is highly ordered. Or as Wright (2011, p18) elaborated: 'contra Reuter (1983), the rejection of industrial organisation as the working paradigm for organised crime does not mean that it is simply "disorganised"'. Perhaps the reality of the situation is that increasing specialisation in response to new criminal opportunities has become a defining tenet of non-street-based criminality:

> Criminal networks are becoming more fluid, extended and flexible, in part due to the use of specialist 'service providers' to assist with money laundering, logistics, documents and other enablers. Meanwhile, the increased availability of information technology has both facilitated various crimes and spawned new forms of criminal activity. (SOCA, 2006-7)

For von Lampe (2008, p8) organised crime can be analysed on three levels as it relates not only to (a) criminal activities and (b) organisations, but it also constitutes (c) a 'systemic condition', whereby power is concentrated in an 'underworld government and/or in the alliance between criminals and economic elites'. We return to the systemic condition in Chapter Four, by considering the overlap between organised crime and state elites in the international drugs trade.

For now, as Albanese (2004, p10) advised, it is possible to produce a working definition of organised crime based on common features identified in the literature: 'Organised crime is a continuing criminal enterprise that rationally works to profit from illegal activities that are often in great public demand. Its continuing existence is maintained through the use of force, threats, monopoly control and/or the corruption of public officials.'

The origins of academic debate on the nature of organised crime are difficult to trace. Although a prominent amount of literature on the issue emerged in the United States towards the middle of the last century (for example Bell, 1953), recent commentators have pointed out how the US 'can claim no legitimacy whatsoever when it comes to the analysis and control of organised crime' (Woodiwiss, 2003, p6). Central to Woodiwiss's thesis was the view that the US-based analyses had tended to operate with a narrow understanding of organised crime, equating it with a national Mafia or with Mafia-style organisations, despite the uncertain evidence for this. In addition, he also suggested that there had been an uneasy relationship in the US between federal law enforcement agencies and organised criminal syndicates, whereby the former have often turned a blind eye to the activities of the latter, who have often exploited other less powerful groups in American society, such as the African American poor. To compound this further, it is precisely these groups that have, as we have seen, been conspicuously in the gaze of US law enforcement agencies, particularly in the last thirty to forty years (Wacquant, 2001, 2009). It is, therefore, in the corruption of officials that the overlap with state and corporate criminality is at its most visible (Whyte, 2015a).

Whereas the US has a distinct history of organised crime, European history has its own trajectory. Returning to von Lampe's (2008) typology, much discussion in British criminology has concentrated on the types of crimes committed, with specific emphasis on how the crimes labelled under organised crime often involve a degree of 'craft' or 'professionalism' and thus can be made distinct from more street-based offending (for example Croall, 2008). Much has been written about professional crimes and criminals with detailed studies forthcoming on the activities of certain gangs in the UK, most notoriously the Krays. In the early to middle decades of the 20th century, organised crime in Britain tended to be very localised and gendered. It mainly consisted of 'firms' from the larger cities, who were engaged in creating monopolies for protection rackets, gambling and prostitution, among other things. According to Hobbs (1994), these organisations tended to be headed by 'elder statesmen', who were like underworld dignitaries with a specific behavioural code based on respect for territory.

There are two things to note here:

- First, this composition of organised criminality began to change in the 1980s with the rapid expansion of drug markets (see Chapter Four). It was thought, although it is the matter of some conjecture, that the drugs trade brought with it higher levels of violence.
- Second, the situation in mainland Britain did diverge from the situation in Northern Ireland, where organised criminality went hand in hand with paramilitary activity. Indeed, continuing the theme of the overlap of criminal enterprises, in a series of articles, Silke (2000a, 2000b) and Horgan and Taylor (1999, 2003) have carried out detailed analyses of the funding streams of paramilitary organisations in Northern Ireland. On the Loyalist side, Silke noted how extortion and blackmail of businesses formed a key funding stream alongside robberies, tax fraud, illegal drinking clubs, smuggling, counterfeiting and drug dealing. On the Republican side, kidnapping for ransom, armed robbery and extortion were widely employed. It has long been a source of contention as to whether

Republican groups participated in drug dealing. Horgan and Taylor (1999, p25) concluded that there was considerable evidence that 'it is highly unlikely' that the Provisional IRA is, or was, involved in direct drug trading. That said, there was also considerable evidence that it did have a sophisticated finance department and was engaged in widespread organised, corporate criminality such as money laundering and lending (Horgan and Taylor, 2003).

Corporate criminality

Despite the pioneering work of thinkers such as Sutherland (1937, 1949), it has only been in the last thirty years or so that awareness has grown on the issue of corporate crime and its associated terms – economic crime, business crime and white-collar crime (for example Clarke, 1990; Ruggiero, 1996; Slapper and Tombs, 1999; Croall, 2001; Nelken, 2007; Benson and Simpson, 2009). This is partly because of a growing appreciation of the issue in both academic and popular circles. Yet what is apparent from this literature is the degree of overlap in the terminology used and the difficulties in distinguishing corporate crime from white-collar crime.

Following Benson and Simpson (2009), one way out of the morass is to state that white-collar crimes are crimes usually committed by middle-class or 'high-status' actors acting independently against an employer. This could take the form of theft or embezzlement, for instance. Corporate crime, meanwhile, relates to crimes carried out by individuals or organisations for the intended benefit of the organisation. From this we arrive at the working definition that corporate crimes are committed by employees on behalf of a corporation, serving the interests of the corporation. They include infringements not just dealt with by criminal courts or the police but also by other agencies such as the inspectorate of taxes or the health and safety regulators, who carry out actions through civil proceedings (Slapper and Tombs, 1999).

In many ways, this is an arbitrary distinction and it is not shared across the entirety of the literature. Nor is there any rationale in the official crime statistics for making such a separation. Bearing these caveats in mind, we maintain that typical corporate crimes are generally economic in nature, and they can also often involve bribery, corruption, espionage, theft of intellectual property, arson, price fixing (by the establishment of cartels), fraud, false labelling, misleading advertising, abuses of the patent system, violation of employment regulations, non-compliance with health and safety guidelines and regulations and pollution and environmental destruction. This, however, is not an exhaustive list.

Deaths and injuries are also significant outcomes of forms of corporate criminality. Nowhere is this better illustrated than in the work associated with Gary Slapper, Steve Tombs and Dave Whyte around the broad area of 'safety crimes' and their overlap with corporate criminality (for example Slapper and Tombs, 1999; Slapper and Tombs, 2002; Tombs and Whyte, 2007, 2010). In terms of mortality rates, human costs of workplace deaths clearly outweigh homicide. Other dangers, such as unsafe products, pollution, unfit food production and their effects on others, are also responsible for the increasing strain placed on healthcare systems in most nations and, as ever, the impact is felt most severely on the disadvantaged, who do not have the resources to act upon their victimisation but who are often also blamed for their situation.

Consistent with all forms of non-conventional criminality, deciphering the true extent of corporate criminality is beset with problems. According to the latest (and last) report (2013-14) from the National Fraud Authority, 'the threat from fraud continues to have a damaging effect on our country with estimated losses of £52 billion per annum (National Fraud Authority, 2014). A further reason for the difficulties in understanding the extent of corporate criminality concerns the role of the mass media. In their famous study, *Manufacturing Consent*, Herman and Chomsky (1988) make a similar point, noting how the mass media in the United States promoted a particular uncritical account of events, aggravated by the fact that much source material cited emanated in the first instance from government sources and, was therefore, little more than propaganda.

For Slapper and Tombs (2002, p107-8), the documentation of crime via the mass media represents and reinforces the 'dominant social constructions of what constitutes the crime problem in contemporary Britain'. In this analysis street crimes thus come to the fore and corporate criminality becomes hidden. There has been some dispute in the literature over this. Nevertheless, Box (1983), as we have witnessed, referred to the 'collective ignorance' of corporate crime in his review of the literature on the topic. The origins of this ignorance lay in the way that corporate crime is 'rendered invisible by its complex and sophisticated planning and execution'. This is buttressed by insipid law enforcement and prosecution as well as by the absence of a critical gaze from the media. Box pointed out how popular crime-based television series at the time, rarely focused on the issue of corporate crime and when the crimes of the more powerful middle classes are considered, it is usually 'the stereotypical conventional crime of murder'. In short, for Box, there is collusion between the media and the state over the representation of corporate crime.

Levi (1987) put forward an alternative explanation, suggesting that there is no conspiracy or collusion between big business and news organisations to hide the truth from the public. In the era of digital social media, Box's argument may seem like something of an oversimplification, but for Levi it was also true of the 1980s. One way this can be illustrated is to draw on Habermas's (1987) concept of 'juridification'. This is the increasing reach of law and regulation into social life to the extent that they affect everyday interactions (Cochrane and Talbot, 2008). One manifestation of the process has been the creation of a new and developing vocabulary associated with corporate criminality. Phenomena such as 'disaster litigation' and 'corporate manslaughter' have become enshrined in law and also in common parlance. The knock-on effect is that with public recognition comes media reportage and increasingly corporate criminality has become fodder for 'Fleet Street'. One can again refer to the issue of MPs' expenses here, but since the 1980s corporate crime has gained more media attention. During this decade this became an additional focus of the media, sitting alongside the more usual concentration on street crime. The change in emphasis arose in part because of a number of spectacular frauds and scandals in the City of London and a number of high-profile disasters leading to major loss of life through alleged criminal neglect of safety regulations and standards. Into the 1990s, the collapse of Barings Bank from insider trading on the futures market by Nick Leeson was indicative of the former and the Zeebrugge ferry disaster was indicative of the latter. In effect, these often spectacular acts served to make more visible the once invisible forms of criminality.

Slapper and Tombs (2002), for their part, suggested that Levi's words of caution were worth heeding, but that his characterisation of Box's account was misleading. They concluded that:

> ... despite the fact that some corporate crimes are represented via mass media, this does not obviate, and in some ways actually reinforces, the fact that dominant representations of crime, law and order issues within various forms of media have the effect of obscuring or removing corporate crimes from such discussions. (Slapper and Tombs, 2002, p108)

This is very much the line we pursue here. In a shorter piece, Tombs and Whyte (2001) went beyond the claim that the reporting of conventional crimes far outnumbers that of corporate crimes in both the tabloid and broadsheet press. Whereas conventional crimes are frequently the stuff of sensational headlines and often accompanied by graphic and spectacular images (Chibnall, 2004), the same is almost never true of corporate crime, which tends to be 'buried' in more specialist business and finance sections of papers (Marsh and Melville, 2009, p97). What is more, in these circumstances the criminality associated with certain acts – for instance health and safety transgressions leading to the loss of lives – is downplayed and the accidental nature of incidents is reinforced.

The utility of statistics: crimes against business

Fitting in with the themes highlighted at the outset, it has become increasingly clear that the crime complex outlined by Garland (2001) operates decidedly unevenly and that those at the bottom of the social heap are not as capable as those at the top in terms of protecting themselves from the scrutiny of their behaviours. Nowhere is this more apparent than when we try to ascertain the extent of corporate criminality from the official crime statistics.

Within criminology, corporate crime remains a specialist area of interest (De Keseredy, 2011). This may be a product of the gaze being applied to the young, disenfranchised, male, urban poor, but it could also be a product of the way that corporate criminality in its various guises is policed and regulated by specialist agencies that extend beyond the police. In the UK, the now defunct Serious and Organised Crime Agency (SOCA) was established for this reason. This amalgamated the National Crime Squad and the National Criminal Intelligence Service (once part of the Customs and Excise). SOCA, as described by Carrabine et al (2009, p343), was an FBI-style law enforcement agency. Along with the British Transport Police, the Ministry of Defence Police, the Royal Parks Police and the UK Atomic Energy Police Authority, SOCA operates as a group of organisations that have monopolised the legitimate use of force in civil society. All of these are specialist forces that operated with the backing of the state to provide them with their legitimacy and authority in relation to their particular private space, but the data generated by these special agencies do not constitute the official crime statistics, as these are the collated data of recorded crimes supplied by the 43 police forces of England and Wales along with the British Transport Police (Home Office, 2011)

Taking our cue from Slapper and Tombs (2002), it is clear that even the most superficial assessment of the category of 'notifiable offences', which makes up the bulk of the official statistics,[1] shows the extent to which it is skewed towards conventional rather than corporate criminality. However, mirroring the discussion on the role of the media, there has been some change in this respect. Isolating two kinds of criminality – violent crime and fraud – the definitions currently employed by the Home Office (2011) in its crime reporting consolidate the hidden nature of corporate crime. With regard to *violent crime*, police recorded data refer to violent crime generally in terms of 'violence against the person' and this contains 'the full spectrum of assaults, from pushing and shoving that result in no physical harm, to murder'.

For the British Crime Survey (now the Crime Survey for England and Wales), violent crime refers to:

- *Wounding*: the incident results in severe or less serious injury, e.g. cuts, severe bruising, chipped teeth, bruising or scratches requiring medical attention or any more serious injuries.
- *Assault with minor injury*: an incident where the victim was punched, kicked, pushed or jostled and the incident resulted in minor injury to the victim, e.g. scratches or bruises.
- *Assault without injury*: an incident (or attempt) where the victim was punched, kicked, pushed or jostled but resulted in no injury.
- *Robbery*: an incident in which force or threat of force is used in a theft or attempted theft.

These primarily relate to what are frequently referred to as 'interpersonal crimes'. In terms of the offender to victim relationship, the data are presented in the following categories:

- *Domestic violence* comprises wounding and assaults which involve partners, ex-partners, other relatives or household members.
- *Stranger violence* includes wounding and assaults in which the victim did not have any information about the offender(s), or did not know and had never seen the offender(s) before.

---

[1]   Here we refer to the official crime statistics as the Police Recorded Data and the data generated by the Crime Survey for England and Wales, hitherto the British Crime Survey.

- *Acquaintance violence* comprises wounding and assaults in which the victim knew one or more of the offenders, at least by sight. It does not include domestic violence.

Here stranger violence could, if interpreted as such, include some forms of corporate crime. One obvious example here would be environmental crimes, but the reality is that this category does not relate to corporate activities.

In terms of *fraud and forgery*, while it is acknowledged that the more accurate data here will be derived from other sources, the bulk of the data concentrate on bank or credit card theft and subsequent misuse; it is, therefore, fairly low-level criminality. It is interesting to consider, however, what Slapper and Tombs (2002) noted in this category back in 2002:

> *Fraud and Forgery* will include some corporate crimes, namely frauds not treated by the Serious Fraud Office. This category is broken down into 'Fraud by a company director', 'False Accounting', 'Other Fraud', 'Forgery, or use of false drug prescription' and 'Other Forgery'. Yet this does not allow us to say anything useful about corporate crime. First, while the two categories 'Other Fraud' and 'Other Forgery' are by far the biggest in terms of numbers of offences, these are the most general and far too vague to be of any use. Second, there is no means of making the distinction based upon this data between occupational and organisational crime. (Slapper and Tombs, 2002, p106)

If, in 2002, we could not say anything useful about corporate crime from the official statistics, then more recently this has been consolidated. From 2006, with the passing of the Fraud Act, fraud was defined as an indivdual or persons:

> ... dishonestly making a false representation to obtain property or money for themselves or another. Recorded crime statistics are collected for: fraud by company director; false accounting; other frauds; failing to disclose information; abuse of position; obtaining services dishonestly; making or supplying articles for use in fraud; possession of articles for use in fraud; bankruptcy and insolvency offences; forgery or use of false drug prescription; other forgery and vehicle/ driver document fraud. (Home Office, 2011, p29)

The Home Office document noted how changes in recording practices to 'a per-account' basis from a 'per-transaction' basis have reduced the number of recorded incidences a year. This, in turn, has reduced the bureaucracy in recording crimes of fraud for both the police and card suppliers. The change has also, according to the Home Office, 'focussed police efforts' and increased greater cooperation between police and financial institutions to combat the problem. It is then suggested that 'the victims of fraud are mainly commercial organisations'. This is a telling point for our purposes, as it switches emphasis of the corporation from perpetrator to victim. This switch was consolidated, as the Fraud Act 2006 created the (now defunct) National Fraud Authority (NFA). The Home Office report emphasised that:

> During 2009/10 the NFA opened a single national point of reporting for a wide range of frauds, in particular those arising from the growing use of the internet and email. This new means of reporting sits outside the police service as a call centre (Action Fraud) with an associated online reporting tool. It is expected that over the next year much of the fraud currently reported to the police will, instead, be reported directly to Action Fraud. At the same time the NFA and police have jointly established a national fraud intelligence bureau (NFIB) to receive reports from action fraud as well as those from the banks and other financial institutions and to analyse them to identify positive investigatory opportunities, which will then be referred to individual forces to follow up. (Home Office, 2011)

These later developments are typical of the processes surrounding white-collar crime identified by Sutherland (1949). One might be forgiven for wondering how it is that business has been constructed as the victim in corporate criminality, when a series of scandals directly and indirectly had an impact on all consumers, such as: the mis-selling of pensions as significant sums were transferred from public to private providers in the 1980s, the mis-selling of endowment mortgages, the mis-selling of Personal Payment Protection Insurance (PPPI) (Tombs, 2015), the rigging of the LIBOR rate (Christensen, 2015) and the role of Private Finance Initiatives (Mair and Jones, 2015). These issues also demonstrated how much white-collar crime is not defined as crime per se, nor is it handled by criminal courts as breaches of criminal law. Indeed, different types of regulation are used for different types of corporate crime. In addition, it is necessary to point out that crime legislation places much more emphasis on crimes committed *against* business rather than *by* business. Again, this significantly underplays the true extent of corporate criminality, and renders the official data of limited value.

State collusion, condolence and acquiescence: the case of corruption

It is pertinent to point out at this stage that crimes such as corruption could quite easily be incorporated under the 'state crime' label. Although usually associated with various forms of violence, and often political in nature, state crime can also be driven by economic imperatives. Corruption serves as a prime example.

As Williams (2010, p747) remonstrated, corruption has traditionally been viewed as an illegitimate abuse of a position of power, frequently for personal gain, and as a result it is usually seen and tried as an individual offence. However, 'much corruption occurs in order to further the interests or goals of the state or is tolerated by state organs because there is some state or institutional interest being served'. It can also occur at every level of government, permeating individuals and collectivities. Williams pointed out that the link between corruption and state crime is convoluted. This is primarily a product of the fact that much state crime is politically motivated and has been committed to promote or fulfil particular goals, such as the promotion of democracy (or free-market capitalism depending on one's stance). Yet this in itself can be counter to democracy through its 'undermining of accountable government' (Williams, 2010, p 747).

One need only think of the CIA funding of the Contras in Nicaragua and their guerrilla warfare against the democratically elected Sandinista government as an example. It is this and other issues pertaining to international drug control that we turn to in Chapter Four.

Summary

By highlighting the various challenges involved in operationalising the concept of state crime, we have potentially set ourselves up to fail in our quest to discover its nature and extent. In this chapter we have been duty bound to return to the issue of terminological overlap and uncertainty. This is something that characterises most of what Braithwaite (1989) has termed crime in 'suites'. We have demonstrated how the tensions and turmoil surrounding the conceptual confusion in non-conventional criminality can be traced back to the work of

Edwin Sutherland. It has been necessary to cover in depth the nature of both corporate and organised crime for two reasons:

- First, unpacking their nature and reach provides a useful frame of reference for understanding the extent and nature of state criminality.
- Second, understanding the contexts in which corporate and organised crime occur and have been described and explained provides the platform for showing how, in frequent scenarios, criminality spans all categories and thus makes it difficult to control.

Yet we are still left with terminological uncertainty. As a way out of the impasse, Friedrichs (1996) has championed a new way of depicting white-collar crime, which he refers to as a multi-stage approach, but which demonstrates the fuzzy boundaries between the kinds of criminality under the microscope in this book. For Friedrichs, there are three distinct aspects to this form of criminality:

1) *The polemical/presentational stage* – which equates to Sutherland's view that criminality cannot solely be explained in terms of poverty and that elite groupings in societies are equally, if not more, criminogenic. This is polemical in the sense that it challenges a more 'mainstream' view that crime is generally committed by the mainly young, male, urban poor and that their crimes involve robbery, burglary and other kinds of often violent disorder. In the polemical stage, the concept is kept brief in order that it avoids the scourge of convolution, which undoubtedly dilutes the potency of the message.

2) *The taxonomic/typological stage* – which seeks to outline the various manifestations of the concept and the key components that make up its constitution. According to Friedrichs (2009, pp 426-7), the key components are:
   a. the setting in which the activity takes place (in an organisation, government agency, professional service etc.) and the level that this happens (individual, workgroup, organisation)
   b. the status/position of the offender (wealthy, middle-class, chief executive, employee)
   c. the primary victims (general public or individual clients)
   d. the principle form of harm (e.g. economic loss or physical injury).

   From this, Friedrichs was able to list the various manifestations of white-collar crime and provide a justification for each:

i. Corporate crime – illegal and harmful acts committed by officers and employees of corporations to promote personal or corporation interests

ii. Occupational crime – illegal or harmful financially driven activity committed within the context of a legitimate, respectable occupation

iii. Governmental crime – an associated form of white-collar crime that relates to the activities of a government, it's agencies or its offices

iv. State-corporate crime, finance crime and techno-crime – hybrid forms of white-collar crime thought to synthesise corporate and governmental crime or corporate and occupational crime; finance crime relates more to crimes committed in the domain of high-finance (e.g. in investment banking and securities; techno-crime takes place at the juncture between 'high technology' and other forms of white collar crime.

v. Enterprise crime; contrepeneurial crime and avocational crime – often crime that takes place at the margins of what is generally thought to be white-collar crime; enterprise crime refers to cooperative enterprises involving syndicates of legitimate and illegitimate business – generally referred to as organised crime; contrepreneurial crime refers to swindles, frauds and scams that take the appearance of legitimate business activity and avocational crimes are crimes often committed by white-collar workers outside an organisational setting, but which may be inspired by the organisational context, for instance, tax evasion or insurance fraud.

3) *The operational/heuristic stage* – which refers to the attempt to provide a working definition of the concept on which empirical research can be conducted.

Friedrich (1996) pointed out, white-collar crime serves as a 'catch-all' term for a range of generally socially harmful activities. In pointing this out, Friedrichs has thus provided us with useful typology, which highlights the many difficulties we have had to face in delineating state crime and, indeed, why there is a need for consideration of a social harm perspective in our definition. For Friedrichs, though, a further key aspect to white-collar criminality centres on the particular violation of trust in the act. In white-collar criminality, this often extends beyond specific individuals (as with interpersonal violence, for instance) to eroding faith in entire systems or institutions. In effect, the numbers of those violated by white-collar offences can be huge and can undermine the public's feelings in the very institutions that govern society – one might think here in terms of the UK parliamentary expenses scandal of 2009 (Whyte, 2015b).

While it is thought that white-collar crimes are unique because they tend to be regulated and monitored by agencies other than the police, it is unclear whether this is because they are technically not 'crimes' or that they are not crimes precisely because they fall under the remit of other agencies. Where one falls in this debate is a probable reflection of where one stands in debates over whether social phenomena can be seen in realist terms or as social constructions. It is not our intention to settle these scores here. For now, suffice to say that the blurry distinction between legality and illegality is one that scholars of all kinds of non-conventional criminality have to grasp.

Ruggiero (1996) demonstrated as much when acknowledging that a high proportion of what is labelled 'organised criminality' is a routine aspect of business life. We stand in firm agreement, but take the analysis further, suggesting that much criminality takes place in the context of routine public administration. For Ruggiero (and for us) there needs to be some integration in the study of organised and corporate crime witnessed by the increasing criminal diversification and increasingly capitalistic enterprises of more renowned organised crime syndicates such as the Mafia and Camorra in Italy or the Triads in China. The same applies to state crime which, due to collusion of various kinds, cannot be understood without some discussion of corporate and organised criminality, however defined. We devote the following chapter to this enterprise.

State crimes can often have single, recognisable victims whose victimisation is severe, but one further point worthy of note, and one that supports the organisational deviance perspective, is that many variants of state crime are long-running episodes of criminality. As a result, explanations of state or organised crimes which equate the activities with a 'few bad apples' have shortcomings, in that one would expect the criminality to cease once those individuals move on (Kauzlarich et al, 2001). As there is clear crossover in explanations pertaining to the possibility of state crime and organised crime, it should be of little surprise that there are examples of criminality that span the two and other (somewhat arbitrary) categories. Indeed, the mix of state-organised deviance and corporate criminality is brought into focus in the case of HSBC money laundering and Mexican drug trafficking (Monaghan, 2014), described in the introduction to this book (Chapter One).

In the following chapter we pick up the theme of overlapping boundaries, by considering the interplay between the international illicit drugs trade and criminality, including terrorism.

FOUR

Drugs and thugs: examples of organised crime, state collusion and limited responses

Chapter Three introduced some of the key themes and issues surrounding corporate crime, organised crime and their cross-fertilisation with state crime and immorality. We demonstrated how the construction of organised crime and, by association, drug prohibition has facilitated opportunities for state crimes through the enforcement of legislation.

In this chapter we develop this idea in two main ways:

- First, via a closer examination of international drug control legislation and the way that this has been selectively enforced over time. This often means that states have been in breach of human rights legislation or have perpetrated (to use Kauzlarich et al's (2001) terminology) international to domestic governmental crimes, whereby criminality takes place beyond the geographic confines of a state, but entails actions in contravention of international criminal, regulatory or procedural laws or codes. We also consider the role of the state in facilitating drug trafficking, drawing on evidence from broad case studies on US foreign policy. In particular, the activities of the US government and its agencies in Central America in the 1980s will be discussed. Government collusion at worst or government toleration at best (from the perspective of prominent politicians and government officials) will also be highlighted.
- Second, we discuss the limitations of the state in controlling elite crimes. This is demonstrated in a discussion of the extent of international drug trade and trafficking, before we consider the response to the issue in the form of 'narco-terror'. This is where the 'war on drugs' meets the 'war on terror', and where the former has been fought sporadically to accommodate the goals of the latter, often to the detriment of both, and has created a situation where state criminality is justified on the grounds of exceptionalism.

The selective enforcement of international drug legislation: state collusion, inactivity or ineptitude?

Three main conventions govern UN drugs policy:

- the 1961 Single Convention on Narcotic Drugs
- the 1971 UN Convention on Psychotropic Drugs
- the 1988 United Nations Convention against Illicit Traffic in Narcotic Drugs and Psychotropic Substances (the Vienna Convention).

The 1961 Convention attempted to standardise the control of narcotics across nations, so that certain drugs could be used only for scientific, medical and, in some cases, industrial purposes. This was achieved by arranging drugs into schedules and applying appropriate controls based on notions of harm and toxicity. Any article in contravention of the convention was a punishable offence, with a custodial term for serious breaches. Crucially, this meant that recreational drug possession invariably became a criminal offence within the signatory states (Barton, 2003). The 1971 UN Convention on Psychotropic Drugs focused mainly on hallucinogens and stimulants but also restricted the use of many drugs for scientific or medical purposes and some were outlawed totally, not even for use in medicine. The 1988 United Nations Convention against Illicit Traffic in Narcotic Drugs and Psychotropic Substances (the Vienna Convention) was used to smooth out some legal grey areas raised by the 1971 Convention regarding offences of possession, purchase and cultivation for personal use.

It is generally contended that global drug prohibition can be traced back to the 1909 Shanghai drug conference 'World War on Opium Traffic', which eventually resulted in the Hague Convention of 1912. As Mills (2003, p166) noted, the 1912 convention aimed to: 'enact effective laws or regulations for the control of the production and distribution of raw opium and coca leaves so that there will be no surplus available for purposes not strictly medical or scientific'. Overall emphasis was placed on the repression of the abuse of drugs such as morphine, opium and cocaine, by placing laws and regulations on the manufacturing countries. Fortson (2005) added that the 1912 Hague Convention proposed that the possession and sale of opiates to unauthorised persons should become punishable offences. It is here where the accretion of prohibition as the favoured regulatory stance can be identified.

Since its establishment in the aftermath of the Second World War, the United Nations (UN) has overseen the development, implementation and monitoring of international drug controls through its various agencies. It has become accepted wisdom that the US has been the driving force behind global drug prohibition through its self-given function of global police force (Andreas and Nadelmann, 2006). Windle (2013) demonstrated, however, that although the US has undoubtedly been responsible for 'globalising' prohibition, it is the case that prohibitionist policies had organically developed across Indochina hundreds of years before the passing of the Harrison Act 1905, which served as the first major piece of legislation outlawing heroin and cocaine in the United States.

Nevertheless, it was in the aftermath of the Second World War that the globalisation of prohibition gathered momentum. Bewley-Taylor (1999) suggested that during the post-1945 era global drug policy was heavily influenced by the then head of the Federal Bureau of Narcotics, Harry Anslinger – the embodiment of what Becker (1963) termed a 'moral entrepreneur'. Anslinger's understanding of the 'drug menace' was heavily xenophobic, portraying marijuana use – his primary concern – as anti-American. Blackman (2004, p16) observed how, in various key publications, Anslinger managed to portray marijuana use as a foreign threat, by arguing that the drug was used first by 'Ancient Egyptians, Persians and the military order of the Assassins', the purpose of which was 'to turn young men into swine and under the influence of hashish engage in violent and bloody deeds'. Consequently, marijuana was reified as a 'killer weed'. Anslinger backed up his assertions with carefully selected evidence suggesting that it was proven that marijuana use led to rape, insanity, and the murder of children, young people, parents and police officers. The frequent inclusion of these stories in the popular press meant that they became 'everyday' accounts of drug use (Becker, 1963).

It was such 'evidence' that came to influence international drug control. It can be seen in the way that cannabis resides in Schedule IV, the most restrictive of all the UN schedules, containing substances seen to be 'liable for abuse' and without therapeutic benefits. The UN approach has successfully labelled cannabis, cocaine and opium as dangerous for individuals and morally harmful for society. According to Bewley-Taylor (1999, p185), the UN is heavily influenced by the United States in such matters, to the extent that the latter has effectively used the former 'in an effort to create a prohibitive norm for international drug control' and to 'promote its own moral value system towards drug use in other nations'. This model has traditionally been premised on the hitherto utopian dream of creating a drug-free society.

The goal of the drug-free society is a useful tool for the UN, because of its relative simplicity on paper. In the opinion of Blackman (2004):

> any nation which is seen as rejecting such a clear and apparently straightforward policy against drugs is condemned and publicly presented as immoral, criminal and a threat to the 'free-world'. This criticism quickly turns to enforcement as nations are required to accept international drug policies. Countries which are reluctant to agree to American policy wholesale experience withdrawal of financial support from the World Bank, IMF and WHO. (Blackman, 2004, p50)

The danger here is that this, in turn, could lead to the collapse of an economy and to widespread political and social turmoil.

One of the determining features of the UN approach to drug control, then, is the fact that drug legalisation is precluded for all those who are signed up to the conventions. There is some irony to the fact, therefore, that some of the biggest challenges to the existing global drug policy infrastructure are coming from within the United States, as cannabis legalisation has been implemented at the state level in both Colorado and Washington and with others legislating to follow suit. This legalisation policy covers the recreational use of cannabis. The legal use of cannabis for medical purposes is also a widespread practice across the US.

Although the UN Conventions do allow for a range of interpretations and are being challenged like never before, in many ways they are sacrosanct. Despite this, the legislation enacted in various jurisdictions has been enforced unevenly since inception. Nowhere is this more apparent than in the history of the US war on drugs and its interlinking with other aspects of foreign policy. Before we go on to illustrate these points in relation to the concept of 'narco-terror', it is worth pausing to consider how other political and economic imperatives have shaped discretion in the administration of global drug policy.

We have demonstrated in earlier chapters the many difficulties entailed in providing definitions of state crime, not least among these being that the kinds of criminality in question merge with, overlap or consist entirely of other kinds of criminality. Corruption provides a useful example. As we have witnessed, corruption has traditionally been viewed as an illegitimate abuse of a position of power frequently for personal gain, and as a result it is usually seen and tried as an individual offence. However, 'much corruption occurs in order to further the interests or goals of the state or is tolerated by state organs because there is some state or institutional interest being served' (Williams, 2010, p747). It can also occur at every level of government, permeating individuals and collectives. Williams went on, though, to point out that the link between corruption and state crime is convoluted. This was primarily a product of the fact that much state crime is politically motivated and has been committed to promote or fulfil particular goals, such as the promotion of democracy (or free-market capitalism, depending on one's stance) in the world where it is yet to flourish. In this respect, von Lampe (2008) showed how organised criminal groups also serve quasi-governmental functions, by enforcing the rules and regulations in markets and communities where the state is weak. Yet, it is also the case that this in itself can be counter to democracy, as it has the effect of undermining accountable government. One need only think of the CIA funding of the Contras in Nicaragua and their guerrilla warfare against the democratically elected Sandinista government and the collusion between US authorities and leading organised crime figures or the control over the activities of the communities exerted by Loyalist and Republican paramilitary groups in Northern Ireland (see Chapter Seven) as examples here.

Arguably, one of the most notorious expositions of the interlinking of states with organised criminal groups comes from the work of Alfred McCoy. McCoy's (1991) thesis, originally published in 1972, outlined the way in which US intelligence agencies, throughout the period described as the globalisation of drug prohibition, had backchannels to criminal organisations, with the CIA (in its current guise) and the Office for Naval Intelligence being complicit in the international drugs trade as a means of helping to reinforce right-wing governments. In other words, they were providing illicit support for US allies in the war against communism. The pattern for such relationships was established sometime before as US intelligence chiefs secured the release from custody of the notorious gangster Charles 'Lucky' Luciano in a bid to bolster national security during the Second World War. In return, Luciano supplied information to the authorities, to aid with the pending invasion of Sicily. Referring to Luciano's release, Cockburn and St Clair (1998, p134) stated:

> US intelligence agencies arranged for the release from prison of the world's preeminent drug lord, allowed him to rebuild his narcotics empire, watched the flow of drugs

into the largely black ghettos of New York and Washington D.C. escalate and then lied about what they had done. This founding saga of the relationship between American spies and gangsters set patterns that would be repeated from Laos and Burma to Marseilles and Panama. (Cited in Blackman, 2004, p35)

The consolidation of 'drugs problems' in black ghettos has been an enduring legacy of the US 'war on drugs' (Tonry, 1995; Wacquant, 2009), yet for McCoy (1991), the twin fears of communism and drugs dominated US foreign policy thinking in the middle decades of the 20th century. Mirroring the contemporary situation, where communism has been replaced by 'terror' (to be discussed later), the 'war on drugs' was always subservient to the geo-political goals of curbing the spread of communism and promoting democracy around the world. The particular brand of democracy, as manifest in the Marshall Plan, is often seen as the promotion of free-market capitalism rather than democracy per se (Klein, 2007).

Examples abound of the inconsistent application of the US 'war on drugs'. Certain countries have been (and are) condemned for allowing the cultivation of substances or movement across their borders. Peru, Bolivia, Columbia and Mexico are prime examples. In other countries, such as Pakistan, the cultivation of drugs has been 'passively' ignored when an alternative US national interest is at stake. Thus, support and cooperation in the war on terror is often felt to outweigh the national interest in controlling narcotics. In other circumstances, the drug trade in a nation state is 'actively' ignored or even encouraged. According to Blackman, but echoing McCoy:

> A key accusation is that American foreign policy has supported right-wing insurgency movements against democratically elected governments where there have been large scale violations of human rights ... Corrupt regimes are propped up by the US government with financial and material assistance to military dictatorships providing they improve investment opportunities for American corporate companies. US foreign policy turns a blind eye to drug production where the profits finance the regime it supports. (Blackman, 2004, p35)

Perhaps the prime example of the selectivity of US foreign policy can be seen in Nicaragua in the 1980s and relates to what is widely known as the Iran-Contra affair or 'Irangate'. Drawing on the definitions raised in previous chapters, this represents a form of 'international to domestic' state criminality and culminated in a political scandal that engulfed the Ronald Reagan administration.

The Nicaraguan Contras were a right-wing insurgency group in conflict with the democratically elected left-wing Sandinista government. The Sandinistas had close ties with both the Cubans and the Soviet Union. The US supported the right-wing insurgency group, who were at the time actively engaged in cocaine trafficking into the US. Doig (2011, p51) provided a succinct account of the affair. For Doig, the US National Security Council had tried to initiate talks with moderate members of the Iranian regime partly in the hope of being able to avoid Soviet influence in the succession of power from Ayatollah Khomeini and partly to engage the Iranians to help free US hostages being held by the Iranian-supported Lebanese group Hezbollah.

Ronald Reagan advised the National Security Council that he would sanction moderate arms sales to Iran, provided it would not tip the balance in the ongoing Iran–Iraq war. The Democrats controlled Congress and had previously outlawed any arms sales. At the same time, Reagan wanted to secure funding for the Contra insurgency in Nicaragua, but this had also been banned by the Democrats in Congress. The figure in charge of both the US–Iran and US Contra relations was Oliver North in his role as head of anti-terrorism policy. He oversaw various shipments of arms to Iran, via Israel, with the profits being hidden in Swiss bank accounts. Some US$12 million was then channelled from the accounts to the Contras in direct contravention of Congressional law. In terms of the hostage situation, the policy was a disaster, as three were released but another three captured. More tellingly, though, was that the policy called into question the US government's official position of not negotiating with terrorists, which Hezbollah were seen to be. The scandal emerged from a leak inside Iran to a Lebanese newspaper. The 'Irangate' affair was the subject of three major inquiries, from the last of which the 1987 Congressional report (United States Government, 1987) condemned Reagan for not knowing the true extent of what was happening while subsequently creating a situation in which members of the National Security Council were seen to be carrying out his orders.

The international market for illicit drugs

The Iran-Contra scandal gives some indication of the financial extent of the global narcotics market. Often seen to be the quintessential form of organised criminality, there is some debate in the literature about the illicit drugs trade operating with business-like principles. Indeed, contrary to dramatised accounts of drug markets in the media, researchers have stressed how it is not uncommon for the amount of violent criminal activity associated with the drug trade to be kept to a minimum by those involved, in order to avoid the unnecessary gaze of law enforcement agencies (Coomber, 2010).

Drugs are usually viewed as addictive substances deleterious to one's health, but when viewed in socioeconomic terms, they are 'principally valued commodities, moreover, valued commodities with a global reach, and drug markets are a classic form of "commodity chain"' (Pearson, 2007, p76-7). The commodity chain is the connective path from which goods travel from producers to consumers. Drug dealers, when looked at as a socioeconomic phenomenon, are entrepreneurial in their pursuit of profits. They operate like many other 'legitimate' small businesses. This is not the picture that emerges in the media, in particular the tabloid press. It is also difficult to portray drug users as such, in light of the illegal (and thus hidden) nature of their activities.

Although it is difficult to conduct research on drug trafficking, it is nonetheless considered to be one of the planet's most lucrative 'businesses' and almost definitively the most lucrative illicit business (Ruggiero and South, 1995). Despite difficulties of measurement, the United Nations *World Drug Report* (United Nations Office on Drugs and Crime (UNODC), 2005) stated that the size of the illicit global drugs market was an estimated US$321.6 billion. When measured at retail prices, this is higher than the GDP of 88% of the countries of the world (Paoli et al, 2010, p627). The United Nations do not release these figures every year, but there is no reason to suspect that this figure has dramatically risen or fallen in recent years.

Attempts to monitor the size of the global drugs trade in terms of turnover of the contemporary drugs market were also produced in 2005 and are listed in Table 4.1. These are based on figures from the UNODC (2005). As Paoli et al (2010, p627) stressed, these figures are at best 'guesstimates' as the data needed for such calculations depend on receiving accurate data on production, prices, quantities exported, quantities imported and quantities consumed. Ultimately, the task of finding accurate measures of all these is hindered by the illegal (and therefore hidden) nature of the market.

Table 4.1: Annual turnover of global drug markets (UNODC, 2005)

Drug type	Turnover in US$ billion
Cannabis[1]	142
Cocaine	71
Opiates[2]	65
Synthetic drugs[3]	44
All illicit drugs	322[4]

Notes: [1] This is the combined total of cannabis herb (often referred to as 'marijuana') US$113 billion and cannabis resin (often referred to as 'hashish') US$29billion. [2] Including raw opium and its derivatives including heroin. [3] Usually referred to as 'amphetamine-type stimulants' this includes methamphetamine, amphetamine and ecstasy. [4] This was the figure for 2003 for retail sales. The figure for wholesale revenues was US$94 billion and US$13 billion in producer sales.

Source: adapted from Paoli et al, 2010, p627

A further way of analysing the range of the illicit global drugs market is to offer further points of comparison:

> Compared with global licit exports or global gross domestic product (GDP) (US$ 7,503bn and US$ 35,765bn respectively in 2003), the estimated size of the global illicit drug market may not seem very large. Total retail drug expenditures correspond to 0.9 per cent of global GDP and drug wholesale revenues represent 1.3 per cent of global export measures. The size of the global illicit drug market is not insubstantial, however. Illicit drug wholesale revenues account for 14 per cent of global agricultural products and are much higher than the export value of most licit agricultural commodities. (Paoli et al, 2010, p627-8)

To fully understand why the supply of illicit drugs is such a lucrative business, it is necessary to consider the demand for the products. The UNODC (2014, p1) estimated that in 2012 between 162 million and 324 million people had used an illicit drug in the past year. Cannabis users constituted by far the largest proportion of global drug users, but the number is decreasing in many Western countries with the exception of the US (Caulkins et al, 2014). Although there is an increasing proportion of drug users in Asia, the bulk of the market activity is concentrated in the traditionally high-demand areas of North America and Europe.

Drug smuggling and trafficking is not new, but this public problem has been exacerbated by changing global processes over the last few years of the 20th century and into the 21st. Various national barriers were broken down to allow easier access for the movement of people, goods and services across the globe. One obvious manifestation of this is the reduction of customs and excise controls across states in the European Union. According to Seddon and colleagues (2008, p823):

> A major feature of late modernity has been the extension and expansion of global flows and networks of capital and commodities. Although this is not an entirely new development ... globalizing processes have developed with a distinctive intensity and rapidity in the late twentieth century ... One consequence of this has been that the transit and trafficking of drugs as commodities have been made much easier and this is a key factor behind their greatly increased availability in Britain in recent decades. To take the example of heroin, an illegally imported supply only began to appear in Britain in the late 1960s and it was not until the early 1980s that this started to expand significantly as new supply routes opened up from south-west Asia. The 1980s heroin 'epidemic' simply would not have been possible without this transformation in global trafficking patterns. (Seddon et al, 2008, p823)

It is almost impossible to explain the myriad of ways in which drugs leave source countries and arrive in their destinations. So inevitably, what follows draws on some of the more established practices and procedures in the global cocaine and heroin markets. This is not to downplay the significance of the trade in the major synthetic drugs, new psychoactive substances and cannabis across the world. In addition, the subsequent focus on 'narco-terror' concentrates on its origins in South America and its grim manifestation in present-day Afghanistan. However, as the discussion of production and supply of cocaine and heroin shows, the drug trade is truly global and as a consequence, the drug war and its associated impacts are felt keenly across the globe (Chouvy, 2011; Klantschnig, 2011; Felbab-Brown, 2011).

The international heroin trade

Heroin is a semi-synthetic opioid. It is synthesised from morphine, which is in turn a derivative of the opium poppy. Over the past 30 years, there has been significant movement in the hotbeds of opium production. At one time, the Golden Triangle of Burma (Myanmar),

Cambodia and Laos were responsible for a significant proportion of global heroin production (Chouvy, 2011; Felbab-Brown, 2011), but this has since been replaced by the Golden Crescent of Afghanistan, Pakistan and Iran (Friesendorf, 2007). There were two main reasons for this:

- According to Felbab-Brown (2011), the fall of governments in Vietnam and Laos disrupted the supply chain stemming from the region to the US.
- Additionally, a prolonged drought in the 1970s and 1980s curtailed supply-side operations in the region at precisely the point where demand was increasing across the globe. Afghanistan proved to be a logical destination for an emerging opium trade on the grounds that throughout the 1970s its agricultural and irrigation infrastructure had been decimated by the Soviets, leaving large swathes of the Afghan populace barely able to subsist. Opium harvesting does not require advanced irrigation and agricultural infrastructure, and thus proved the ideal crop to cultivate. In doing so, participation in the illicit opium trade was a lifeline to large segments of the population (Felbab-Brown, 2011).

As should be apparent, this displacement process is, therefore, complex and is rarely a sole consequence of supply-side enforcement interventions. There is some dispute among scholars as to the efficacy of supply-side control strategies such as crop eradication and interdiction. Windle and Farrell (2012) demonstrated this through a discussion of the 'balloon effect', which refers to the way control merely serves to displace the illicit trade without impacting on its size and scale. For Windle and Farrell (2012), this downplays the fact that control efforts can lead to a 'diffusion of benefits', which provides a counter-argument to the standard view that control leads to displacement. While not denying that displacement occurs, Windle and Farrell (2012) suggested that displacement effects can have a mirror reading. To give one example, the most widely discussed effect of drug control is spatial displacement, whereby control efforts in one location do not eradicate the trade, but relocate it elsewhere. What this downplays, according to the authors, is that this process of relocation can have a significant knock-on effect for drug producers. As they pointed out, forced relocation of drug trafficking means additional costs are incurred and often a new *modus operandi* (with new kinds of risk assessment) are needed. In other words, traffickers were not located in the new location in the first place for good reason. This could be because the new locations and routes are not as financially viable for infrastructural and temporal reasons, and control can, therefore, impact upon trade.

Although drug control strategies can have some impact on the markets, it is also the case that where heroin is concerned, these efforts have probably not had net gains over time in terms of curbing supply. To summarise the current situation, Paoli et al (2010, p 630) noted that since 1980 Afghanistan and Myanmar have been responsible for between 70% and 95% of global heroin supply. Recent data from the UN *World Drug Report* (UNODC, 2014, p x) demonstrated how for three years running, the area used for opium cultivation has increased and, as of 2013, stands at 209,000 hectares out of a global area of 296,720 hectares. There is also evidence that heroin of Afghan origin is reaching new parts of the globe. After 2001, Afghanistan accounted for an estimated 92% of global heroin production, meaning that of the entire drug-producing countries it is the Afghan economy that is 'by far the most dependent on the illegal drug industry' (UNODC, 2014, p x). Numerous facts and figures can be used to support this assertion. For instance, 14.3% of the total Afghan population (3 million people) are directly involved in opium cultivation, with many hundreds of thousands indirectly profiting from the trade. This could be via cultivating opium poppies, refining the raw opium into heroin or trafficking.

Paoli and colleagues (2010, p 635) showed how there are two primary routes for the trafficking of heroin into Europe:

- The oldest and largest is the 'Balkan route', which primarily caters for the market in Western Europe. Prior to the fall of the Eastern bloc, this route navigated from Turkey through Bulgaria and the former Yugoslavia. Physical proximity to producer (farm-gate) countries and to final destinations explains the significance of Turkey as a strategically important transit route for the smuggling of heroin. Via its land boundary with Bulgaria, Turkey borders the EU, and most of the heroin from Afghanistan makes its way into Europe through Turkey. Turkey also has a porous land border with Iran, which in turn shares a border with Afghanistan. Since 1989, various options have opened up for traffickers, including northern and southern routes. There is one route that operates via sea through Greece, Albania and into southern Italy. This is unique, as in other cases heroin is transported over land. The UNODC (2014) highlighted how the Balkan route remains a key transit pathway for Afghan heroin into the markets of Central and Western Europe, but a shrinking cohort of drug users in this region may account for its declining significance. Meanwhile, the southern route is, according to estimates, expanding to cater for the still substantial markets that exist in this subregion.

- A newer 'Silk route' emerged around 1991 to supply the emerging market in post-communist Eastern Europe and central Asia. Paoli et al (2010, p636) also revealed the way in which Tajikistan 'now rivals Afghanistan for the unenviable title of the country most dependent on the illicit drug industry'. Furthermore, Paoli and colleagues also stipulated that there is a tangible change in the way that heroin is being smuggled into central Asia, with larger shipments increasingly replacing the smaller amounts trafficked by so-called 'mules'.

In terms of other regional supply routes, the US and Canada are mainly served by Mexico and Colombia, whereas the African market is served by heroin smuggled out of Afghanistan through Pakistan and India. Meanwhile, the Chinese, East Asian and Australasian markets are supplied by sources in South-East Asia, although Paoli et al speculated that the decline in heroin production in the region may mean that Afghanistan becomes the main source for these areas too.

In addition, a 2008 report by the UNODC highlighted how 'the total export of opiates to neighbouring countries, estimated at about US$4bn, added over 50 percent to Afghanistan's legitimate GDP' (cited in Paoli et al, 2010, p630). In Afghanistan, it is particularly difficult to measure this accurately, as decades of war have ravaged its national economic infrastructure, its industrial sector and other service sector activities. Moreover, no detailed economic records were compiled by the Taliban when they were in control from 1996 to 2001. It is the best guess that money from the opium trade buttresses the licit agricultural sector. One way would be through the purchasing of fertiliser for the intensive opium cultivation that takes place in Afghanistan. Profits from opium sales are also more than likely used to pay for the growing of wheat, the country's main legal crop. What is clear, however, is that sustained attempts to eradicate the opium poppy in Afghanistan, if successful, could have a serious knock-on effect for the legitimate economy which, if it happened, would have serious implications for Afghanistan's future development as a stable economy and nation (Felbab-Brown, 2010, 2011). The eradication of opium in Afghanistan could also have other unintended consequences, as we shall see.

Cocaine production and supply

Globally, cocaine cultivation takes place in a relatively small geographical area, centred on three countries in the Andes, South America: Bolivia, Peru and Colombia. Ecuador is also thought to be a producer as it is the natural habitat to the coca plant, of which cocaine is a derivative. According to the UNODC (2007, p70), cocaine trafficking is increasingly taking on a globalised appearance. Thus in 2005, '131 countries reported seizures of cocaine, from 69 countries two decades earlier now nearly 80 per cent of all countries reporting drug seizures report some seizures of cocaine'. Although this is the case, the bulk of cocaine arriving in any destination has its origins in Colombia.

More recently, data from the UNODC (2014, p34) indicated how globally the availability of cocaine seems to be on the wane. By association, the geographical area where the coca bush is cultivated has, as of December 2012, declined to 133,700 hectares – the lowest level since estimates were first collated in 1990. Felbab-Brown (2010) demonstrated how this could, in part, be down to changes in the Peruvian political landscape and the decoupling of cocaine as a funding stream for various insurgent and belligerent groups such as the Sendero Luminoso (Shining Path). Despite this, it can be claimed that the intensity of cultivation could be increasing, in that 671 tonnes of cocaine were seized across the globe in 2012 in comparison to 634 tonnes the previous year.

The major markets for cocaine are still the 'traditional' ones of the US and Western Europe, although the UNODC (2014) refers to emerging markets in Brazil and Oceania. The US market is served in two main ways:

- The first is the overland or aerial route through Central America to Northern Mexico, where it is broken down and smuggled across the approximately 4,000 km US–Mexico border.
- The second route is over water where Colombian and Mexican smugglers have set up various smuggling operations through the Caribbean to reach the mainland US (predominantly Florida). According to the UNODC (2007, p73-4), the US Department of State estimated that between 74% and 90% of the cocaine which enters US soil is transited through Mexico. This proportion is believed to have increased over the last few years as the Caribbean route has declined. The main entry point into the US is over the border between Mexico and southern Texas, followed by southern California, Arizona and western Texas.

Elsewhere, Klantschnig (2011) has noted the way in which West Africa has become a key staging post in the international cocaine (and heroin) markets. He stated that, according to Interpol, somewhere in the region of 330 tonnes of cocaine are routed through West African ports, particularly transit hubs in The Gambia, Guinea and Guinea Bissau. For Klantschnig, this smuggling is mainly carried out by foreign operators from Europe and/or Latin America seeking to benefit from the lucrative European markets.

Research conducted into the traffickers themselves demonstrated the heterogeneity of traffickers as a group. For instance, in Colombia they came from a range of socioeconomic backgrounds and their 'businesses' range in size, scale and networks (Zaitch, 2001; Felbab-Brown, 2010). In February 2011, the technological skill and wherewithal of international drug traffickers was again made clear as the Columbian navy seized a US$2 million submarine, which was believed to have been built to smuggle cocaine into Mexico. The submarine was undoubtedly sophisticated and capable of travelling at 30 feet below the surface of the water. It was also fortified with sophisticated navigational technology, enabling the crew to travel long distances, including the 2,000–3,000 km journey from South America to Central America (BBC, 2011).

Paoli et al (2010, p636) showed how larger quantities of cocaine are transited by sea using ordinary cargo vessels. They pointed out that 'smugglers are highly creative' in the way that cocaine is disguised or hidden in other legitimate goods, ranging from other foodstuffs to white goods and electrical equipment. Sometimes private yachts are used for the transit of cocaine.

Fleetwood (2011), meanwhile, revealed the use of drug mules, who are employed to carry smaller quantities of drugs over international territories. Mules are individuals who generally carry drugs paid for by someone else. They may or may not operate in groups. The main techniques employed are: 'body packing', whereby drugs are stored on the body; ballooning, where drugs are concealed in the body, for instance by wrapping them in latex and then swallowing them; and stowing them away in luggage (Paoli et al, 2010, p637). Drug mules engage in high-risk activities. Recent research has shown that they are typically the focus of the gaze of law enforcement agencies, despite being responsible for the importation of relatively small amounts of drugs.

'Narco-terror'

It is widely thought that drug money is used to corrupt officials at all levels and across a range of institutions such as the police, the military, the judiciary and politics. According to Rolles et al (2006, p11) illegal drug profits, it is estimated, pay for the US$100 million each year it takes Colombian cartels to bribe officials. Furthermore, Grabosky and Stohl (2010) asserted that the profits generated from the international narcotics trade help to fund paramilitary groups, guerrilla groups and terrorist organisations across the world, although this is notoriously difficult to prove and far from straightforward (Felbab-Brown, 2010). In recent years this connection has been referred to as 'narco-terror'.

Usage of the term 'narco-terror' dates back to the 1980s. Grabosky and Stohl (2010, p7) pointed out how the phrase was developed to describe the practices of various Latin American drugs cartels. As we have seen, it is now widely acknowledged that the Nicaraguan Contras engaged in drug trafficking, particularly the trafficking of cocaine, to finance their insurgency. By way of a further explanation, Björnehed (2004) suggested that:

> The term narco-terrorism was first used to describe campaigns by drug traffickers using terrorist methods, such as the use of car bombs, assassinations and kidnappings, against anti-narcotics police in Colombia and Peru ... Narco-terrorists in this context refers to individuals such as the drug lord Pablo Escobar from the Medellín cartel in Colombia and other members of drug cartels, mafia or other criminal organisations, whose actions were defined as the attempts of narcotics traffickers to influence the policies of government by the systematic threat or use of violence. (Björnehed, 2004, p306)

On one level, the concept of 'narco-terror' provides a challenge for scholars of state crime on the grounds that, by their very nature, the targets of terrorist incidents are states. In effect, the concept highlights how states can be both the victims and the perpetrators of state crimes (see Chapters Six, Seven and Eight for a further discussion). What is clear is that the literature on terrorism and its perceived links with organised criminality share some similarities with the literature on the problems of organised crime and its origins. These are almost always depicted as a 'foreign problem'. One is reminded of the deliberations of the Kefauver Committee when reading the literature on the nature of contemporary terror organisations (Chapter Three).

In this respect, Björnehed (2004) pointed out how knowledge of trafficking routes has been put to good use by terror organisations. She demonstrated how the Balkan route has declined in popularity as a primary transit route for narcotics entering Europe because of the war in the former Yugoslavia. In its place a so-called Northern route has emerged:

> allowing narcotics to move from northern Afghanistan through the Central Asian states, predominantly through Tajikistan, Turkmenistan and Uzbekistan, passing into the Caucasus and/through Kazakhstan into Russia, the Baltic states and on toward Scandinavia and Europe. The active use of these routes was apparent following 9/11 when terrorists were smuggled out of Afghanistan through Iran, Central Asia, and Ukraine. (Björnehed, 2004, p310)

Björnehed demonstrated that the connection between the illicit drug trade and terror organisations was not merely financial, yet it is precisely the issue of financing terror that is used most often to consolidate the connection between organised criminality – often in the form of drug trafficking – and terrorism.

There is little by way of agreement on what actually constitutes the crime–terror axis. Yet as Hutchinson and O'Malley (2007) uncovered:

> Paragraph 4 of UN Security Council Resolution 1373 (28 September 2001), notes 'with concern' the close connection between international terrorism and 'illicit drugs, money laundering, illegal arms, trafficking, and illegal movement.' Drug trafficking, for example, is now thought to be the largest source of income for both international organized crime groups and terrorists. (Hutchinson and O'Malley, 2007, p1096)

Yet as Grabosky and Stohl (2010, p7-8) maintained, the connection between the two concepts is far from clear. On the one hand, there are terrorists who turn to criminality to support their cause, more often than not for financial reasons. On the other hand, however, there are also those whose criminality becomes linked to terror. Grabosky and Stohl proceeded to demonstrate the variety of ways in which terror is financed, replete with examples of each. It is interesting to note that whereas billions of dollars are spent by governments and private industry in the global prevention of terror, the actual perpetration of acts, even the most spectacular ones, is by comparison relatively cheap. Thus the authors commented that 'the total cost of the coordinated attacks of September 11, 2001 was approximately US$500,000' (Grabosky and Stohl, 2010, p47–8). Certainly, al Qaeda in its formative years was funded by the family wealth of Osama bin Laden (Burke, 2004); by contrast, much IRA activity in Northern Ireland was heavily dependent on the criminal enterprise of its various members and various levels of the organisation (Coogan, 1995).

As Table 4.2 demonstrates, there are various ways in which terror and/or political violence and criminality can converge, a point reinforced by Levi (2007, p792) with his assertion that 'almost any licit or illicit income-generating activity could finance terrorism'. Levi made a number of interesting observations about the financing of terrorism, suggesting that because terrorism is not homogenous, one must be circumspect about assigning a price tag to its cost. He went on to stress that 'weaponry used for rocket attacks in the Middle East' requires significant expenditure, as does the financing of financial gifts given by Hezbollah to Lebanese residents who had their homes destroyed by Israel in the 2006 war. He also said that prior to 9/11, al Qaeda's largest expense was 'support for the Taliban', which was thought to be in the region of US$20 million per year.

Table 4.2: Means of financing terrorism

Crime type	Brief explanation	Example(s) (organisation and/or country of origin)
Extortion (revolutionary taxes)	Extortion refers to system of crime whereby a premium is paid by individuals and/or organisations to other individuals and/or organisations to both obtain contracts and to avoid harm from regulators and enforcement personnel. A *New York Times report* (Conde, 2004) shows how in the Philippines the New People's Army earned around US$745,000 from mining, agricultural, telecommunications and transportation companies in the first six months of 2004. Companies who refused to pay were usually attacked, which often meant that vital resources essential to the running of the business were destroyed.	Maoists (India); New People's Army (Philippines); FARC (Colombia)

Crime type	Brief explanation	Example(s) (organisation and/or country of origin)
Sale of pornographic material	Bhaumik (2005) notes how armed groups in Tripura (a north-east Indian state) are coercing some tribal women and men into making pornographic films, which are then distributed in India and other countries in the region. The money raised is used to finance the NLFT separatist movement.	National Liberation Front of Tripura (NLFT) (north-east India)
Narco-terrorism	Although a contested term, this generally refers to the selling of illicit narcotics to finance terror activities.	Colombia; Burma; Afghanistan
Ransom kidnapping	This usually involves the kidnapping of foreign tourists and aid workers in order to obtain a ransom. In recent years, this has become a prominent tool adopted by Somali pirates off the east coast of Africa.	FARC (Colombia); Abu Sayyaf (Philippines); violent jihadists (India)
Misuse of charities		Saudi Arabia; Philippines; India; and the West in general
Intellectual property piracy	This generally involves the illegal production of DVDs and video-games	Tri-Border area of South America
Robbery, car re-birthing, general crime		Global
State sponsorship	The Iranian state is known to have provided financial backing to Hezbollah	Pakistan; Iran
Human trafficking	Various groups have engaged in human trafficking and smuggling because it can yield significant profits and carries a reduced chance of detection than drug supply. Human trafficking can involve the supply of 'workers' for the domestic sex industry, but it can also involve moving terror suspects around the globe	Global
Cigarette smuggling	In 2004 it was reported that a Hezbollah cell in North Carolina in the US took advantage of the tax difference on cigarettes sold in North Carolina and Michigan to net over US$7.9 million (Dishman, 2005, p246).	Hezbollah
Legitimate business		Al Qaeda (global)

Source: adapted from Dishman, 2005; Hutchinson and O'Malley, 2007; Levi, 2007; Grabosky and Stohl, 2010

Grabosky and Stohl (2010, p48) disclosed how terrorists often resort to 'conventional criminality' to finance operations, suggesting that 'ransom kidnapping' was a preferred method of various European terror organisations in the 1970s and 1980s, a point supported by Ruggiero's (1996) work in the area. Developments in technology yield opportunities too. The Tamil Tigers of Sri Lanka engaged in credit card and ATM fraud as a key fundraising scheme (Hutchinson and O'Malley, 2007, p1097). Ultimately, as Hutchinson and O'Malley pointed out, 'drug trafficking has been placed at the top of the hierarchy of illegal money raising activities for terrorist groups', but 'robberies, extortion, kidnapping, and arms trading and smuggling are not far down the list'. According to Björnehed (2004):

> [t]he total annual amount of finances emanating from the narcotics trade is estimated to be between US$500 billion-US$1.5 trillion ... Of this total revenue the Executive Director of the UN Office on Drugs and Crime (UNODC), Antonio Maria Costa stated in February 2004 that approximately US$2.3 billion end up in the hands of organisations like al-Qaeda ... In addition, weapons, mainly small-scale arms, became more easily available after the dismantling of the Soviet Union and security protocols and physical security of storage facilities deteriorated ... As a result, a large quantity of weapons circulated on the illegal market and fell into the hands of clandestine organisations at the end of the Cold War ... Drugs and weapons are of interest to both narcotics organisations and terrorist groups for military and economic purposes thus making the illegal arms and drug market a common area of interest where they would have a strong presence. (Björnehed, 2004, p310)

In short, financing terror can be expensive, but not always. Hutchinson and O'Malley (2007) warned that 'this type of analysis can do little more than provide a list of what crimes terrorists have engaged in so far'. It is highly likely that there is not a preferred option for terror organisations, but that criminality is primarily a product of what Pfeffer and Salancik (1978) called 'resource dependency theory'. Broadly speaking, this theory asserted that in order to survive, organisations have to cultivate relationships with others. These relationships may be predatory or symbiotic (Felbab-Brown, 2010). In a predatory relationship, the organisation seeks to somehow colonise or control its collaborators through the exercise of power; this can be physical, economic or ideological. In a symbiotic relationship, attempts are made to demonstrate how relationships between organisations can be mutually beneficial.

For Björnehed, these early definitions unnecessarily polarise those deemed to be criminals and those deemed to be terrorists. Drawing on the work of Makarenko (2004), she suggested that a more useful conceptual device is to consider organised crime and terrorist organisations existing along a continuum. Björnehed (2004, p309) pointed to the similarities between the various illegal organisations, as 'both are forced to operate in the more murky part of society, thus coming into contact or even sharing a common turf'. From Björnehed's perspective, this meant that their various activities may overlap, as might the tangible and intangible resources they need or use.

While undoubtedly the acts and actors at times overlap, there are also elements of each that do not necessarily constitute the other. Mirroring some of the literature explaining the actions of drug dealers, most criminals (like drug dealers) wish to operate under the radar of agencies of state control. This is also true of terrorists, despite their ultimate goal to seek conflict with the state and its agencies. But even then, they do not want their activities to be hindered in the short term.

In addition, it is fair to say that most acts of terrorism involve a non-trivial degree of criminality not just in the perpetration, but often in the preparation. Grabosky and Stohl (2010, p6-7) provided a useful synopsis of the crime–terror interface, which covers a range of ground and shows how the lines of departure between the two become even more blurred when the criminality in question is of the organised variety. Table 4.3 highlights examples of organisations, to show how their *modus operandi* blurs the boundaries between the two phenomena. Of course, even this description requires some unpacking, as terms such as 'political violence' are used interchangeably with 'terrorism', which will not be to everyone's satisfaction. This reiterates our discussion in Chapter Three on the problem of terminological overlap.

Responding to (narco-) terrorism: pre-emption and exceptionalism and the limitations of the state

Although complex, it is still a widely accepted assertion that 'drug trafficking is thought to be the largest source of income for both international organized crime groups and terrorists' (Hutchinson and O'Malley, 2007, p1096). Combating drug trafficking can be useful in the war on terror, in that most terrorism is funded from involvement in the trafficking of narcotics. Certain policies and technological

Table 4.3: The crime–terror nexus: blurring the boundaries

Terrorists engaging in 'conventional criminality'	Organised crime gangs engaging in political violence
• Drug trafficking is carried out by various organisations including Al Qaeda, the Kosovo Liberation Army and Islamic Movement of Uzbekistan • Al Qaeda engages in credit card fraud as a sauce of funding, as have the Tamil Tigers • Abu Sayyaf has undertaken random kidnappings • Hezbollah have made profits from cigarette smuggling in the United States	• Mafia 'hits' of leading investigators (judges and police) are often as much political as violent (see murders of Giovanni Falcone and Paolo Borsellino)
Terrorists become criminals • The Northern Ireland bank robbery of 2004 – one of the UK's largest – was blamed on retiring IRA activists who needed to fund their retirement in the aftermath of the Irish peace process	**Ordinary criminals becoming politicised** • Jose Padilla convicted of aiding terrorists post 9/11 was a member of a Chicago street gang in his youth • Mohammed Bouyeri, who assassinated Dutch filmmaker Theo Van Gogh, was a petty criminal before he turned to political violence in 2004
Terrorists and criminal organisations exchange knowledge/commodities for mutual gain • Marriages of convenience between FARC and Colombian drug cartels	**Hybrid organisations engaging in crime and terrorism** • The Indian organised crime syndicate D-Company is alleged to have been involved in drug trafficking, money laundering and a Mumbai bombing in 1993, killing 257 people • Hezbollah has justified its participation in drug trafficking as part of its jihad on the grounds that it believes drug consumption is potentially just as dangerous for its enemies as its more conventional weaponry • Jamal Ahmidan, one of the cell leaders who orchestrated the Madrid bombings of 2006, is thought to have run a cell who counted six drug traffickers among their number. Indeed, the fact that some of the cell were known drug traffickers provided a smokescreen for the terrorist activities they were planning at the time

Source: adapted from Dishman, 2005; Hutchinson and O'Malley, 2007; Grabosky and Stohl, 2010.

developments can be mutually reinforcing. 'Investments in security devices and customs apparatuses can be used for the dual purpose of detecting bombs as well as narcotics' (Björnehed, 2004, p317). Furthermore, law enforcement and security equipment have versatile uses. Thus scanners that detect hidden compartments are useful regardless of what is being hidden, and databases at airports capable of crosschecking passports and outstanding warrants with international criminal databases alert officials to narcotics traffickers as well as terrorists.

That said, as Felbab-Brown (2010) demonstrated, policies focusing primarily on supply-side interdiction of drug supply can yield problems for counter-terror. This goes back to the economics of supply and demand. In her detailed account of the links between drug traffickers and belligerent groups, Felbab-Brown (2010) postulated that it is necessary not to be drawn into the trap of thinking about the relationship between terror organisations and organised crime groups or drug traffickers in purely economic terms. This 'conventional narcoterrorism view', which states that as terror organisations – or 'belligerents' as she refers to them – obtain their finances from participation in the illicit economy, effectively meaning that terror groups and drug traffickers are one and the same. This has been one of the significant mistakes in attempts to tackle drugs by tackling terror.

In a discussion about the policy of crop eradication as a means of combating the international drug trade, Björnehed (2004) noted how on one level such a policy may appear compatible with the control of international terror, but this may not always be the case:

> This objective for the war on drugs is arguably compatible with the objectives of the war on terror since it could reduce the availability of narcotics and simultaneously reduce finances for terrorist organisations. However, eradicating or replacing the growing of coca and poppies for illegal use actually increases the price of the product, in this case cocaine and heroin, thanks to market forces as a diminution of supply is not coupled with any reduction in demand. This was actually the observed effect after the ban on poppy cultivation set in place by the Taliban in 2000, when the prices of Afghan opium drastically increased in the region. If supply had been further reduced prices were expected to have increased also in Western Europe ... Hence a decreased supply of narcotics, although possibly a partial victory in the war on drugs, could actually increase the revenue made

by terrorist organisations involved in the narcotics trade.
(Björnehed, 2004, p315-6)

In short, if supply-side interventions are successful, but demand-side
levels remain the same, the policy becomes self-defeating as the cost
of drugs rises. This means that there are more profits to be made from
trafficking scarcer substances and thus more funds find their way into
the accounts of terror organisations (Björnehed, 2004). Ultimately for
Björnehed, the key drawback with the narco-terrorism concept is that
it leads to confused, often contradictory, policy aims, not least because
the connection between terrorists and drug traffickers is overstated as
their motivations and objectives diverge:

> Consider an ethnic separatist group with a Marxist-Leninist
> ideological foundation such as the Kurdish PKK, or an
> essentially religiously-based group such as al-Qaeda. Their
> objective, although vastly different in character, is to change
> society and the state, to a state-run economy or a society
> based on strict religious laws and codes. They want to
> rebuild the state in the image that fits their sense of the
> proper order and organisation. In contrast, drug traffickers
> and producers want to exist within the state structure with
> minimum state intervention in the economy. (Björnehed,
> 2004, p312)

Björnehed (2004, p320) also pointed to the existence of a clear 'pecking
order' in the allocation of resources to the war on terror and the war on
drugs, whereby the former frequently trumps the latter. She drew on
the example of Plan Colombia to demonstrate this, showing how prior
to 9/11 the US made a clear distinction in its aid packages for Colombia
to highlight how they would not fund Colombian counter-insurgency
efforts. Since 9/11, however, a clause in a key piece of Colombian
legislation (HR 4775) determined how 'a unified campaign against
narcotics trafficking and against activities by organisations designated as
terrorist organisations' (Björnehed, 2004, p319) is permissible. When
a transfer of resources is required, this is still a one-way street as, post
9/11, 'the US Coast Guard reports that 75% of their personnel and
boats earmarked for drug interdiction were transferred to anti terrorist
patrols' (Björnehed, 2004, p319). Additionally:

> ... there have been reports of a 25% increase in drug
> trafficking in the Caribbean after 9/11. It is advocated that

this increase in drug trade to the US is due to the fact that national and international law enforcement is occupied with countering potential terrorism threats. This focus of agencies on terrorism can be seen in the inter-agency cooperation between the DEA [Drug Enforcement Administration] and the FBI for example, which shows the unevenness with which the cooperation is taking place. Drug Enforcement Administrator Asa Hutchinson remarked in a statement that DEA resources had been 'stretched thin' since 9/11. (Björnehed, 2004, p320)

It is this often overlooked divergence that has led to confusing policy directions and to policy makers taking their eye of the ball in relation to some of the other challenges posed by contemporary terror cells, not least in terms of the decentralised structure and organisation of many terror networks. Indeed, the challenges for law and order agencies posed by the decentralisation of terror networks cannot be underestimated. As Dishman (2005, p248) effectively demonstrated: 'Decentralized organizations leave few evidentiary trails between the leadership and its cells, and between the cells themselves'. This is because many of the cells themselves have no knowledge of who forms part of the other like-minded units

There are also differing schools of thought as to whether the connection between organised crime and terror groups is fleeting or a more permanent feature of certain groups' activities. According to Dishman (2005), because of the 'cell'-like structure of various transglobal organisations, there is frequently a lack of direction, or 'leaderless nexus', in the goals of organisations. As a result, activities that were once seen to be off-limits are now on the agenda if cells wish to pursue this line of action. Dishman (2005) noted:

International money laundering crackdowns are making it more difficult for terrorist financiers to quickly and continually send money to both their operatives and the more limited bank accounts of the terrorists themselves. Low- to mid-level terrorist and criminal actors are forced to find their funding sources, fraudulent documents, transportation, and safe houses. Mid to lower-level criminals – who have quickly risen to greater levels of prominence in decentralized structures – have few qualms working with terrorists, in spite of the fact their ultimate boss would certainly disapprove of such an arrangement. The result is that a *leadership nexus* has emerged between criminals and terrorists; a phenomenon with far-reaching implications that should be a major concern for law enforcement and intelligence. (Dishman, 2005, p238)

Although much of the response to drug trafficking and terror is retaliatory and involves face-to-face combat, increasingly other pre-emptive measure are being adopted. Nowhere is the complex relationship between drug traffickers, terror organisations and the state more visible than around the poppy fields of Afghanistan. It is here that attempts to disrupt the supply side of the drugs trade, for instance through crop eradication programmes, have become accepted wisdom and standard policy. Yet the tactics being employed on behalf of the 'West' are increasingly extreme. Crop eradication programmes have for a long time been a staple of initiatives to curb the trade in drugs, and these sit alongside other supply-side initiatives such as crop substitution programmes and interdiction.

In Afghanistan, eradication has proved to be enormously difficult. Although once opposed to the opium industry, in contemporary times, the Taliban have become staunch defenders of the opium farmers and have aided in resisting eradication efforts of the Western-backed Afghan government. Pryce (2012, p52) explained the dangers of eradication for the opium farmers on the grounds that it leaves them not only susceptible, as we have seen, to losing their livelihoods, but also at the mercy of ruthless traffickers, who will extract payment from farmers to whom they have advanced loans to grow opium, regardless of whether their crops have been destroyed. Quite often, this means that if farmers cannot pay in cash, their children are taken.

In some cases, farmers are persuaded to voluntarily give up their crops in return for compensation. Such a strategy has been used in the Helmand province of Afghanistan. Pryce (2012) discussed the difficulties of such a strategy, stating that the process of administering the compensation is far from straightforward and that there were examples from 2006 of farmers waiting for four years for compensation payments that had been promised by the British, but which were yet to materialise. Consistent with Felbab-Brown's thesis, this has had the impact of potentially increasing support for the Taliban, who have taken on the role of the protector of the farmers.

One recent development in eradication programmes has been the development of biological technology and weaponry to fight the problem. Pryce (2012) highlighted how scientists in Uzbekistan have been working on a *pleospora* fungus, which is supposed to attack

the target plant – in this case the opium poppy – and leave all other vegetation intact. This fungus is also extremely durable. Not only does it kill the existing plants, but it also prevents subsequent harvests. As Pryce observed:

> the scientists insist that these fungi are harmless to humans, animals and other plants. However, this assertion is unproven … there is no certainty that they could not mutate. Touted as a sensational solution to the heroin problem, there are no guarantees that the method is 100 per cent safe. (Pryce, 2012, p54)

It has been demonstrated how 'narco-terror' became accepted into common parlance, as in the case of Escobar's Medellín cartel. It is in Colombia, then, that responses to the war on drugs have taken on a military veneer, but one that is undoubtedly influenced by tactics of conventional crime prevention and the prevention of terror. Plan Colombia is, as Pryce (2012) noted, the key US anti-drug cooperative strategy with Colombia, whereby in 2000 US$1.3 billion was being spent on the fight against drugs, a high percentage of which went on military aid to the Colombian government in its fight against the FARC rebels who controlled large parts of the country. According to Pryce (2012), Plan Colombia is an example of attempts to curb drug trafficking by targeting the supply side of the market. Its primary goal was to eradicate the raw ingredient of cocaine, but such actions may be the cause of significant social harms.

In most cases, eradication is undertaken by crop-spraying programmes. Although not necessarily carried out for environmental reasons, there could be a rationale for eradicating the cocaine trade on these grounds. The jungle laboratories that produce cocaine hydrochloride use a variety of highly toxic chemicals that eventually end up in local water sources. These chemicals resist biodegradation. In addition, a huge land-clearing programme has been taking in place in Colombia to accommodate the widespread plantation of coca. In an article for *The Observer* newspaper, Doward (2009) explained that the cultivation of illicit crops has led to the destruction of 2.2 million hectares of tropical forest in Colombia, an area slightly larger than Wales. For every hectare of coca grown, three hectares of forest are cut down. This means that for each gram of cocaine used, four square metres of rainforest are cleared (Doward, 2009). The process of cocaine production can be deleterious for the environment. Doward (2009) also revealed that cocaine production is a potentially global social problem, not just for the violence associated with the drug's trade. Colombia – the largest producer of cocaine hydrochloride across the globe – is also one of the most biodiverse countries in the world. It has, however, been complaining about the dangers of 'ecocide' for some time, as the drug cartels, at one time in charge of huge swathes of territory, ransacked the natural environment in cultivating the lucrative coca crop.

There is a clear sense that the destruction of the environment in the supply side of the drug chain is possible as the entire industry is currently unregulated. As a result, there is no sense or necessity for illegal cartels to comply with basic health, safety and environmental regulations as part of their production practice. That said, one of the great ironies of the environmental problems associated with supply-side drug policy interventions is that crop eradication programmes are also contributing to the destruction of the environment:

> Aerial spraying of the crops offers a quicker and, at first sight, a safer alternative to those intent on eradication. In this policy planes fly over targeted fields and spray chemical herbicide. ... Spraying is ... a blunt instrument. The Americans insist that spraying is sharply targeted to affect only drug crops and that the chemicals used are harmless to humans and animals. The farmers, aid workers and those monitoring human rights violations are all equally insistent that the sprays destroy surrounding food crops, degrade the soil and lead to a range of symptoms, such as headaches, sickness and rashes, in those people unfortunate enough to breathe in the spray. (Pryce, 2012, p53)

The herbicides involved are highly toxic. Glyphosates are widely used. They are powerful weedkillers. Studies conducted in Ecuador have demonstrated that they can have significant implications on human health as well as on the fauna of a region. According to Oldham and Massey (2001) in the Southern Colombian Province of Putumayo, 'the Health Department has reported that there have been numerous incidences of serious skin complaints in children as well as complaints of dizziness, diarrhoea, vomiting, red eyes and head aches'. This is despite the fact that the US Embassy in Bogota maintains that the aerial spray eradication programme is 'directly' targeted against the largest coca producers. In addition, because aerial spraying is the chosen method of dispersal, prevailing winds or indeed human error can mean that legitimate crops can be destroyed at the same time as the illegal crops.

There is also the potential that crop eradication, to echo our earlier discussion, is really crop displacement and that the areas of coca plants that are destroyed are subsequently replaced as more and more of the tropical forests are deforested to replace those lost to the drug enforcement teams. The ensuing desertification has serious implications for the biodiversity of Colombia as species face extinction. In addition, it is now widely accepted by scientists of global warming that deforestation on such a scale is a major contributor to climate change.

With seemingly counter-productive results, it is unclear why such policies are persisted with, yet they are part of a broader trend in policy post 9/11. In his thorough exposition on the nature of 'risk' and contemporary responses to terror, Mythen (2014) demonstrated how there has been a 'pre-emptive' drift in responses to situations deemed critical. In effect, as Mythen noted, the magnitude of the terrorist threat 'requires that nation states rethink their security policies and develop a broader range of horizon scanning techniques to identify upcoming terrorist attacks' (Mythen, 2014, p101) such processes are often referred to as exceptionalism. Although the UK had extensive terror legislation as a consequence of the 'Troubles' in Northern Ireland and the running conflict concerning the IRA, Loyalist Paramilitaries and the British state, a 'remarkable' raft of legislation was passed in the first decade of the 21st century, including: the Terrorism Act 2000; the Anti-Terrorism, Crime and Security Act 2001; the Prevention of Terrorism Act 2005; the Terrorism Act 2006; and the Counter-Terrorism Act 2008 (Mythen, 2014, p102).

This extensive legislative activity – or 'juridification' in Habermasian terms – has generated much debate. Exceptional measures such as the 'stop and search' powers of the Terrorism Act, whereby the police can 'stop and search vehicles, people in vehicles and pedestrians for terrorism without reasonable suspicion' (Mythen, 2014, p103), were seen to be necessary because of the exceptional nature of the threat. For critics, though, this was a disproportionate response to an unlikely threat. Mythen pointed out, however, that one unifying theme found in most of this legislation, particularly the 2000, 2005, and 2006 Acts, is their links with the move towards anticipatory risk strategies common in strands of criminology, defined some years ago as the 'New Penology' (Feeley and Simon, 2003).

These anticipatory risk strategies are also indicative of a switch to a pre-crime society (Zedner, 2007; Young, 1999, 2003). For Mythen and Walklate (2008), the rationale behind pre-crime is closely interlinked with the politics of risk and tactics employed by terrorists in their often visible and spectacular acts. Beck (2002, p8) emphasised that 'a suicide bomber can neither commit a suicide act more than once, nor can state authorities convict him. The singularity is marked by the simultaneity of act, confession and self-extinguishment.'

In one instance, then, all principles of social insurance and criminal justice are dispensed forthwith and pre-crime and specific prevention measures *de facto* become the policy option. It is in such an environment that authoritarian policies such as crop eradication become accepted by so-called liberal polities and amount to an example of what Baudrillard (2003) has termed the use of 'terror against terror'. We return to this issue in Chapter Six, when we consider the nature of state-perpetrated violence in the form of what can be labelled 'state terror'.

Summary

This chapter has considered in detail the nature of the international drugs trade as an example of organised criminality, and how this overlaps with various forms of state criminality. It has demonstrated how global drug control legislation has created opportunities for state criminality through the creation of a huge illicit market. States have often sought to cash in on the lucrative spoils of the drug war, as the Iran-Contra case demonstrated. We have also shown how the fusing of the 'war on drugs' with the 'war on terror' has created a situation where states can be seen to be simultaneously the real or potential victim of state crime and political violence, as well as the perpetrator of such actions.

Continuing a theme of this book, the concept of 'narco-terror' also demonstrates effectively the difficulties in policing state- or elite-level criminality. While there seems to be some rationale for assuming that there is collusion between terror organisations and organised crime, it is not always a sensible policy strategy to fuse the two. We have demonstrated how successes in one area of a problem, such as drugs interdiction, can arguably have a detrimental effect on another – increasing the prices of commodities and thus the profits for terror organisations.

In addition, it has become apparent that in addressing the threat of terrorism – perceived or otherwise – states have frequently resorted to tactics that are in themselves of dubious legality and questionable morality, often resulting in widespread social harm. This often goes unnoticed or receives limited critical attention in much of the mainstream press. The example of Plan Colombia revealed a consistent theme in attempts to combat crime, in that the resort to exceptional methods can be considered as criminal as the crimes it is attempting

to curb. In this sense, it mirrors tactics employed in contemporary conventional crime prevention and the prevention of terror also.

We pick up the themes of exceptionalism, pre-emption and precaution in subsequent chapters, as we look to unpack the case of the Iraq War. Before that, however, our attention turns in Chapter Five to a key arbiter in determining the success or failure of policy: the role of the media and its relationship with the state.

FIVE

The media as both an influential and a supportive arm of the state

In Chapter Two, in our discussion of state maintenance and the formulation of key alliances, we flagged the issue of the significance of media as being a key agency in shaping public opinion. On the one hand, the media particularly in jurisdictions with a developed regulatory regime (are supposed to) have a duty to the citizenry for the portrayal of current affairs. On the other hand, however, as private enterprises they have a duty towards shareholders and owners. This creates some confusion as to their purpose. This chapter picks up on these issues and links to a discussion of the often hidden nature of state criminality due to the occupational functions of the (mainly) print media in the UK and, more specifically, publications associated with the media mogul Rupert Murdoch.

Nonetheless, this chapter does not confine itself to how widespread and powerful Murdoch and his growing media platforms became within the British political arena. It also charts similar activities to gain influence in the US and beyond. To do this, we consider briefly the origins of the so-called Murdoch 'empire', before highlighting how, through its business model, Murdoch has become a powerful influence in social and political life across the globe. Here we consider the facilitators that have made this possible, such as Murdoch himself, and how he exercised dictatorial control over the 'empire'. We then go on to consider the morality behind how Murdoch has continuously courted political favours, for example through making significant political US campaign contributions to politicians of various hues and, through the HarperCollins publishing house, offering book contracts to key and strategically placed political figures, despite the knowledge that (on Murdoch's part at least) the extent of the advances offered could not be recouped through book sales alone (McKnight and Hobbs, 2011). Such examples are indicative of how for decades, as Chenoweth (2001) noted, the Murdoch 'empire' had existed and acted in the borderlands between legality and illegality. Indeed, the book deals may be legal but the chapter moves on to investigate what Murdoch demanded in return and whether these demands were criminal, deviant or immoral.

In recent times, it has become apparent how employees in the various platforms owned by Murdoch have been engaged in activity that has encroached into the illegal. Nowhere is this more apparent than in the phone-hacking scandal that engulfed his UK-based News International Company from 2007 onwards, but which gathered pace over the succeeding years. What has been downplayed in the ensuing commentary, but is of primary significance to us, is the role that News International played in acquiring information from the Metropolitan Police in return for cash payments. This has been the subject of an official investigation, Operation Elveden, and it is this that we concentrate on here, as it acts as a microcosm of the travails of law enforcement and regulation in state criminality, and highlights the complexities of the relationship between the state and the media.

This chapter provides a neat introduction to Chapter Six, which picks up on some these themes, in part considering Murdoch and his media platforms' influence over the invasion of Iraq, which in itself can be seen both as an affront to UK and US democracy and as an example of bipartite state terrorism.

The rise (and fall) and durability of the Murdoch 'empire'

According to Hallin and Mancini (2004), the US and UK print medias are part of the 'liberal model' of journalism, which has at its core a commitment to self-regulation; deemed by the industry to be a more efficacious mode of governance. Yet there are clear differences between the US and UK in this context.

Carlson and Berkowitz (2014) noted how, as a result of smaller geographical area and centralised political power, the UK newspaper industry is primarily one of 'national distribution among a dozen or so competing newspapers', which in turn is segmented along class and political lines. There is a local presence, but these focus primarily on localised issues. Deacon (2004) commented on how with nine daily and weekly upmarket broadsheet titles and with 10 tabloids, the British newspaper industry constituted a crowded marketplace. By contrast, the US industry is characterised by 'geographic dispersion', whereby 'publishers have strong incentives to pursue a general audience and to avoid a political slant outside the editorial pages'. The only national outlets are 'supermarket tabloids' which specialise in 'celebrity news, personal interest stories and offbeat topics' (Carlson and Berkowitz, 2014, p393).

The knock-on effect of such organisation is a different approach to professional ethics on the part of UK and US journalists. For Hallin and Mancini (2004, p222), notions of journalistic 'public service' are weaker in the British press, as is 'ethical self-regulation'. In effect, there is a primary concern for the bottom line. Furthermore, in the UK the tabloids are more popular than the broadsheets and, because of such, journalists are seemingly less forthright in their observance of professional values (Aldridge and Evetts, 2003; Sanders and Hanna, 2012). It is in such an environment that the media in the UK came to influence public opinion from 1968 onwards. Indeed, this was particularly apparent when Murdoch acquired the now-defunct *News of the World*.

For an organisation so ubiquitous, there is proportionately little coverage of the Murdoch 'empire' in academic literature, although there is now an ever-increasing array of material that sheds light into Murdoch's life and organisation from an investigative journalism perspective. It is safe to suggest that Murdoch's 'empire' was, and in a modified way still is, centred on NewsCorp, of which the Murdoch family are the majority shareholders. Arsenault and Castells (2008, p491) consider how NewsCorp parallels many other large media conglomerates, in that it is a product of various mergers, buyouts, hostile takeovers and other forms of restructuring, but unlike its major competitors it has maintained constant leadership throughout its nearly 60 years of expansion, dating from when Rupert Murdoch inherited the *Adelaide News* from his father in 1952. A major reshuffle – at least by the standards of NewsCorp – did occur in 2011 as NewsCorp split into two separate entities: 21st Century Fox has primarily taken over the film and television platforms once controlled by NewsCorp; and the reworked NewsCorp – technically a new company – broadly oversees the print and social media profiles.

Murdoch's business model

To speak of a single business model in relation to the practices of the Murdoch conglomerate is misleading. There are a number of factors that serve to typify the *modus operandi* of the organisation. Taking a lead from Arsenault and Castells (2008), we concentrate on three overlapping strategies:

- Murdoch has maintained dictatorial control or a 'vertical organisational structure' throughout his time as head of NewsCorp. This has enabled him to make decisions quickly and also to minimise the risk of a hostile takeover.

- It has also helped the strategy of his courting of political personnel. Frequently, this has led to endorsements in his widely read news outlets and to favourable coverage on his satellite and cable TV stations.
- He has supplemented this power through brokering deals with key political personnel, either via offering senior roles within his organisation or through other means.

These strategies have contributed to the rapid expansion of the 'empire' through time and location.

Dictatorial control

A common thread running through descriptions of Murdoch's practice is that he has taken great pains to routinely enforce policies that maximise his control. In essence, Murdoch has deliberately avoided expanding the number of NewsCorp institutional investors (of which there are far fewer in comparison to other media conglomerates) so that his family remain the custodians of the business. With this in mind, a defining feature of the organisation of the Murdoch 'empire' concerns its vertical and horizontal structures. In effect, as Arsenault and Castells pointed out, this maximised the ability of his executives to beat out competitors by making split-second decisions, since they faced few bureaucratic hurdles once Murdoch's approval had been obtained. To demonstrate this, Arsenault and Castells cited the example of how NewsCorp was able to edge out its rival Viacom in the acquisition of two critical digital properties, IGN.com and MySpace.com, on the basis that it was able to broker favourable deals more quickly (Arsenault and Castells, 2008, p493).

But what is vertical control? According to Gomery (1986, p84-5), vertical control is best thought of alongside 'vertical integration' which, in turn, was described as 'the expansion of a business enterprise by gaining control of operations from the acquisition of fundamental raw materials to the sale of the final product'. More specifically in terms of the film and television arms of the media, 'a fully integrated system would include the production of the programme, its distribution, and its final presentation'. Where the print media are concerned, Murdoch's corporate control facilitates and is facilitated by his ability to intervene in the editorial policies of his vast holdings typified in the way that all 175 NewsCorp controlled papers followed Murdoch in his support for the 2003 US-led invasion of Iraq (Greenslade, 2003) (see also Chapter Six).

On the one hand, the support of the Murdoch press for the Iraq War made sense. Murdoch was an ideological ally of the former US President, George W. Bush. On the other hand, ideological sympathies often come second to the clamour for profit and market domination. Jones (2014) observed how, around the time of the Iraq War, the Murdoch 'empire' had suffered some setbacks in trying to break into the lucrative Chinese markets, despite trying to appease the Chinese government by withdrawing BBC programming from the packages he supplied – the BBC being a long-time critic of China. Murdoch viewed the Middle East as a 'new potential frontier for his newspaper and television channels' (Jones, 2014, p94).

This could only be realised, however, if 'stability' was brought to the region. In this sense, stability was a byword for free-market capitalism (Klein, 2007). Jones quoted Chris Bryant, a one-time Minister in the Foreign Office, who stated that it was unlikely that the Iraq War would have happened, if the Murdoch papers had been against it.

Courting political favour and 'making kings'

The ability of the media to shape public opinion is the subject of much speculation and conjecture. Theorists have rightly become sceptical of a direct causal association between media outputs and the actions of the public; as premised in the hypodermic needle. What is beyond doubt, however, is that there can be influence in some shape or form. As Arsenault and Castells (2008, p504) suggested, it is clear that the media can leverage public opinion.

To reiterate, in the UK such issues were brought into sharp focus from 1968 onwards when Murdoch's influence on politicians and the electorate began to grow. Other titles and platforms followed the purchase of the *News of the World* and *The Sun*, to secure his influence even further. Indeed, his support helped to secure the election of Margaret Thatcher on the Right, demonising the so-called 'underclass' with an overtly neo-liberal agenda. It also helped the Conservative government to consolidate power after Thatcher's demise. As Jones (2014) explained, the 1992 General Election was the most marginal campaign for decades. After 13 years out of office, Labour under their leader Neil Kinnock were close to re-entering government:

> On the 2 April – a week before voters were due to march to schools and village halls to cast their ballots – one poll projected that Labour was on course for a 6-point win. But the creeping jubilation of the party's grassroots was matched

only by the horror of Britain's media elite at the prospect of a Labour victory. After playing a crucial role in cementing Thatcherism and demolishing its opponents, Fleet Street was not about to risk any of the grand achievements of the 1980s being stripped away. Labour – and its leader – were subject to one of the most vitriolic media campaigns in post-war political history. (Jones, 2014, p88)

This reached its denouement on the day of the election as *The Sun* ran an image of Labour leader Neil Kinnock's face superimposed on a light bulb under the headline: 'If Kinnock Wins Today Will The Last Person to Leave Britain Please Turn Out the Lights'; the Conservatives won. Deacon (2004, p12) noted that, in the aftermath of their surprise defeat in 1992, the Labour Party started to develop policy proposals that would have led to the break-up of large media conglomerates.

Determined not to make the same mistake as Kinnock, one of Tony Blair's first acts on becoming Labour leader in 1994 was to court Murdoch (Shawcross, 1993; Crainer, 2002; Watson and Hickman, 2012). As Kellner (2012) remarked, Blair had a well-known meeting in 1995 with Murdoch in Australia and he would become very friendly with the Murdoch family. The early outcome of their 1995 meeting, however, was to lead the Murdoch press to switch its allegiance from supporting the John Major Conservative government, as it had done in 1992, to Blair's New Labour in 1997. According to Kellner, it was this meeting, and the friendship it cemented, which enabled Murdoch to 'expand his media 'empire' by avoiding 'meaningful regulation', as well as giving Murdoch access to the British government (Kellner, 2012, p1177).

To suggest that this was a fundamental realignment of the media towards the political Left would be misleading. Deacon (2004, p12) highlighted how the core political values expressed in editorials have remained consistent for a number of years. They have been consistently and traditionally aligned to the policies of the Conservative Party, in that 'they express views that are antagonistic towards increased public expenditure, progressive taxation, trade unions and European integration'. Furthermore, they stand foursquare behind the goals of the free market. Deacon went on to note that in the 2001 General Election, New Labour enjoyed 72% of national press support, but this says more about the 'Blairite' shift to the centre or even right of centre (Prideaux, 2005) rather than any seismic movement in the ideological positions of most of the media. One other revealing episode of the shift in support to Blair's Labour at this time was that it showed how 'conditional and tepid' (Deacon, 2004, p12) media support for political parties has actually become, and how this is a fickle world.

In a chapter on *'Mediaocracy'*, Jones (2014) secured and reported on some remarkably frank conversations with leading political insiders. Particularly revealing was a discussion with Damian McBride, the former Prime Minister Gordon Brown's special adviser. McBride recounted how, under Gordon Brown's leadership and somewhat contrary to established civil service protocol, Brown would have various 'off-the-record' meetings with powerful media personnel. McBride noted that Brown had never done a complete volte-face on an issue subsequent to a meeting, but undoubtedly, as Jones highlighted: 'the wishes and desires of these unelected media tycoons did help craft the policies of an elected government' (Jones, 2014, p96).

Although Murdoch was not implicated in this decision, an example of this practice related to Gordon Brown's (and his then Home Secretary Jacqui Smith's) decision to change the classification of cannabis under the Misuse of Drugs Act 1971 from Class C to Class B, reversing the previous Labour government. Daly and Sampson (2013, unpaginated) revealed that the media's power to impact on the direction of drug policy was 'undoubted' and this was brought to bear in the 'mutually beneficial meeting of minds between' Gordon Brown and the proprietor of the *Daily Mail*, Paul Dacre mid-2007. Brown, 'gearing up to lead the Labour Party and take over from Tony Blair, was eager to ensure he had continued support from the influential mid-market tabloid. Dacre was eager to see a triumphant end to his personal, three year mission to return cannabis to being a Class B drug' (Daly and Sampson, 2013, unpaginated).

Within weeks of assuming the premiership of the land, Brown implemented the change in policy. This was symbolic for a number of reasons. Not only did it mark a departure from the direction of travel in drug policy under Tony Blair, but it also dispatched any remaining notion that the Labour government was committed to developing evidence-based policies (Monaghan, 2011). The decision to amend the cannabis legislation was in direct contrast to the advice of the government's Advisory Council on the Misuse of Drugs (2002, 2005, 2008), which had consistently argued that cannabis should reside in Class C. For Daly and Sampson (2013), Brown's decision was welcomed as 'a major victory' for the *Daily Mail*, with many claiming Dacre to be the real inspiration behind the move.

The episode is indicative of a broader issue in the UK media. According to Jones (2014), the opinions expressed by newspapers often reflect, to a degree, those held by their owners. Jones (2014, p98) also maintained that Murdoch has at no time tried to hide the fact that through his vertical control he wields enormous power over his organisation and 'did not disguise the fact he is hands on both economically and editorially'. If this was true at *The Sun* and the *News of the World*, it was not quite as visible at *The Times* or *Sunday Times*. As Jones illustrated, even though Murdoch claimed not to have such power here, he would ring the editors to ask 'What are you doing?' It hardly seems likely that, with Murdoch on the other end of the phone, his editors would be inclined to do anything other than agree with him.

This points to a particularly revealing situation in the traditional British press: where 'anyone rich enough to own a newspaper has a vested interest in an order that protects wealth and power' (Jones, 2014, p97). Certainly, it is an order that Murdoch has continually used to his advantage, especially when circumnavigating media regulation as his 'empire' grew. While this growth and circumnavigation have been achieved in numerous ways, a key facet has been the supporting and rewarding of political figures of various hues as part of his overall business model.

Supporting/rewarding political figures

In many senses, Rupert Murdoch can be said to be a complex and often contradictory figure. Thought to be socially conservative and, thus, sharing a natural affinity with the Conservative and Republican parties in the UK and the US respectively, the reality is that Murdoch has been proven to be more *homo economicus* than an ideological outrider. It is apparent that his organisation's bottom line, rather than its political leanings, drives decisions, but this does not preclude action that fails to yield a profit.

For Arsenault and Castells (2008, p497), this is frequently evidenced in his 'political gamesmanship'. They observed that Murdoch's support for the Iraq War came from potential economic benefits rather than political ideology. One notorious manifestation of the political gamesmanship in question concerns donations to political parties and the offering of book contracts to key political figures via the HarperCollins publishing house. With regard to the latter, Arsenault and Castells commented on how key political figures such as Tony Blair, Margaret Thatcher, Mikhail Gorbachev, Raisa Gorbachev, Dan Quayle, Boris Yeltsin and John Major signed lucrative deals with HarperCollins. The late Robin Cook, a vocal opponent of the Iraq War but a key force in UK politics, also signed a US$400,000 book contract with the company. Significantly, these advances were typically much larger sums than the book was likely to recoup. For example, Newt Gingrich was offered US$4.5 million for *To Renew America*, yet it barely recouped its printing costs (Arsenault and Castells, 2008, p499–500).

With regard to political/campaign donations, Murdoch's financial endowments to key political figures are revealing. Table 5.1 highlights the top 10 political individual recipients of NewsCorp political contributions between 1998 and 2006.

Table 5.1: Top 10 political recipients of NewsCorp political contributions in the US between 1998 and 2006

Name	Amount received in US$
Kerry, John (Democrat - Massachusetts)	140,086
Bush, George W (Republican)	59,544
Schumer, Charles E. (Democrat - New York)	54,250
Stevens, Ted (Republican - Arkansas)	49,250
Harman, Jane (Democrat - California)	45,500
Berman, Howard L. (Democrat - California)	44,250
McCain, John (Republic - Arizona)	40,900
Hollings, Fritz (Democrat - South Carolina)	40,474
Markey, Edward J. (Democrat - Massachusetts)	38,000
Waxman, Henry (Democrat - California)	36,969

Source: Arsenault and Castells (2008, p499)

It is somewhat surprising to see Democratic Senator John Kerry at the top of this list. Kerry was the unsuccessful Democratic presidential candidate in the 2004 US elections, losing out to George W. Bush. Murdoch's support for Bush was often seen to be unwavering; a fact most visible in debates over the Iraq War. As Greenslade (2003, unpaginated) pointed out, Murdoch had been at his most forthright when declaring that: 'we can't back down now, where you hand over the whole of the Middle East to Saddam … . I think Bush is acting very morally, very correctly.' Although subsequently Secretary of State under Barack Obama, Kerry has had a number of high-profile political appointments throughout his career. Why, then, would Murdoch be a key donor to Kerry, a frequent critic of Bush and his main challenger for the White House? The answer, for Arsenault and Castells, lay with the fact that Kerry was an erstwhile Chair of the Senate Commerce Subcommittee on Science, Technology and Innovation and, as a consequence, a key broker in 'shaping regulatory decisions critical to NewsCorp's bottom line' (p498). With the exception of Bush, as Arsenault and Castells demonstrated, the remaining nine top recipients of financial support 'all served on the House or Senate Commerce or Judiciary Committees' (p499), which provide legislative oversight of media ownership in the US.

If NewsCorp's donations reflected a trend, then as Arsenault and Castells also noted, so too did Murdoch's personal contributions. In a telling piece of evidence of his political pragmatism

> Murdoch ... donated US$2100 Clinton's Senate Primary Campaign and US$2100 to her general re-election campaign, and hosted a fundraiser for her in May 2006. In 2006, the *NYP* [*New York Post*], commonly regarded as the most direct channel for Murdoch's political views, endorsed Hillary Clinton over conservative John Spencer for Senator of New York. During the same period, Hillary Clinton stood as one of the most vocal opponents of changes to the Nielsen USTV rating system, changes that severely threatened NewsCorp's advertising revenue. (Arsenault and Castells, 2008, p499-50)

Calling in the dues: circumventing competition laws

Primarily as a product of Murdoch's vertical and horizontal integration, NewsCorp has been particularly adept at manipulating regulatory frameworks to its own ends. Consequently, it has often been the first conglomerate to break into new markets. As an indicator of its influence, NewsCorp remains the only broadcaster ever to receive a waiver on US foreign ownership restrictions. Arsenault and Castells (2008, p505) revealed how, in 1994, NBC (National Broadcasting Company) and NAACP (National Association for the Advancement of Colored People) complained to the Federal Communications Commission (FCC) – the independent communications regulatory agency – stating that the Murdoch-owned Fox Network 'violated FCC regulations that foreign entities may own no more than 24.9 per cent of any broadcaster'. Murdoch had opted not to relocate from his native Australia, where he enjoyed more beneficial tax arrangements, but he used his influence to successfully achieve a waiver. 'The FCC granted the waiver on the basis of arguments made by FCC commissioner James Quello, a personal friend of Murdoch's, that the provision of a fourth network served the common good' (Arsenault and Castells,

2008, p505). This was, however, in direct contrast to the reports filed by the staff at the FCC.

According to Kellner (2012, p1173), the ownership restrictions in question were part of a raft of measures that sought to ensure that a democratic society was maintained. In the context of the US, the free press was sacrosanct in that, as indicated at the outset of this chapter, it had a 'dual function': to 'provide a check against excessive power' and to 'inform the people concerning major issues of public interest'. Kellner cited the Federal Communications Act 1934 as being a pivotal buttress of press control. This extended the concept of a free press to the broadcast media. Or in this context, broadcasting, like the print media, 'was conceived as a public utility, with the airwaves established as part of the public domain, subject to regulation by the government to assure that broadcasting would meet its democratic responsibilities' (p1173).

Kellner (2012, p1174) also remarked on how much of the regulatory apparatus was eroded during the Thatcher and Reagan administrations of the 1980s and continued throughout the 1990s to the present. It culminated with an 'overwhelming concentration of power in the hands of corporate groups that now own powerful media empires, which they use to promote their own interests and agendas'. In Britain, for example, Tony Blair gave his support to a Communications Bill that contained a provision relaxing television and newspaper cross-ownership restrictions so that NewsCorp could assume ownership of Channel 5,[1] Britain's fifth national broadcaster. This became widely known as the 'Murdoch Clause', in that it applied only to NewsCorp. According to a report in *The Guardian* (Leigh and Evans, 2005) on 2 April 2005, executives from the Murdoch-owned Sky met with the then government minister Tessa Jowell to 'set out their concerns about the Bill. The primary sticking point concerned a clause which 'imposed a specific duty on the new regulator Ofcom to maintain a diverse range of owners of television and radio stations' (Leigh and Evans, unpaginated). The minutes from the meeting reveal how Jowell reassured the Sky representatives that the clause would not be used to block any merger.

Of course, none of this was new. Back in 1981, as Jones (2014, p90) remarked, there had been a 'secret meeting' between Margaret Thatcher and Rupert Murdoch at Chequers (the Prime Minister's country

---

[1]   There is some confusion in the literature here. Arsenault and Castells discuss this in the context of the Sky buyout of ITV. Sky did eventually acquire a stake in ITV and not Channel 5.

residence). Here, 'Murdoch had done a deal to buy *The Times* and *The Sunday Times*. Murdoch had briefed Thatcher about his plans, including taking on the trade unions and slashing the workforce by 25 per cent. After this meeting, the Thatcher government did not refer Murdoch's takeover bid to the Monopolies and Mergers Commission, which could have blocked what became Britain's largest newspaper group'. As Jones went on to note, this meeting was very much about power. This was politics courting the media, with the knowing realisation that the latter had the power to 'make or break' the former.

State and media collusion: corrupt payments and complex relations

Reaffirming a line of argument that we have pursued throughout concerning the revolving door of what Mills (1956) termed the 'power elite', it is clear that the Murdoch 'empire' has been both a supporter of, and supported by, political individuals and parties that have facilitated opportunities for the expansion of his 'empire'.

The revolving door between the media and the state is nowhere better expressed than in the career of Andy Coulson, one-time editor of the *News of the World*, who went on to become Prime Minister David Cameron's Director of Communications, and who was a central figure in the scandal to engulf the Murdoch 'empire' from 2007. We return to this issue in due course; for now it is necessary to point out how the relationship between the press and the state (in this case the print media and the criminal justice system) has been the subject of much discussion.

In a chapter discussing the mystification of the police through media representation, Reiner (1992, p171) quoted the one-time Commissioner of the Metropolitan Police, Sir Robert Mark, as stating that the relationship between journalists and the police is 'enduring' if not 'an ecstatically happy marriage'. The case of Operation Elveden, to be discussed later, brings this into focus. As Reiner insightfully pointed out:

> Overall the treatment of the Police by the news media has been such as to legitimate their role and activities. But this outcome has been neither smooth nor unruffled. Conflict has frequently arisen between police and journalists over specific issues, and many police officers have a genuine sense of the media as biased against them. These perceptions are not unfounded. The media, even while reproducing

perspectives fundamentally legitimating the police role, none the less criticise particular police actions and individual officers. As long as this is not carried too far, the existence of the media as apparently independent, impartial and ever-vigilant watchdogs over state agencies on behalf of the public interest is conducive to the legitimation of these apparatuses (but not individuals working within them). (Reiner, 1992, p171-2)

A closer look at the workings of the Murdoch press lends weight to Reiner's observations. The activities of the Murdoch 'empire' also reveal the often fuzzy line between criminality, deviance and (im)morality. If this was true in the 1980s and 1990s, things began to change in the 2000s as various high-profile scandals relating to the organisation came to light. They were scandals that extended beyond the bending of competition rules to outright criminality. Details surrounding the latter came to light in the aftermath of the phone-hacking scandal. In many ways, this proved to be a decisive break with other activities associated with the Murdoch 'empire', in that it clearly breached legal codes and regulations.

Although the scandal is still unfurling at the time of writing and the response of the state has been complex for reasons that will become clear, there are critics who are unequivocal in their view of the activities of the Murdoch press:

> For the past 30 years, the Murdoch 'empire' has sought to undermine and destabilise elected governments, and independent regulators, in pursuit of a political agenda that, while hiding behind a smokescreen of free market orthodoxy, is in the end nothing less than a sophisticated attempt to optimise the power and influence of News Corporation and its populist, right wing agenda. (Puttnam, cited in Kellner, 2012, p1174)

In addition, Kellner also noted how:

> Murdoch's 'empire' were employing the vilest methods to get stories and were kingmakers in the British system while the state, police and legal system were complicit in the Murdoch media 'empire' amassing media and political power wielded in their own partisan and corporate interests, often operating outside the law. (Kellner, 2012, p1177)

The 'sophisticated attempts' and 'vile methods' to optimise power were brought to the public's attention from 2011 onwards in the aftermath of the phone-hacking scandal that engulfed the *News of the World* and subsequently News International. This sparked a series of further investigations into the UK's print media (see Table 5.2). Although the scandal broke some years later, the Murdoch papers had been implicated in illegal activity for some time. On 11 March 2003, Rebekah Brooks (Rebekah Wade as she was then known) and Andy Coulson appeared before the UK House of Commons Culture, Media and Sport Select Committee (2003). After a detailed exposition on Brooks and Wade's views regarding the Press Complaints Commission (the self-regulatory organisation responsible for press propriety), the Labour MP Chris Bryant moved the conversation on to the issue of information retrieval. The following is an abridged transcript of the hearing:

> 466. (*Mr Bryant*) The issue of how you set about getting information is also, of course, a matter of importance. There have been a series of stories over the last couple of years suggesting that *The Sun*, *The Mirror*, *The Express*, the *News of the World*, use private detectives, pay people to provide them with information which they should not legally have, pay the police to make sure they know things before they are rightfully public. In the case of Sarah Payne, *The Sun*, *The Mirror* and *The Express* all paid £5,000 to somebody to steal sensitive documents and sell them in their newspaper. Do either of your newspapers ever use private detectives, ever bug or pay the police? (*Ms Wade*) All those things you have mentioned like private detectives and listening devices and so on come under those two umbrellas…. If I give you one example, and we are talking about ordinary people here and I will keep it to that in the context of the Committee, on a council estate in Birmingham there was a woman that had four daughters all under the age of 16, and we were told she was selling her daughters to local, if you like, paedophiles, because they were well under the age of 16, as I explained, so we were called to look at this story and we did not know whether it was true or not … We sent somebody in who had a listening device on them, and the woman who was selling her daughters did not know that. The reporter came out, rang me and said, 'This story is true. It is absolutely horrendous and I have not seen anything like it'. We immediately

called the police; we got her arrested; we got the children
protected; all the agencies were called in; and the thought
of even publishing that story did not come into our heads

In addressing Bryant's questions, Wade then discusses the issue of
subterfuge

> The fact is that subterfuge was used, the man got in contact
> with the woman on the estate and said he had been put
> in touch by a local paedophile – that was subterfuge. He
> is a reporter but he did not declare he was a reporter. He
> needed to get into the house and the listening device was
> then used, and sometimes that is necessary. So to answer
> your question, yes, but if you want me to sit here and go
> through all of the situations where that happens, it would be
> ridiculous. The most important thing is that it is only ever
> used in the public interest in the sense of what that means.

This exchange provides us with a neat microcosm of the mechanics of
NewsCorp/News International journalism. It highlights the extent to
which reporters would go for novel stories, but there is a moral stance
and a belief in being on the side of the 'just' that underpins Wade's
decision about whether or not to publish the story. The discussion in
the Committee then turns to the payment of public officals

> 467. And on the element of whether you ever pay the
> police for information?
> (*Ms Wade*) We have paid the police for information in the
> past.

> 468. And will you do it in the future?
> (*Ms Wade*) It depends
> (*Mr Coulson*) We operate within the code and within the
> law and if there is a clear public interest then we will. The
> same holds for private detectives, subterfuge, a video bag
> – whatever you want to talk about.

> 469. It is illegal for police officers to receive payments.
> (*Mr Coulson*) No. I just said, within the law.

For our purposes, there was also an admission of the payment of serving
police officers for information. When this was pointed out, there was

a swift rebuttal and a retreat into technicalities and operating within established codes of practice. Nevertheless, Scott (2013) argued that, at the time, the act of paying public officials may not necessarily have been a criminal offence. The legislation in question was the Prevention of Corruption Act 1906, which was very much of its time. Payments to public officials, therefore, were likely to contravene the common law of misconduct in a public office.

What became apparent, however, is that the practices of the Murdoch 'empire' (and indeed those of other outlets such as those associated with the Trinity Mirror Group and Express Newspapers) continued unabated, while the legislation changed around them. Thus the Bribery Act 2010 sought to tighten up the legislation surrounding payments to officials, but the practice continued.

Inquiries into the British media since 2005

A useful insight into the extent of criminal and immoral activity in the British media can be gleaned from the number of inquiries initiated by Scotland Yard over recent years. The list in Table 5.2 demonstrates the size and scale of the investigations, which at the time of writing are yet to reach their conclusions. There are 11 interlinked operations stemming from the phone-hacking inquiry, with the highest-profile conviction being for Andy Coulson and acquittal for Rebekah Brooks in Operation Weeting. In all, over 210 people have been arrested, with more being interviewed under caution. The investigations are listed in Table 5.2.

Table 5.2: Inquiries into the British media since 2005

Name	Details
Operation Weeting	News of the World hacking
Operation Elveden	Corrupt payments to public officials involving various newspapers
Operation Pinetree	Second News of the World hacking
Operation Golding	Alleged Mirror Group Newspaper hacking
Operation Sacha	Alleged attempt to conceal evidence
Operation Tuleta	Alleged computer hacking
Operation Kalmyk	Computer misuse inquiry
Operation Sabinas	Computer misuse inquiry
Operation Carrizo	Computer misuse inquiry
Operation Kerville	Computer misuse inquiry
Operation Caryatid	Original 2005-06 hacking inquiry

Source: adapted from Casciani, 2014

It is interesting to draw a parallel between the top two police operations on this list. As noted by the Turvill (2013), Operations Weeting and Elveden along with Operation Tuleta had, as of April 2013, cost over £19 million. Since the *Press Gazette* is the trade magazine for the profession of journalism, it was of little surprise that the focus was on the cost of the inquiries. That said, Operation Weeting had concentrated mainly on the hacking of phones of figures in the public eye. These have included celebrities of various kinds, but also political figures and members of the British royal family and, most infamously, the hacking of the mobile phone of a teenager, Milly Dowler.

Milly Dowler went missing in March 2002 on her way home from school. Her body was found in September of that year. Levi Bellfield was convicted of her murder in 2011. It is the case of Milly Dowler that has drawn much comment. In 2011, *The Guardian* newspaper published allegations that Milly Dowler's phone had been hacked by journalists from the *News of the World* (Davies and Hill, 2011). In doing so, some voice messages had been deleted, giving the Dowler family false hope that Milly was still alive. An entire chapter of the report into phone-hacking on the behalf of *News International* by the House of Commons Culture, Media and Sport Select Committee (2012) was reserved for this episode. The chapter detailed the intricacies of the case and the to-ing and fro-ing of correspondence between the *News of the World* and Surrey Police, the force responsible for investigating Milly Dowler's disappearance. The conclusions drawn by the committee gave some insight into the practices employed by the *News of the World*, which contrasted with the moral stance enunciated by Brooks in 2003:

> Rebekah Brooks was Editor of the *News of the World* at the time that reporters from that paper illegally accessed Milly Dowler's voicemail in 2002. She told us that she only became aware of the hacking of Milly Dowler's telephone in early July 2011. In support of this, we note that she has stated that she was on holiday between 9 and 13 April 2002, the period over which Surrey Police had most contact with the *News of the World* about the Milly Dowler story, although she had returned by the following week, and contact with Surrey Police continued until 20 April 2002. Impersonating members of a missing girl's family; besieging an employment agency; falsely asserting cooperation with the police; falsely quoting the police; and, according to their own account, obtaining Milly Dowler's mobile telephone number from her school friends are hardly the actions of a

respectful and responsible news outlet. For those actions, and the culture which permitted them, the Editor should accept responsibility. (House of Commons Culture, Media and Sport Select Committee, 2012, unpaginated)

The timeframe between 9 and 13 April 2002 is significant, as these were the times when intensive reporting of the Milly Dowler case was taking place by the paper. Indeed, the committee noted how a story printed in early editions of the *News of the World* on 14 April 2002 'made detailed reference to three voicemails messages left on Milly Dowler's telephone', but that these had all but disappeared in the final edition that made it to press. So what happened? The committee concluded that:

> Tom Crone was Legal Manager of News Group Newspapers in 2002 and was on duty on the night of 13 April 2002, when the *News of the World* was engaged in producing an article based on information gleaned from the illegal accessing of Milly Dowler's voicemail. He has said that he does not remember the article in question. It is, however, very unlikely that he had no sight of at least the first edition article before he left on the night of 13 April 2002. It is indeed highly probable, in view of his role at the newspaper, that he was responsible for checking the original article's content, at the very least. Anybody who saw that article will have been aware that the information came from Milly Dowler's voicemail account. Any competent newspaper lawyer could reasonably have been expected to ask questions about how that information had been obtained. In this context, we are astonished that Tom Crone should have decided to present to the Committee the hypothesis that the information was provided – and subsequently retracted – by the police. We note that his hypothesis bears some resemblance to the process by which Surrey Police ensured that later editions of the *News of the World* contained a quotation that they had approved instead of the falsely attributed quotation that appeared in the early edition. (House of Commons Culture, Media and Sport Select Committee, 2012, unpaginated)

The two Select Committee inquiries discussed in this chapter have concentrated on the issue of payments for information, and it is this that provided the backdrop to the ongoing Metropolitan Police investigation known as Operation Elveden. Elveden sheds light on the close relationship between the police and the media, but as the subsequent convictions and appeals highlight, this is a relationship of murk and unpredictability – and one that casts some doubt on the cosy marriage of the state and media thesis.

On most measures, Operation Elveden has proved to be problematic. Although, as pointed out, attempts had been made to modernise the legislation in relation to the corrupting of public officials, the charges brought under Operation Elveden related primarily to the 1906 legislation and the common law legislation of misconduct in a public office (Scott, 2013). In a rare success for the Crown Prosecution Service, in May 2015, *The Sun* journalist Anthony France was found guilty of cultivating a 'corrupt relationship' with PC Timothy Edwards. According to the *Independent* newspaper, Edwards had previously pleaded guilty to 'misconduct in public office' and had been jailed for two years in 2014 (Pennink, 2015). At the time of writing (August 2015), Anthony France was one of only three successful convictions under Operation Elveden; of the other two, *News of the World* crime reporter Lucy Panton has since had her conviction quashed, and reporter Ryan Sabey has the right of appeal. The U-turn of the decision against Panton coincided with the Crown Prosecution Service dropping cases against Andy Coulson and eight other journalists in April 2015 for making payments to public officials.

This episode created a furious backlash from the journalists and calls for a public inquiry into the expenditure on Operation Elveden vis-à-vis its impact on the lives of journalists, many of whom remained on bail for over two years. Journalists also suggested that the operation was politically motivated and an attack on the freedom of the press (Press Association, 2015). As it stands, Operation Elveden is currently under review by the Crown Prosecution Service but there is still the intention to pursue cases against a range of public officials. For our purposes, the case reveals the complexities of the relationship between the state and the media. Although the case of the Murdoch 'empire' reveals that the media can be a supportive arm of the state, this is a claim that does need to be treated with some caution.

Summary

Ultimately, an underlying philosophy of the expansion for Murdoch was that 'growth begets growth'. By currying favour with key power brokers, particularly those with the bailiwick of media regulation and governance, Murdoch was able to expand his 'empire' and enter new markets. In turn, entering new markets creates expanding avenues for advertising and consumer purchases, thus generating increased revenues, which allowed Murdoch to curry more favour and, ultimately, to wield even more power and subsequently influence policy agendas. The strategy is to not only influence lawmakers and regulators regarding policies that could constrict the network's expansion, but also to promote a political agenda that serves his overarching business goals. This is clear in the business model he has cultivated over time and the broader political missions he has supported, as the case of the Iraq War reveals (see Chapter Six).

Yet this strategy was also implicated in the near downfall of the 'empire'. Carlson and Berkowitz (2014, p392) referred to the phone-hacking scandal as an episode of 'synecdochic deviance'. In their words, synecdoche: 'refers to a figure of speech in which a part stands for the whole. Thus, synecdochic deviance denotes the extension of a deviant act as indicative of a widespread problem rather than its amelioration as an individualised occurrence.' This analysis stands to reason and can be explained by the vertical and horizontal management structures employed by Murdoch across his 'empire' where, as Anand and Attea (2003, p14) maintained, many employees of News Corporation 'think that Rupert is their boss' (cited in Arsenault and Castells, 2008, p493).

There is a sense that the sensationalist reporting that was a hallmark of various News International outlets and that was at the heart of Murdoch's growth strategy was also a key part of the scandal surrounding his 'empire'. The particular aspect of reporting that crossed the boundary into illegality relates to what Chibnall (2004) referred to as the search for novelty. It was not the need for novelty itself, but the means by which this was to be realised that lay at the heart of the scandal and resulted in Murdoch becoming the scapegoat for what has transpired to be a structural moral malaise in the media – or in other words, a rotten press.

Carlson and Berkowitz (2014) also noted how the reporting of the Murdoch scandal contained the perfect amount of symmetry as the predators became the prey. They commented on the reporting of the phone-hacking scandal by Joe Nocera of the *New York Times*, a rival newspaper to NewsCorp. Nocera was concerned that the *Wall Street Journal*, a thoroughbred of the Murdoch 'empire', had taken steps to defend the practices of its UK counterparts on the *News of the World* and *The Sun* and Murdoch himself, accusing rival publications of competitive *schadenfreude*. Nocera stated:

The whole thing reminds me a little of the ending of Ian McEwan's wonderful novel 'Solar' in which the many awful things that the central character has done in his long life suddenly come together to bury him in an avalanche of comeuppance. I'm OK with that. (Nocera, 2011, cited in Carlson and Berkowitz, 2012, p401)

It was not just Murdoch's publications that went on the offensive. The man himself took to social media to express exasperation at his treatment and the lack of balance associated with reporting on social media. Murdoch lamented how 'ignorant and vicious abuse lowers whole society' and that it might even show real 'social decay' (Hutchinson, 2012). In sum, Kellner notes how:

It was clear that the Murdoch Corporation had corrupted the British media, the political system, and ... the police and the legal system, all of which had failed to investigate and prosecute its earlier wrongdoings. Murdoch's media were employing the vilest methods to get stories and were kingmakers in the British system while the state, police and legal system were complicit in the Murdoch media 'empire' amassing media and political power wielded in their own partisan and corporate interests, often operating outside the law. (Kellner, 2012, p1177)

There is, then, some irony that the largest threat to the Murdoch 'empire' came from a media scandal, the stock-in-trade of the organisation for decades. Overall, the analysis of the Murdoch empire presented in this chapter leads to a potential conclusion of collusion between the political system and the legislature and a powerful media conglomeration. It is clear that the former had abrogated its responsibility to thoroughly investigate the workings of the latter by sidestepping the monopolies and mergers committees for example, and in return, they had reaped the benefits of Murdoch's endorsements. However, as the case of Operation Elveden has revealed so far, this relationship has been – and looks as if it will continue to be – tumultuous.

Beyond the borders: state terrorism from without and against the 'other'

Chapter Six turns to the issue of state-sanctioned violence, discussing how this is frequently achieved with the acquiescence of the media. It will be acknowledged that violence is a widespread resort utilised by people and governments around the world to achieve political ends. Numerous groups and, indeed, individuals believe that existing political systems will refuse to recognise and respond to their political ambitions and demands. Violence – in the form of terrorism, for example – can thus be justified and deemed necessary by many groups and individuals in their pursuit of differing political agendas.

In a similar vein, this chapter points out that many governments around the world also resort to the use of violence. On the one hand, governments may use violence to intimidate their own population into acquiescence (see Chapter Eight for a more detailed discussion). On the other hand, governments may also use (exceptional) force to defend their country from outside invasion or other threats such as terrorist bombings (see also Chapter Four). Drawing on some of the discussion in Chapters Two and Three, this chapter outlines the different forms that political violence can take, and explains why the commission of state violence can be deemed necessary by the perpetrators (possibly as a last resort) or why such violence can be viewed as the preferred option to take.

In particular, this chapter introduces the invasion of Iraq by a 'coalition of the willing' (the United States, the United Kingdom and Australia) on 20 March 2003 (Bellamy, 2004; Graham and Luke, 2005; Patman, 2006; Hobbs, 2010). The significance of this example is threefold:

- First, it demonstrates how governments or nation states attempt to justify their actions on the grounds of pre-empting a potential threat against their interests despite the failure of their justifications to materialise (Patman, 2006).
- Second, the chapter highlights how a government can utilise its justifications and media support not only to ignore mass public demonstrations against such invasive action, but also to condone

the perpetration of violence on another state despite the lack of electoral domestic support and despite international approval from the United Nations (UN) and others.

• Third, the neo–liberal/capitalist drive is also revealed, with the exposure of lucrative contracts being awarded to major corporate players regardless of the devastation and social harm caused by the invasion, war and an uncoordinated, unplanned aftermath.

Returning to earlier themes, the chapter moves on to discuss the interpretation of international laws and regulations, before commenting on the devastation wreaked by political violence in Iraq, including the absence of long-term planning in its reconstruction.

The Iraq invasion and the Iraq War

The Iraq War, which was named as 'Operation Iraqi Freedom', began on 20 March 2003, when the United States launched – with the support of the United Kingdom and, to a lesser extent, partners such as Australia – a missile attack intended to incapacitate the Iraqi government led by Saddam Hussein's Ba'ath Party (Kellner, 2005; Hobbs, 2010). Thereafter, a force of some 300,000 to 400,000 military personnel flooded into Iraq from Kuwait.

The conflict was decidedly one-sided. The previous US and UK strikes in the 1990s (coincidently conducted under the auspices of the then US President George Bush Sr, the father of George W. Bush) had rendered the Iraq military incapable of matching the coalition's hi-tech forces. Under relentless US bombing, around 8,000 Iraqi civilians were killed, 20,000 injured and maimed, alongside countless numbers of Iraqi military personnel (Iraq Body Count, 2003; Sundar, 2004). Only pockets of resistance appeared, usually from the Republican Guard. Besides these pockets of resistance, many of the regular Iraqi soldiers had abandoned their posts prior to and during the ground invasion (Hobbs, 2010). Advances upon Baghdad were relatively swift.

Legitimising invasion and war

In preparing for the invasion of – and war with – Iraq, the central arguments put forward by the major protagonists (George W. Bush, the US President; Tony Blair, the UK Prime Minister; and John Howard, the Australian Prime Minister) suggested that 'there was enough authority in existing UN Security Council Resolutions to justify the use of force against Iraq' (Bellamy, 2004, p134).

Essentially, the legitimation of war and invasion was based on the arguments put forward by the Attorney Generals of the UK and Australia which, in turn, rested on particular interpretations of Resolutions 660, 678, 687 and 1441 of the UN Charter. Each was conceived and implemented from 1990 to 2002 respectively (Lowe, 2003; Bellamy, 2004). It was argued that Resolution 660 – which was formulated on the invasion of Kuwait by Iraq – justified the three protagonists' proposed invasion of Iraq, by reviving the authorisation given to 'Member States co-operating with the Government of Kuwait ... to use all necessary means to uphold and implement resolution 660 ... and all subsequent resolutions and restore international peace and security in the area' (Resolution 660, 1990, cited in Lowe, 2003, p865).

Primarily, Resolution 1441 was said to be the force behind this revival of Resolution 660. Under Resolution 1441 it was determined that Iraq was in 'material breach of its disarmament obligations under Resolution 687' (Lowe, 2003, p865).

To legitimise the invasion and subsequent war even further, the argument continued to point towards the later Resolutions of 1154 (1998) and 1158 (1998), whereby Iraqi non-compliance constituted a threat to international security and peace (Bellamy, 2004). Thus the UK and Australian governments put forward the argument that the initial invasion and subsequent war with Iraq were legitimated by the Resolutions of the Security Council.

Naturally, the US agreed with this stance, yet they added a third argument to the case. Bush and his administration stressed a belief that a war with Iraq would be a continuation of the 'war against terrorism' (Bellamy, 2004), which invoked sentiments of the atrocities committed in the 9/11 aeroplane attack on the Twin Towers of the World Trade Center in New York and the partial attack on the Pentagon, Washington DC. In this latter respect, the major legitimising theme was the 'enemy as terrorist' (Sundar, 2004; Patman, 2006), with Iraq – along with Iran and North Korea – being part of an 'axis of evil' (Patman, 2006) and in possession of weapons of mass destruction (WMD) intended to be used against the West. As Altheide and Grimes (2005, p626) succinctly pointed out, a major aspect of the case against Iraq during the war, 'consisted of numerous messages about Iraq's stockpile of WMD, Saddam Hussein's support for terrorists, and the likelihood that terrorists would use such weapons against the United States'.

Pre-emption of such was, therefore, deemed to be the best and preferred course of action. Indeed, confirmation of intent came from *The National Security Strategy of the United States of America*, which was issued by the Bush administration in 2002 (Callinicos, 2005). This document emphasised the willingness of the US to take unilateral pre-emptive action of self-defence (Bellamy, 2004; Callinicos, 2005) if it needed to. Yet:

> ... this report took the idea of pre-emption even further. Not only those nations or groups visibly preparing to launch an attack should be in the cross-hairs – any group with access to weapons of mass destruction and the ability to deliver them against the USA should be considered targets, even if it was not known whether they would actually launch an attack. (Patman, 2006, p975)

To add to the mounting case of the terrorist threat, the personality of Saddam Hussein and the violation of human rights came under scrutiny, in particular the genocide of Iraqi Kurds. This had been a long process that had also occupied previous regimes. Under the title *Saddam's Chemical Weapons Campaign: Halabja* (1988), for example, the US Department of State had accused Saddam Hussein of being 'the first world leader in modern times to have brutally used chemical weapons against his own people' (US Department of State, 1988, p1, cited in Lin, 2007, p3625). The focus on Saddam as an evil individual continued:

> His goals were to systematically terrorise and exterminate the Kurdish population in northern Iraq, to silence his critics, and to test the effects of his chemical and biological weapons. Hussein launched chemical attacks against 40 Kurdish villages and thousands of innocent civilians in 1987-88, using them as testing grounds. (US Department of State, 1988, p1, cited in Lin, 2007, p3625)

Although this document predates George W. Bush's administration, it did, nonetheless, still have relevance to the 2003 invasion of Iraq. Halabja – and the gassing of other Kurdish towns and villages – became yet another of the pretexts for the 'coalition of the willing' to rally behind and invade Iraq and remove Saddam Hussein (Lin, 2007). Clearly, the character assassination of Saddam Hussein was designed to demonstrate how untrustworthy and dictatorial he was. A pre-emptive attack was thus painted as the only viable way in which further heinous acts could be prevented (see also Chapter Four).

By contrast, the US, UK and Australian leaders painted a more positive picture of each other and their alliance. During the actual 21 days of conflict, the leaders of the US and the UK tried to justify their actions under the banner of 'the coalition of the willing' and with a personal affirmation of each other's abilities and objectivity. Of Tony Blair, George W. Bush said:

> [he] is a friend, he is a strong leader, we are bound by the strong conviction that freedom belongs to everybody and we have got to work together to make the world a more peaceful place ... In order to achieve peace all countries in our region must take responsibility to do their best to fight off terror, and I know the Prime Minister joins me as we mourn the loss of life. (George W. Bush cited in Graham and Luke, 2005, p22)

Besides the camaraderie expressed through the use of 'friend', 'a strong leader' and that they were 'bound', there were other inferences and assumptions which served as a means to justify the war. The concept of making 'the world a more peaceful place' appeared, at face value, to be honourable, to say the least – likewise, notions of 'freedom' and that our region (the Western world of neo-liberalism) had to fight off terror. The use of the word 'terror' was yet another attempt to gain justification on the basis of a pre-emptive strike.

In response to Bush on a visit to the UK, Blair stated that he wanted to:

> ... thank President Bush for coming here ... as well as our own pride in our own forces during the course of this conflict we have watched with immense admiration the skill and tenacity and professionalism of the American forces. This is a strong alliance, we are strong allies and I think day by day the proof of that wisdom of that alliance grows. (Tony Blair, cited in Graham and Luke, 2005, p22)

In this speech, the bond between Blair and Bush – and by implication the two nations – was clearly expressed through his declaration that they had formed a 'strong alliance' and that there was an 'immense admiration' for the US forces deployed. Moreover, the use of the word 'wisdom' could be applied to the choice of alliance partners and the decision to wage war. In both scenarios, a sense of thoughtful deliberation and objective decision-making were invoked as a form of legitimation that was growing 'day by day' throughout the UK and the US. Yet there were also hints of justification on the basis of neo-liberalism through the use of the term 'professionalism' – 'the key word of corporatist business here applied to organised and massive violence' (Graham and Luke, 2005, p22).

The third leader in the 'coalition of the willing', the Australian Prime Minister, John Howard, expressed deference to the leadership of both Bush and Blair. Not only did he point out how powerful the US was, but also how they 'were an easy mark for all the critics and all the people who have grumbles'. He also declared 'as a fellow participant ... how much I admire the leadership of Tony Blair on this issue' (John Howard, cited in Graham and Luke, 2005, p22-3). Respect and fellowship resonated with the statements of Bush and Blair, while the Iraq conflict was reduced to an 'issue' in an attempt to play down what some would have called an atrocity. In a way, Howard's speech reflected the unity of a willing triumvirate by voicing legitimation through sanitisation, fellowship, respect and strong leadership. Once again, the 'issue' of Iraq was presented as a neo-liberal 'management problem that had to be solved through strong *leadership*' (Graham and Luke, 2005, p23), designed to provide freedom, peace and the promotion of democratic values that the 'coalition' – and the US in particular – can introduce and thereby reform the Middle East region at large.

Media support for the war

The justification for waging war on Iraq became manifest in an international propaganda exercise based on the claims that:

> Saddam Hussein was implicated in the 9/11 attacks on the United States, had not complied with the United Nations (UN) requirements about weapons inspections, and still harboured numerous weapons of mass destruction (WMD) that he planned to use against the United States ... [and others] as well as deliver to terrorists. (Altheide and Grimes, 2005, p618; see also Patman, 2006)

Nowhere more than in the US was this propaganda justification more apparent. And no-one was more prominent than Rupert Murdoch in purveying this form of reasoning to the general public. As discussed in Chapter Five, Murdoch's world media empire put him in prime position to promote the agendas of both his political associates and, of course, himself. In the US, for instance, Murdoch's cable news service (FOX News) set the standards and formula for the build-up to the Iraq invasion and the reporting of events during the war. As such,

Murdoch exerted his powerful position to use his news and reporting platforms as key cultural engines capable of simultaneously shaping and interpreting so-called 'reality' (Hobbs, 2010).

In the pursuit of ratings and increased revenue (see also Chapter Five), objective and politically neutral reporting was abandoned by presenters on FOX News. Instead a more aggressive interviewing style was deployed to introduce the tried-and-tested Murdoch formula of entertainment and sensationalism (Halper and Clark, 2004; Hobbs, 2010). Indeed, during the 2003 invasion of Iraq, FOX News became the most watched cable news service, thus setting the standards for patriotic television by echoing the Bush administration's official stance. Furthermore, any challenges to the White House's position were robustly rebuffed and even made to appear tantamount to treason (Calabrese, 2005; Hobbs, 2010). Other news services followed suit in an attempt to reverse their dwindling ratings.

Known as the 'FOX effect' (Greenwald, 2004, cited in Hobbs, 2010), this 'infotainment' appeal to attract/gain viewers became anchored around threats to invade nations to prevent the future attacks or threats to safety of the US, UK and, indeed, Australia. With reference to 9/11, these threatening nations – who were referred to as the 'axis of evil' and which included Iraq – essentially helped to inflame a climate of fear based on the theme of the enemy as 'terrorist' (Altheide and Grimes, 2005). Crucially, fear was the first part of a triad of factors (the others being consumption and international intervention), which transformed the meaning of terrorism into more than a tactic, but into an idea, a lifestyle and the state of the world (Kellner, 2004; Altheide and Grimes, 2005).

In addition, the new style of reporting in an entertaining way enhanced this process by:

1. fear supporting consumption as a tangible way for the audience to maintain an identity of substance and character
2. the symbolic joining of giving and consumption as governmental and business propaganda to emphasise the common themes of spending and buying
3. the construction of broad symbolic enemies and goals in the absence of a clear target for reprisals (that is Iraq). (Adapted from Kellner, 2004; Altheide and Grimes, 2005)

In practice, all of this meant that the war and invasion of Iraq gained support in the US at least in a 'jingoistic', nationalist patriotic form. Democratic support for the invasion from the major protagonist in the 'coalition' was almost guaranteed. Indeed, that was also a conviction/ interpretation of Blair in the UK, which was also subject to a Murdoch media barrage.

In a similar vein, the same was expected in Australia, not least because of an inherent bias in the reporting of Murdoch newspapers – specifically, in the reporting of *The Australian*, founded by Murdoch in 1964. Other papers in his empire and subject to his views on the war were the *Herald Sun*, Melbourne's most widely read tabloid, and the *Daily Telegraph*, Sydney's most widely read tabloid (Hobbs, 2010). When comparing *The Australian* to the reporting of the *Sydney Morning Herald* (the biggest rival to *The Australian* in New South Wales if not further afield), Hobbs (2010) found that between 21 February and 21 March 2003 *The Australian* was far more likely to use the key coalition phrase 'weapons of mass destruction' than the *Sydney Morning Herald*. Over the aforementioned period, the ratio of usage of this phrase was 181/120 out of the word total for Iraq War news items respectively. For the phrase 'coalition of the willing', the ratio was 42/31, while the use of the words 'terrorism' or 'terrorists' was 287/247 (Hobbs, 2010, p198). By contrast, the same comparison discovered that *The Australian* was less likely to refer to the action in Iraq as an 'invasion', which has aggressive connotations (93 words as opposed to 226 in the *Sydney Morning Herald*) (Hobbs, 2010, p198). Mention of 'oil' or 'oilfields' was 125/218 (p198), which could be of relevance to Murdoch's neo-liberal bent and the importance of oil in the West (see later).

Just on this quantitative analysis alone, it is possible to see how the media – disproportionately owned and directed by Murdoch – purveyed (and influenced) the views of the coalition leaders. In this respect, the media can, with a few exceptions, be viewed as a powerful ally of neo-liberalism and the neo-liberal state in which they have a vested interest.

The role and subversion of Western capitalist interest

Naturally, this media coverage was partly a symptom of, and partly a vehicle for, capitalist interests. As in the case of Murdoch's empire it was also a reflection of personal vested interest. Likewise, the interests of capital can be further demonstrated as the periods building up to the Iraq invasion, during the war and as the aftermath unfolded.

In relation to these three distinct periods, it is worth noting the vested interests of Halliburton an American multinational cooperation and one of the largest oil field services companies in the world and US Vice-President Dick Cheney. Cheney's position represents a significant example of how corporate interest operated around and within the discussions, drive and strategic positioning relating to the invasion of Iraq. Specifically, Cheney 'received a million dollars per year in "deferred compensation" payments ... since retiring as the corporation's CEO immediately after his nomination as Bush's running mate in 2000' (Graham and Luke, 2005, p25). Halliburton became the recipient of post-war reconstruction contracts worth billions of US dollars (Graham and Luke, 2005). Moreover, the pre-invasion, pre-war vested interests of capital and Halliburton were also demonstrated by the post-war revelation that the Bush administration had, before the war began, allocated reconstruction to Halliburton (culminating in the eventual sum of $12 billion) and also to the Bechtel Corporation, which negotiated around $2.8 billion worth of contracts (Juhasz, 2007, unpaginated). The timing of these allocations was crucial. Clear financial incentives were there for corporations to not only compete for but also, arguably, to hasten along the process of invasive action and its completion. In other words, the invasion and war were in their interest and, if conflict was to happen, substantial financial rewards would be reaped from repairing the damage that the invasion and war had inflicted (Graham and Luke, 2005; Klein, 2007).

Certainly it is true that 'the occupation has paid some big dividends – to the American companies that won a clean sweep of contracts to rebuild Iraq's physical infrastructure, health, education, transport and political systems' (Medani, 2004, p28). Despite this, Paul Bremer – the head of the Coalition Provisional Authority responsible for issuing reconstruction contracts – announced, in 2003 after the contracts to Halliburton and Bechtel had been awarded, the Bush administration's plans to rebuild Iraq along the lines of neo-liberal, free market principles. Bremer stated that: 'For a free Iraq to thrive, its economy must be transformed – and this will require the wholesale reallocation of resources and people from state control to private enterprise, the promotion of free trade, and the mobilization of domestic and foreign capital' (Bremer, 2003, cited in Medani, 2004, p28).

Of prime interest here was the mention of 'domestic capital', yet little of Bremer's transformation has become evident to Iraqis. Moreover, free trade can hardly be said to have been created or encouraged. What little competition for contracts there was tended to favour US companies by virtue of a restricted tendering process (if indeed there was a tender at all). Poignantly, US contractors were, and still are, contracted for work that should have been the preserve of the Iraqi interim authorities. In March 2003, for example, 'the Research Triangle Institute of North Carolina was the sole bidder for a one-year, $167.9 million deal to set up 108 local and provincial town councils. It retained its contract in 2004' (Medani, 2004, p31). After the handover of 'sovereignty', Creative Associates International, another USAID contractor, still earned millions to increase the recruitment and 'quality' of primary and secondary schools (Medani, 2004).

DynCorp was another winner of exclusive contracts. It was also guilty of being exclusive in who it employed. When it was recruiting security personnel, the advertisement stipulated:

> On behalf of the United States Department of States, Bureau of International Narcotics and Law Enforcement Affairs, DynCorp … is seeking individuals with appropriate experience and expertise to participate in an international effort to re-establish police, justice and prison functions in post-conflict Iraq. Interested applicants must be active duty, retired or recently separated sworn police officers, correctional officers or experienced judicial experts. US citizenship is required. (DynCorp, 2003, cited in Graham and Luke, 2005, p24)

Taken as a whole, the examples of the Research Triangle Institute, Creative Associates International and DynCorp demonstrated the monopoly that US companies had and, to some extent, still have in Iraq. To reiterate, little of Bremer's (2003) laissez-faire vision was on display with these contractors and contracts. To make matters worse, DynCorp's insistence on US citizenship was a deliberate attempt to exclude Iraqis from securing and running their own country.

Prior to reconstruction, however, and during the actual war – which, to reiterate, lasted only around 21 days (Hobbs, 2010) – other corporations profited: they received revenues from the weaponry and military facilities used in the conflict (Graham and Luke, 2005). Ironically, the weapons and military hardware provided allowed for the reconstruction contracts through the damage and destruction they caused. Again, the links between war and private capital are inevitably intertwined – more so, when one realises that some of the world's largest personal finance companies, IT firms, telecommunications organisations, media and entertainment companies, aerospace manufacturers and car makers are among the largest corporate manufacturers of military hardware and software. Prominent names include General Electric, Siemens, IBM, Toshiba, Boeing, Lockheed, British Aerospace, CBS, General Motors, Ford and Mitsubishi to name but a few (Graham and Luke, 2005).

Klein (2007) provided a detailed synopsis on the ideology behind the reconstruction of Iraq. At its core was an anti-statist and 'radical experiment in hollow governance'. She identified a deliberate ploy, where there was a distinct absence of senior civil servants in the Green Zone – the heavily fortified area of Baghdad which served as the headquarters for the reconstruction under the aegis of the Coalition Provisional Authority:

> By the time the think-tank lifers arrived in Baghdad, the crucial roles in the reconstruction had already all been outsourced to Halliburton and KPMG. Their job as public servants was simply to administer the petty cash, which in Iraq took the form of handing shrink-wrapped bricks of hundred dollar bills to contractors. It was a graphic glimpse into the acceptable role of government in a corporatist state. (Klein, 2007)

At least the public servants could satiate themselves with a meal from Pizza Hut or Burger King after their day's work, as these companies were contracted to run franchises for catering facilities. Finally – and without dwelling too heavily on one of the most frequent accusations levelled against the proposed invasion (that the war was solely about oil capture/control) – it has to be noted that the oilfields of Iraq were of interest and did, indeed, provide a motivating factor. When it came to oil, however, both private corporations and governmental interests would be served by an invasion of Iraq. In May 2001, for example, Vice-President Dick Cheney and his advisory team reported on the future energy needs of the US (Callinicos, 2005). It was estimated that by the year 2020, the US would be dependent on importing two-thirds of its oil needs. Naturally, big oil conglomerates stood to benefit from control of the oilfields with a massive market waiting in the US alone. Nevertheless, political interests were just as crucial. The heavy reliance on imported oil meant that the US would be tied 'even more closely to unstable and potentially hostile regions – the Middle East, Latin America, Central Asia, Russia and West Africa' (Callinicos, 2005, p599).

Although Middle Eastern oil was more important in other countries (most notably in the EU, Japan, China and India), the dilemma facing the US was still undesirable in the eyes of the Bush administration. An invasion of Iraq would, then, be in the best interests of both the private and political spheres. In terms of the political, control of Iraq's oilfields – the second largest in the world – would put the US in a more secure position. It would also free the US from depending on Saudi Arabia, which had the largest oil reserves in the world. In addition, control of Iraq and the military presence of the US would, it was believed, make them less reliant on Saudi military power in the Middle East. This was particularly acute as relations between the US and Saudi Arabia were deteriorating – especially since 9/11, where 15 out of the 19 suicide hijackers were Saudi subjects (Callinicos, 2005, p599). Harvey, writing in 2003, summarised the situation astutely:

> Europe and Japan, as well as East and South-East Asia (now crucially including China) are heavily dependent on Gulf oil, and these are regional configurations of political-economic power that now pose a challenge to US global hegemony in the worlds of production and finance. What better way for the United States to ward off that competition and secure its own hegemonic position than to control the prices, conditions, and distribution of the key economic resources upon which those competitors rely? And what better way to do that than to use the one line of force where the US still remain all-powerful – military might? (Harvey, 2003, p25, cited in Callinicos, 2005, p599-60)

From this discussion, it is clear that neo-liberal capitalist interests had a vested interest in the invasion of Iraq. Even when putting the invasion of Iraq to one side for a moment, it is reasonable to conclude that war in general tends to be profitable for private enterprises and it reflects what could be called a 'military-industrial complex' which we are all tied to, whether directly or indirectly (Graham and Luke, 2005): a complex that has a great deal of sway with the workings of a neo-liberal democracy.

Erroneous mass interpretations of international law, misleading representations and ignorance of the democratic

If the notion of profit as a motivational factor for going to war with Iraq was not enough, then the interpretation of international law adds to the suspicion that there was another agenda on the table besides the need for a pre-emptive strike. As this chapter has shown, the 'willing coalition' rested most of its case on the basis that they were acting in self-defence and/or preventing a humanitarian catastrophe.

Under international law, though, there was no legal justification for such invasive acts (Lowe, 2003). The so-called 'revival' of Resolution 660 by Resolution 1441, which allowed member states of the UN to cooperate with Kuwait and 'use all necessary means to uphold and implement resolution 1660 and subsequent resolutions ... to restore international peace and security in the area' was at best a misunderstanding or at worse a misrepresentation (Lowe, 2003, p865). To reiterate, the 'revival', issue was interpreted by the US, the UK and Australia on the grounds that Resolution 1441 determined Iraq to be in material breach of its arms regulations set out in Resolution 687 (Bellamy, 2004). Resolution 1441 did not, however, authorise the use of force against Iraq and it definitely did not authorise a 'revival' of its contents to those states acting in coalition with Kuwait during 1991.

Furthermore, the conveniently overlooked caveats in Resolutions 686 and 687 suggested that the authorisation to use force was only valid during the military operation to expel Iraq from Kuwait. Any further action – should there be any – had to be decided and agreed upon by the UN Security Council. Indeed, the Security Council had not abandoned or lost interest in matters relating to Iraq. In fact, it was active at all critical times after 1991. Crucially, Resolution 1441 made it clear that some members actually needed a second resolution to grant the necessary authorisation to use force against Iraq. This was a direct contradiction of the interpretation adopted by the US (Lowe, 2003). As a consequence, the invasion of Iraq in 2003 lacked any legal justification which, in turn, rendered the actions of the 'willing coalition' illegal (Bellamy, 2004).

Besides the misunderstanding of international law – whether deliberate or not – there were a number of other false claims made by the three main protagonists against Iraq before and during the war. For example:

> The exhaustive debates in the US and Britain on the intelligence used to justify the invasion and conquest of Iraq ... established beyond any doubt that the official pretext for the war – the continued possession by the Iraqi Ba'athist regime of weapons of mass destruction – had no basis in fact. (Callinicos, 2005, p593)

Moreover, even before the invasion and war, US governmental agencies seriously questioned Iraq's possession of WMD (Altheide and Grimes, 2005). Arguably, the idea that Iraq possessed such weaponry was a smokescreen devised to 'manage' public opinion in the 'coalition of the willing'. Behind that façade was the intention to impose a regime change, depose Saddam Hussein and enforce a neo-liberal democratic revolution. These accusations are further substantiated when a closer look is taken at the claims that Hussein was linked to 9/11 and supported terrorism. Yet again, there were further doubts about their validity, thus casting a shadow over the purported reasons for going to war. Despite constant reiteration of the links with 9/11 and the support of terrorism, evidence refuted the connections being made; prior to 9/11, for instance, the Bush administration had stated that Iraq was not a major threat to the US (Callinicos, 2005).

Given these doubts, it is not unreasonable to conclude that along with economic and geopolitical interests there was – and still is – an ideological neo-liberal agenda that the Bush administration and their 'willing coalition' wanted to implement (Callinicos, 2005). It was an agenda that would be pursued whether public support had been secured or not. Indeed, on 15 February 2003 there was a global demonstration – across 600 cities throughout the world – against an upcoming war against Iraq. In many of these countries, the marches broke all attendance records (Walgrave and Verhulst, 2009). Slogans such as 'Not in my name' and 'No blood for oil' predominated in a concerted worldwide resistance to a potential invasion of Iraq. The demonstrators were not, as the most cynical would suspect, homogeneous – in culture, age and political persuasions – and, therefore, the size and composition of the crowds perplexed respective leaders and commentators in terms of the effect that the proposed war had on its own citizens. In the UK, for instance, *The Times* (2003) described the London marches as:

> Groups representing their local churches and mosques, university students, parents with young children ... People who have never been on a demonstration before ... grandmothers, ranging in age from the later 40s to a frail 86. Cooks, teachers, doctors, computer programmers ... Virgin marchers, elderly, the young, families: people from all walks of life ... [were there demonstrating]. (Cited in Walgrave and Verhulst, 2009, p1359)

Not insignificantly, there were over one million (some would say two million) marchers united against the imminent war and invasion in London. Elsewhere, three million marched in Rome, one million or more in Barcelona and around two hundred thousand in both San Francisco and New York City (Tharoor, 2013, unpaginated).

Partly because of a general underreporting of the actual numbers involved in the marches (the Metropolitan Police, for example, estimated that seven hundred and fifty thousand took part – Gordon, 2003; Walgrave and Verhulst, 2009), leaders of the warring coalition seemed remarkably dismissive of the protests. In Glasgow, on the same day as the march in London, Tony Blair, to name but one leader, responded to the marchers by saying:

> The moral case against the war has a moral answer: it is the moral case for removing Saddam … it is the reason, frankly, why if we do have to act, we should do so with a clear conscience. Yes, there are consequences of war. If we remove Saddam by force, people will die and some will be innocent … But I ask the marchers to understand this … If there are 500,000 on that march, that is still less than the number of people whose deaths Saddam has been responsible for. If there are one million, that is still less than the number of people who died in the wars he started. (Blair, 2003, cited in Gordon, 2003, p1117)

As previously discussed, Blair continued with the demonisation of Saddam Hussein, but this was only part of the justification for war. The moral case Blair put forward rested on the assumption that there would be fewer deaths and less suffering of ordinary Iraqi people (a claim that will be disputed later in this chapter). For the time being, though, it is important to ask: what happened to the 'wisdom' and the sense of 'objectivity' that Blair spoke of in support of the alliance with Bush? Where, also, was the respect of democracy in terms of the will of the people who clearly did not want the invasion to go ahead?

To make matters worse, the earlier assertion that the reasons for going to war fit with a neo-liberal ideological agenda – as opposed to listening to the democratic will of the British population – is substantiated further by Blair's 'morality' response to the march in London. As the quotation demonstrates, Blair's moral case rested on the assumption that fewer would die and suffer if the war and defeat of Saddam occurred, as opposed to his being left in power. Nevertheless, a look back to the events after the first war against Saddam – orchestrated by George Bush Sr – depicted a very different scenario. After that war, it was estimated that 'in excess of half a million innocent young children … [had] died and mass poverty … [had] befallen the Iraqi population' (Gordon, 2003, p1119).

Where, then, is the 'morality' behind such logic? The inability to consider or learn from past events hardly constituted excusable behaviour. It was a neglect/negligence that suggested other, ulterior motives for going to war. Rather than constructing a 'moral' case for war, evidence could, and for many does, suggest that this was an 'immoral' case, based on our definition and built on Western interests as outlined earlier in this chapter.

The devastating effects of political violence, torture and state terrorism

The political violence inflicted on Iraq by the US in particular and its allies in general is easily demonstrable. Regardless of the political or socioeconomic reasoning that propelled the bombings and subsequent invasion, none of the already depicted justifications can excuse the deaths and injuries of thousands of civilians. Civilian deaths and injuries cannot be reasonably accounted for in terms of a pre-emptive strike against a ruthless dictator supposedly in possession of WMD. The idea of enriching Iraqi society through the imposition of neo-liberal ideology, economy and society does not represent any morally justifiable position either; nor does the mass destruction of the country's infrastructure, civilian homes and urban areas. All that has happened in Iraq is that the oppression of Saddam Hussein has been replaced with mass devastation and a loss of relatively – in comparison to the situation today – stable communities, living standards and livelihoods (discussed in more detail later) in an atrocious example of political violence in the name of 'liberation'.

Yet going beyond these politically violent atrocities, there was also the grim spectre of Abu Ghraib prison in Iraq during and after the invasion. Despite the revelation that US soldiers were guilty of torturing Iraqi detainees, General Paul D. Clement reaffirmed on 28 April 2004 the Bush administration's pledge to abide 'by its obligations under the Convention Against Torture – including prevention of 'acts of cruel, inhuman or degrading treatment or punishment which did not amount to torture" (Amann, 2005, p2090). Hours later, that same day, viewers of *60 Minutes II* were presented with 'the image of a black-hooded figure standing atop a box. He … [was] naked beneath the black robe that … [draped] outstretched arms, from which wires … [ran] to some unseen source of electricity' (Amann, 2005, p2091). In the same programme, pictures showed uniformed American men and women posing with naked Iraqi prisoners, shots of prisoners piled in a pyramid and photographs of the US military personnel laughing, pointing and posing. Viewers then witnessed Brigadier General Mark Kimmitt (deputy director of the US-led coalition) telling the American people to not judge their army of 150,000 'on the actions of a few' (Amann, 2005, p2091). More revelations followed, which countered the suggestion that these were acts of only a few. Coincidently, one might argue, many of the recorded abuses occurred after a visit to Abu Ghraib from Major Geoffrey D. Miller, the commander of the Joint Task Force at Guantanamo.[1]

When turning to the accusation of state terrorism, it is reasonable to argue that this form of terrorism is a product of all the actions described earlier. Civilian deaths, the destruction of the country's infrastructure, torture and loss of livelihood combine to create feelings of insecurity, fear and a sense of terror. Continued conflicts after the invasion did not help either. As the next section will clarify, such feelings have not dissipated; rather, they have been exacerbated when the effects of the social harm inflicted on the population are considered in more detail. Suffice to say now, though, that the disregard on behalf of the 'willing coalition' to respect the culture and communities of Iraq, by implementing a new, 'liberating' agenda of neo-liberal politics and economics, only served to heighten such feelings (Ismael and Ismael, 2005).

Lack of reconstruction, lack of long-term awareness and the prevalence of social harm

As this chapter has shown so far, the invasion of Iraq has had devastating effects on the general population of the country and its infrastructure. However, the devastation has not ended with the conflict. Devastation continued (and still continues) with the promised but inadequately planned reconstruction and repair of the damage inflicted by the war on Iraq.

To fully explore this – and to fully make a case about the immorality behind such an invasion – the attempts at reconstruction are best examined through the lens of social harm. As Brown (2005) pointed out, there has been no consistent, systemic strategy for addressing important environmental concerns relating to the political, economic, social and/or technological situation after the conflict. More specifically, the effects on the environment from the damaged infrastructure were virtually ignored at worse or overlooked at best. In particular, little was

---

[1] Guantanamo Bay detention camp is a US military prison in Cuba and, because of its location, is considered to be outside US legal jurisdiction.

done to counter the pre-2003 'staining of large areas of the desert by irregular oil discharges, widespread oil contamination of surface water and ground-water and the destruction by draining of the Mesopotamian Marshlands in the South (and the consequent displacement and migration of the Madan (Marsh Arabs)' (Brown, 2005, p764).

During the actual war, however, things were made even worse. One prime example was the use of depleted uranium (DU) weapons. In a report released by the Dutch peace group PAX, US forces fired nearly 10,000 DU rounds, most of which were aimed at targets near or in heavily populated areas that included As Samawah, Nasiriyah and Basrah (Edwards, 2014, unpaginated). This was despite official warnings at the time and despite knowledge of the long-term cancerous effects of DU use.

Notwithstanding the failure to rectify or consider much of the health and ecological implications of actions committed before, during and after the conflict/war, the invasion of Iraq also had other devastating social consequences. At the time of writing this book, conflict, assassinations (of specific religious groups) and the entire destruction of cities and ways of life still continue. Yet reducing such divides as internal religious conflicts between Sunni and Shia Muslims is rather simplistic and misses the wider picture. Social upheaval and the interests and fears of Iran, Saudi Arabia and Qatar in the area also have to be concern: a substantial area of consideration that was overlooked when invading Iraq and which will become apparent when looking at the problems within Iraq after invasion of the 'willing coalition'.

Initially, then, external interests have to be taken aside for one moment. It has to be noted that the internal divisions unleashed by the invasion created a security vacuum (Dodge, 2006). As we have commented on earlier, George W. Bush committed the US to build a neo-liberal government in the wake of the invasion. This was a 'top down' operation that was 'driven by dynamics, personnel and ideologies completely outside the society they … [were] operating in' (Dodge, 2006, p190). Fundamental to the success of this new order was the new state's ability to monopolise the legitimate use of violence, whereby order can be imposed. In the longer term, order would allow for the emergence of a non-coercive bureaucracy to implement state decisions and changes across the entire country. Indeed, 'This evolution of state power would be closely linked to the ability of state institutions to penetrate society in a regularised fashion and become central to the population's ongoing and daily "strategies of survival" (Dodge, 2006, p191).

With the benefit of hindsight, it has become clear that order was not imposed in any meaningful way across Iraq. Nor was there an effective plan to develop Iraqi involvement in the reconstruction of Iraq after 2003. As Brown (2005) pointed out, what was missing from the development strategy were the three vital functions of:

- instilling Iraqi dignity
- mobilising the Iraqi people as problem solvers in their own social environment
- facilitating Iraqi access to the higher levels of decision-making.

All three of these vital functions represented necessary prerequisites to building a participatory approach that would bring 'development alive and ensure that initiatives lean[ed] towards being people focussed' (Brown, 2005, p762), as opposed to being project focused: thus allowing for sustainable reconstruction. Of course, with a sustainable reconstruction of the infrastructure comes economic security and by implication human security, yet the exclusion of Iraqi involvement in the reconstruction contracts (as depicted earlier) deprived Iraqis of wealth-generating opportunities and, therefore, the restoration of their livelihoods.

The loss of livelihood was to have devastating consequences. Areas were left 'to fester with high unemployment and unfulfilled dreams of receiving even the most basic of essential services in power, water and sanitation' (Brown, 2005, p768). In the Sadr City area of Baghdad, for instance, over two million people lived in squatter conditions (Brown, 2005, p768). Malnutrition rates for Iraqi children 'increased from 4% before the US invasion to 7.7% after more than a year of occupation' (Ismael and Ismael, 2005, p616). Not surprisingly, resentment arose and areas like Sadr City became fertile recruiting grounds for disaffected youth by rebel groups, not least by Moqtada al-Sadr's Mehdi Army. Insurgency proliferated as latent conflicts became apparent. Security and order were not achieved, while human security and livelihood were jeopardised even further as internal conflicts targeted the US-oriented reconstruction.

More worryingly, the conflicts and violent insurgency in Iraq allowed for the growth of the extreme Sunni fundamentalist group known as Islamic State (IS) to exploit a growing security vacuum and foster their declared ambition to establish a caliphate (named after the perceived natural political and religious successor to Mohammed, Caliph) in parts of northern Iraq and Syria (BBC, 2014). In order to achieve this, killing and warfare has continued – and still continues – in Iraq alongside a number of well-publicised beheadings. Furthermore, the predominantly Shia nation of Iran, the Hanbali Sunnis of Saudi Arabia and the Wahhabi-dominated nation of Qatar are extremely ill at ease with this fundamentalist IS caliphate, which could threaten their borders, interests and possibly internal security. So much so, that the latter two nations are now (at the time of writing) involved in bombing campaigns alongside Bahrain, Jordan and the United Arab Emirates within Syria in the struggle to thwart IS (Kovessy, 2014).

As before, the neglect by the US and its allies to look at long-term consequences of the invasion has created a destabilised Middle East that could result in more devastating examples of social harm, should the instability continue. Again, accountability for the situation have not been held accountable for the US- and UK-led invasion of Iraq.

A final word

Throughout this chapter the immoral – if not criminal – acts of states, governments and the media have been charted. Despite neo-liberal corruption in the pursuit of profit, the contravention of international legislation and the violation of human rights (through violence and torture), none of the 'willing coalition' (primarily the US, the UK and Australia) have been held to account.

As the final part of the chapter has demonstrated, the lens of social harm is a powerful analytical tool by which the extent and gravity of the illegal invasion of Iraq can be truly measured. That said, any criminal prosecutions that have gone ahead have not reached beyond the individual and have been contained within the old adage of a 'rotten apple in a barrel' scenario. To reiterate, no head of state or state agency of the US, the UK or Australia has been legally deemed culpable. To add insult to injury, state culpability itself is:

> concealed by the work of relatively autonomous institutions that ... [attempt to] engender public sanctions or complicity in violence against minorities and distant others. For far too long, anthropology [and criminology/sociology] have specialized in culturalist explanations of violence that inevitably set up hierarchies between cultures without looking at the transnational flow of ideas of security, terror and 'normal' states of the economy and the global reach of a few media organisations. (Sundar, 2004, p157)

To view the perpetrators and supporters of such violence as warped individuals merely distorts the bigger picture. It is myopic to say the least. Social harm, however, overcomes that myopia and broadens the panorama to help confront these discourses of hate, destruction and neo-liberal profiteering, by exposing the immorality and crimes of the state and the powerful. Indeed, Chapter Eight also explores the utility of social harm as a means of highlighting such immoral behaviour: but in this instance it is in relation to how illegal/immoral acts affected the civilian population in Argentina and the mining communities in the UK.

SEVEN

Without and within: state crime in Northern Ireland (violence, collusion and the paramilitaries)

So far we have witnessed the difficulties in defining state crime stemming from difficulties in determining the nature of the ideal state and the terminological crossover between state crime and other forms of non-conventional criminality. We have considered the ways in which state crime moves beyond borders via the international drugs trade and also how states have acted in criminal ways towards other states. In this chapter, we consider how analysing state crime as external pressure exerted from one regime towards another can break down.

Following on from Chapter Six, this chapter depicts a case study of state crime/terrorism in the UK and Ireland, by considering the issue of collusion between various paramilitary groups in Northern Ireland and the British and Irish Police (Guardai). There are many features of the period known as the 'Troubles' that may fall under the rubric of state crime; we have chosen to concentrate our discussion on the role of collusion between state agencies in paramilitary organisations and the perpetration of episodes of often extreme violence. We contend that actions undertaken by the then Royal Ulster Constabulary (RUC) could be deemed to be examples of state crime/terrorism from within, as they occurred on UK territory. On this basis, and despite the claim made by many in the nationalist and Republican communities that Northern Ireland is part of a united Ireland, the actions of the Guardai can be interpreted as state crime/terrorism from without. Whichever side of the argument one prefers, there can be little dispute that actions taken from both sides constitute state criminality on the basis that such collusion with paramilitary groups was undertaken by organisations of the state, whether it be of the UK or Eire (Taylor, 1998, 2000, 2002).

The case of Northern Ireland is used here, then, to highlight how definitions of state crime are very much contingent on political standpoints, on issues of identity and citizenship which, in turn, influence how the labels of state terrorism and state crime can be applied. To fully draw out the nuances of such distinctions – and to present the case that collusion represents both criminal and terroristic activity – the chapter covers some of the background to the 'Troubles' in Northern Ireland, by introducing key terminology and symbolism surrounding the dispute along with the main protagonists involved. The issue of sectarianism and the role of the state are also discussed. The next part of the chapter looks at the issue of collusion in terms of how agencies of law enforcement are suspected of facilitating murder in the province over a number of years (Mulcahy, 2006). This is done through the examination of a number of high-profile cases. The final section examines the findings of the Saville and Smethwick inquiries into collusion, concluding that it has been a key feature of the 'Troubles', with both the British and Irish states being complicit.

Background to the 'Troubles'

The 'Troubles' generally refer to the period stretching from the late 1960s to the late 1990s. As with most issues relating to Northern Ireland, this is a matter of some debate. McAuley (2003) suggested that even referring to the Northern Ireland situation as 'the Troubles' is misleading, as it implies that there is a solution waiting to be found. Since its creation (under force) in 1922, Northern Ireland has remained a key challenge for politicians and policy makers alike. Even the term 'Northern Ireland' carries with it ideological baggage, so much so that in her memoirs, the former Secretary of State for Northern Ireland, Mo Mowlam, preferred 'N. Ireland' as her chosen descriptor. Referring to her role in the run-up to the Belfast agreement (often referred to as the 'Good Friday Agreement'), Mowlam (2002) insisted that:

> I have written this book from my own perspective. I could find no other way to do it. It is my perspective on the marches and the talks and how we got to where we have. One of the difficulties is illustrated by my use of N. Ireland throughout the book. North is preferred by the nationalists as it suggests the north of the whole of Ireland; Northern is preferred by the unionists, signifying that it is part of the UK. (Mowlam, 2002, pxvi)

Although this is inevitably something of a caricature, 'nationalists' refers mainly to those who identify as Irish and who frequently celebrate and participate in Irish cultures and traditions. Nationalists are predominantly Catholic. The term is often used interchangeably with 'Republican', although many nationalists would not consider themselves Republicans. The latter term tends to refer to the more militant tendencies of the Catholic/nationalist communities. 'Unionists', meanwhile, are those who wish to remain loyal to the United Kingdom. They are traditionally from the Protestant communities in the North. Many Unionists are members of anti-Catholic organisations, such as the Orange Order, and the more militant are, or were, part of Loyalist paramilitary organisations.

Although there is much debate as to the origins of the dispute, what is clear is that 'the most contested expression of politics and of political identity within the United Kingdom still surrounds that of the six counties of Northern Ireland' (McAuley, 2003, p135). Underpinning much of this contestation and identity politics is debate around whether the six counties are and/or should be part of the United Kingdom. One line of argument dates the genesis of the 'Troubles' back at least 800 years, with the Norman invasion of Ireland. Another suggests that the Tudor conquest of Ireland by England under Henry VIII marked a key episode. Considered to be one of the bloodiest times in the history of Ireland, the 17th century is also a pivotal period. At this time, Catholic landowners were increasingly disenfranchised in the aftermath of the Protestant 'plantation' of the north-east of the island, whereby many rich Protestant landowners, from England and the west of Scotland, confiscated land from Irish rebels and imported tenants from their own estates onto this new land. McAuley (2003) effectively distilled the complex history of the island:

> In Northern Ireland, British unionists and Irish nationalists hold conflicting views on the origins of the conflict, its causes and its solutions. History is often recycled to interpret contemporary events and to highlight continuities with the past. Events such as the 'plantation of Ireland', Cromwell's arrival in 1641, the Williamite victory in 1690 or the rebellion of 1798 (to name but a few) are often invoked when discussing contemporary political events. (McAuley, 2003, p136)

The process known as 'Partition' was also a central development. Since the Act of Union 1801, Ireland had been governed from mainland Britain. 'Partition' refers to the creation of Northern Ireland and the emergence of two separate states on the island of Ireland. The two-state island emerged in 1920 with the passing of the Government of Ireland Act, which effectively was a product of the aftermath of the 1916 Rebellion and Easter Uprising followed by the 1919 Irish War of Independence between the Irish Republican Army (IRA) and the United Kingdom. In line with an agreed political settlement in 1922, the political entity of Northern Ireland comprises six of the nine counties of Ulster.[1] The terms Ulster and Northern Ireland are often used interchangeably. A legacy of the plantations is that Northern Ireland has a majority Protestant population, but a large Catholic minority. Southern Ireland, as it was known after partition, became the Irish Free State and was (and still is in its present form) largely Catholic. In times of increasing secularisation, there is some debate as to the accuracy and wisdom of these depictions, but for current purposes they will suffice.

The Irish Free Sate remained part of the British Commonwealth until 1949, when the final formal link with the United Kingdom was quashed and when the Irish Parliament (Oireachtas) passed the Republic of Ireland Act. It was significant that in the drafting of the constitution of the Republic, Articles 2 and 3 laid claim to the North. In many senses, this is a key foundation stone of the 'Troubles'. When examining the complexities of the case, Edwards (2011) suggested that:

> Such was the determinism to resist incorporation into the southern state that the Unionist administration began to equate its own dominance over local politics, society and culture with the survival of Northern Ireland itself ... When de Valera declared Eire to be 'a Catholic state for Catholic people', Sir James Craig ... Northern Ireland's first prime minister, responded with the (often misquoted) adage about Northern Ireland having 'a Protestant people and a Protestant parliament'. (Edwards, 2011, p16)

McAuley (2003, p136-7) reasoned that the origins of the conflict in Northern Ireland can be explained by the process where in most developed societies 'political structure and organisation is reinforced by the transmission of a set of reasonably consensual values from generation to generation', whereas Northern Ireland was and is different: different because 'political socialization' is very much a product of one's community, cultures and traditions. These create self-perpetuating discourses, which are backed up with careful selective readings of key events in history, which are then used to exacerbate tensions in contemporary society. In short, the process of socialisation in Northern Ireland has involved the early recognition of division and the danger of the 'other'. This is an issue to which we shall return.

---

[1] Ulster is one of four ancient provinces of Ireland, along with Connacht to the west, Munster to the south and Leinster to the east.

It is now widely accepted, and more contemporaneous accounts testify, that the Unionist governments in the period 1961-68 under the leadership of various figures starting with James Craig and culminating with Brian Faulkner oversaw a regime that practised a non-trivial degree of discrimination to nationalist Catholics. Yet this is still the source of debate. The perceived or real (depending on one's viewpoint) political and economic discrimination practised by the Protestant majority against the Catholic minority was largely ignored by politicians in mainland Britain. This may have been down to ignorance and repeated warnings by politicians to junior colleagues telling them to stay clear of the 'Irish issue' and that the question was too difficult to answer. Indeed, in his memoirs James Callaghan (1973, p98) recollected how, on becoming British Home Secretary in 1967, his despatch box contained papers on various pressing issues of the day, such as prisons, race relations and the police as well as the reform of the House of Lords. There was not, however, 'a single word about Northern Ireland'.

In his review of the issues, Whyte (1983, p2) believed a case can be made that discriminatory practices – seen as the source of much of the Nationalist grievance – were neither as malign nor benign as the two opposing sides maintained. Focusing on six main areas of social life, Whyte listed the order of discrimination in the following way, with the most serious first: '(1) Electoral practice; (2) Public employment; (3) Private employment; (4) Public housing; (5) Regional policy); (6) Policing'. He then went on to suggest that this list alone is somewhat redundant, as there have been great variations within these categories. With this in mind:

[a] more helpful classification might be geographical. A group of local authorities in the west of the province provide a startlingly high proportion of the total number of complaints. All the accusations of gerrymandering, practically all the complaints about housing and regional policy, and a disproportionate amount of the charges about public and private employment come from this area. The area – which consisted of Counties Tyrone and Fermanagh, Londonderry County Borough, and portions of Counties Londonderry and Armagh – had less than a quarter of the total population of Northern Ireland yet generated not far short of three-quarters of the complaints of discrimination. Elsewhere, discrimination occurred. The USC [Ulster Special Constabulary] was everywhere a Protestant militia;

> some police decisions betrayed partisanship; there were
> fewer Catholics in the higher reaches of the public service
> than were willing and qualified to serve; some private firms
> discriminated against Catholics. But when all this is said,
> the prominence of an area in the west remains. (Whyte,
> 1983, p30-1)

Although Whyte was probably correct, it is now widely acknowledged that the Northern Irish state practised discrimination against the minority Catholic nationalist population. One decisive piece of evidence for this came from the fact that this was actually recognised by the state itself. In 1963, when Terrence O'Neill became Prime Minister of Northern Ireland, he set about a process of reforming Stormont as the devolved Parliament in the province was known. McAuley (2003, p138) documented how 'this marked an attempt by sections of the unionist leadership to move away from an overtly discriminatory state and towards the notions of political and economic modernity finding expression in the rest of the United Kingdom'.

Such discrimination manifested itself in a variety of ways, although as the debates in the *British Journal of Sociology* throughout the 1980s testify, this (as with most things concerning the Northern Irish situation) was not without controversy. The initial dispute in the journal between Hewitt (1981, 1983, 1985) and O'Hearn (1983, 1985) revealed the extent of the issue of discrimination and violence in the province, but also the degree of disagreement surrounding its nature and prevalence and, in the case of violence, its cause or causes. Later, Kovalcheck (1987) tried to adjudicate, thus prompting further comment from Hewitt (1987). The debate was at times vitriolic. Hewitt's main assertion was that the extent of discrimination against the Catholic nationalist community as a spur for the 'Troubles' was considerably exaggerated. O'Hearn (1985), however, maintained that it was systematic and pervasive especially in terms of: the franchise; gerrymandering; the allocation of housing by local councils; and discrimination in the public and private sectors leading to high Catholic unemployment. These issues had been identified by the Cameron Commission (1969) as being a major factor in the outbreak of civil unrest in the late 1960s (Birrell, 1994). It was also apparent that these issues were a catalyst for the formation of the Northern Irish Civil Rights Association (NICRA), whose promotion of the concerns prompted the response by O'Neill's government which created fertile ground for the civil unrest that was to follow.

The aforementioned franchise referred to the particular voting arrangements in the province. One of the main points of contention was the block vote for businesses in local government elections, effectively disenfranchising a substantial number of Catholics due to their higher rates of unemployment. In addition, the vote was only extended to those who owned their own property and to their spouses. As many more Catholics were in rented accommodation, a higher proportion than Protestants were denied the vote. The issue of the franchise in local councils was closely tied to the issue of gerrymandering. Both often combined to give Unionists control of councils, even when the majority of the population were nationalists. The most cited and infamous example of this was in Londonderry/Derry City council. Londonderry/Derry is a city with a nationalist majority, but frequently returned a Unionist council due to the way that seats were allocated (Whyte, 1983, p5-7).

In terms of housing allocation, Birrell (1994) noticed that root and branch reorganisation of the administration of public sector housing in 1971 was undertaken to remedy the shortage of housing in the Province and to make sure that allocation was fair (with the obvious assumption that until this point it had not been). The Northern Ireland Housing Executive was created to this end and quickly introduced a model allocation scheme, based on fairness and need alongside the principle that housing resources should be distributed equally throughout the community. Birrell suggested that the creation of the Housing Executive served to depoliticise the issue of housing and thus sought to overcome allegations of sectarianism in this domain. On one level, this seemed to work, as housing allocation appeared to be more equal across religious groups. Importantly, however, and echoing the debates of the 1980s in the *British Journal of Sociology*, there is no clear evidence that discrimination was being practised. Birrell (1994) commented, therefore, that the allegations of the Cameron Commission were somewhat exaggerated and there was little statistical evidence of discrimination based on census data at the time.

The final grievance related to discrimination in employment. It had long been recognised that the main employers in the Province were more likely to employ Protestants over Catholics. This was particularly true in the shipyards of Belfast, where Harland Wolff employed a total of 10,000 workers in 1970, of whom only 400 were Catholic (O'Hearn, 1983, p444). There were also suggestions that the decision to locate the New University of Ulster in Coleraine as opposed to Londonderry/Derry in 1968 was an act of systematic discrimination, as the Stormont government did not want to locate a university in a primarily nationalist area. The flip side of this argument is that on one level, because of Catholic non-engagement with the institutions of the state, it made little sense to locate a university in Londonderry/Derry.

According to Amnesty International (1994, p2): 'In a period of over 20 years, the Republican armed groups have been responsible for over half the total number of deaths, the Loyalist groups for more than a quarter, and the security forces for about 11 per cent'. For a number of years in the early 1990s, Loyalist groups carried out more killings than Republicans (Taylor, 2000). There are countless and useful research materials documenting most aspects of the Northern Irish crisis – from policing and prisons to paramilitary activity and politics. Malcolm Sutton has been recording the details of deaths arising out of the conflict by triangulating evidence from newspaper cuttings, coroners' reports, observing funerals and studying books and pamphlets from 1969 to 2001. Although it was published in 2001, a website hosted by the University of Ulster[2] has continually updated Sutton's work. As of December 2009, the date of the most recent additional death added to the index, the total number of deaths in the conflict was 3,527. Moreover, when outlining the background to the conflict in Northern Ireland, McEvoy (2001, p9) emphasised that in addition to the number of killings from 1969 onwards (which he lists as over 3,600), over '40,000 people have been injured in a conflict which has cost the British and Northern Irish economy several billion pounds'. The Amnesty International (1994) report stated that the picture of the killings in Northern Ireland is complex and is not just a result of armed encounters between armed political groups and the security forces; on the contrary, since 1969, 'the largest numbers of deaths have been civilians; almost a third of members of the security forces; and the rest are reported to have been members of armed political groups' (Amnesty International, 1994, p1).

The two communities of Northern Ireland and the British state

Following the work of others (Taylor, 1998, 2000, 2002; McEvoy, 2001; Edwards, 2011), three sets of protagonists can be identified as being central to the public problems of Northern Ireland. The main focus of the chapter is, however, to consider the relationship between Loyalist paramilitary organisations and British state agencies in light of accusations of collusion made against them and, likewise, to consider

[2] www.cain.ulst.ac.uk/sutton/updates.html

the role of the main Republican groups such as the IRA and the Irish State in the same respect.

From its inception, Northern Ireland was constitutionally unique in the UK, as it had its own devolved parliament – often referred to as 'Stormont' – from partition until 1972. The Northern Irish parliament had no control over external matters such as foreign policy, foreign trade and defence, which came under the bailiwick of Westminster, but it did have control over internal political matters including law and order, local government representation, agriculture, social services and education among others. Within the UK, the limitations on public spending have also been more fluidly applied in Northern Ireland in comparison to England, Wales and Scotland, perhaps reflecting a need stemming from its more tumultuous recent history (Birrell, 1994).

From the outset, many from the Catholic/nationalist community refused to engage with the state. Northern Ireland was a political entity they did not recognise, and they did not want to bequeath any degree of legitimacy by doing so. As the 'Troubles' progressed, employees of the state came to be considered 'legitimate targets' for Republican paramilitary groups. Although this was so, McAuley (2003, p 138) noted that the Stormont institutions 'did little to encourage participation from the Catholic community'. Indeed, Stormont has been criticised for being a 'Unionist' parliament for Unionist people. Certainly, every Prime Minister of Northern Ireland came from the Ulster Unionist Party which, at the time, was the largest of the Unionist parties.

Yet it was religion as much as politics that provided a dividing line between the communities. Although we need to be wary about caricaturing entire populations and communities, religious difference at the very least provides a useful heuristic device in which to explain the complex history of the Province. The minority Catholic population of the North felt embittered by partition, feeling that they had been 'sold out' by those in the South. Terms associated with elements of the Catholic population in Ireland are 'Republicans' and 'nationalists'. Broadly speaking, Republicanism is a political doctrine aligning the Catholic population of the North with the Republic of Ireland. Nationalism, meanwhile, is more a celebration of Irish culture, language and identity.

Today, many Catholic Republicans in the North derogatorily refer to their counterparts in the south as 'Freestaters', yet they hold out the hope of one day living in a united Ireland. Although often referred to as the Irish Republican Army (IRA), the main republican movement throughout the time of the troubles was the Provisional IRA (PIRA), with its political wing known as Sinn Fein ('Ourselves Alone'). The extent to which these are one and the same remains a source of consternation, but undoubtedly they were, at their origin, separate organisations (Coogan, 1995). The history of Irish Republicanism is long and complex, and various splits and factions have emerged over time. The Republican movement in the north of Ireland is drawn primarily from the Catholic population. The PIRA emerged from the dormant official IRA, who were all but disbanded in the aftermath of the border campaign (1956-62). In effect, this was guerrilla action on behalf of a relatively small group of armed campaigners, whose aim was to overthrow British rule on the island of Ireland and create a unitary Irish state. In military and political terms, the border campaign was unsuccessful, making few gains and enjoying little support from the majority nationalist community in the South. In practical terms, however, the border campaign did show that militant republicanism was not moribund, and it ensured that a further generation would emerge in the spirit of republicanism.

The main legacy of the border campaign was, however, to foster a split within Republicanism itself as the IRA chief of staff, Cathal Goulding, tried to align the goals of republicanism with left-wing militarism and Marxist politics. Those who followed this route became part of the Official IRA, while those who chose to follow the previous path became the Provisional IRA. The former chose to engage in Parliamentary politics through promoting their political wing, Official Sinn Fein, as a revolutionary party. Meanwhile, the Provisional IRA, under the leadership of Ruairí Ó Brádaigh, chose to maintain the policy of abstentionism; disengaging in Parliamentary politics in Northern Ireland, the Republic of Ireland and the United Kingdom. Furthermore, the Provisional wing declared itself as the defenders of the Catholic, nationalist population of the North with the onset of increasing sectarian violence towards the end of the 1960s and into the 1970s (Taylor, 1998, 2000; Moloney, 2002).

The next split in Irish Republicanism arose in response to the policy that has now become known as 'The Armalite and the Ballot Box'. This arose out of a feeling that the previous strategy of the 'Long War' with the British was draining resources and that fresh impetus could be gained by simultaneously pursuing political and paramilitary means. The precursor to the development of this strategy was the political success of the 1981 Hunger Strikers. Crucially, in terms of political engagement, two of the Hunger Strikers – Bobby Sands in the UK and Keiran Doherty in the Irish Republic – were elected Parliamentarians. Under the leadership of Gerry Adams and Martin McGuinness, this new strategy required an end to abstentionism (one of the key tenets of republicanism) and some recognition of the parliamentary institutions north and south of the border. Those rejecting this approach broke away to form Republican Sinn Fein and the Continuity IRA. Nevertheless, the Adams/McGuinness leadership still advocated what has become known as the IRA's need to fight the 'Long War'. As Dudai (2012, p35) explained, this involved, in part, a transition from a British army-style, 'battalion-based' structure to one based on 'small cells'. Essentially, this was in order to diminish the damage that informers could reap on the organisation in terms of its missions being compromised.

The manifestation of two states on one Ireland undoubtedly created a great deal of political and social instability and insecurity. The Protestant, Unionist majority in the North in the early years of the state feared the outbreak of violence just as much as the Catholic minority. As the Republic of Ireland in its constitution laid claim to the territory occupied by the six counties of Northern Ireland, Unionists lived in fear of a kind of ethnic cleansing, whereby the six counties would be absorbed into the Republic and they would find themselves a minority on the island of Ireland. Such a fear underpinned Unionist opposition to the 1985 Anglo-Irish Agreement and is best expressed in the infamous Unionist slogan 'not an inch'; a rallying cry that Unionists would not secede any territory to the Republic.

There were traditionally two main Loyalist organisations: the Ulster Volunteer Force (UVF) and the Ulster Defence Association (UDA). The Ulster Freedom Fighters (UFF) are often cited as a third key group, but there is some debate as to their independence and genesis. It is now widely accepted that they constituted a militant, 'hard core' wing of the UDA. The UDA was for a long time the largest Loyalist organisation. According to Taylor (2000, p2) it was initially an 'umbrella' organisation of various vigilante groups that had sprung up across Belfast in the early 1970s in response to an upsurge in IRA sectarian attacks.

Bruce (2004, p504-5) recounted how 'the UVF have always been smaller and more centralised and had a stable leadership', whereas the UDA 'has always been a "Federal organisation" whose brigades have enjoyed a large amount of autonomy'. In many ways it is the UDA who mirror the Provisional IRA. A defining feature of the larger organisation, the UDA, was a desire to have an Independent Ulster free of British and Irish rule, but many of the rank and file identified as British. More recently, the UVF along with its political wing the Progressive Unionist Party (PUP) has been more supportive of the Peace Process. Indeed, the PUP enjoyed some electoral success in contrast to the political front of the UDA – the Ulster Democratic

Party who, as Bruce (2004, p505) highlighted, 'failed to win any seats in the Northern Ireland assembly and dissolved in acrimony in 2001'.

The history of Loyalist paramilitary activity, like most terrorist organisations including the IRA, is one of internecine disputes and splits. As Bruce (2004) explained:

> When men acquire positions of leadership by being 'harder bastards' than their rivals, it is no surprise that succession often involves murder or the threat of it. When murdering political enemies is one of the accepted ways in which an organization achieves its goals, we must expect that competition within the organization will also become murderous. (Bruce, 2004, p507)

Despite the desire of certain Loyalists to see an independent Ulster, it has been a long-held view in Republican circles that the British were using the Loyalists to 'do some of their dirty work for them'. 'British' here refers to the presence in Northern Ireland of what Althusser (1971) referred to as members of the 'Repressive State Apparatus'; this is the army in its many guises and the police force – the RUC now rebranded as the Police Service for Northern Ireland (PSNI) – and the Special Branch, which was described as a 'force within a force' (Rolston and Scraton, 2005, p558). As we shall see, there has lingered a suggestion that the British state was involved in illegal activities in Ireland as well as trying to eradicate Republican paramilitaries. But as Rolston and Scraton (2005) also demonstrated, Northern Ireland is often an anomaly in discussions about the social and political nature of the United Kingdom on the grounds that the exceptional policies discussed in the previous chapter have been a mainstay of governance in Northern Ireland to the extent that:

> British state intervention in the North of Ireland cannot be considered in the same light as the application of its policies and laws within Britain. Since partition, and the formation of the Irish Free State, the six northern counties have experienced exceptional state powers as the norm ... The due process of the rule of law has been regularly suspended, internment without trial repeatedly used, paramilitary policing consolidated and military rule imposed. In this neo-colonialist context, the democratic process has been partial, weak and suspended. (Rolston and Scraton, 2005, p548)

Curtis (1984) gave a critical portrayal of the role of the British state in society, suggesting that they entered the province in 1969 as 'disinterested' and 'above the fray', intervening between 'warring factions' to prevent a bloodbath. Consequently:

> The British authorities, aided by the media, presented a topsy-turvy picture of events in order to sustain the image of British impartiality. They played down the atrocities committed by the British forces, minimised Loyalist responsibility for violence, and depicted the situation as one long succession of violent acts committed by republicans. They portrayed the IRA as the cause – rather than a product of the conflict, and did their utmost to exclude nationalist political views from the media. They refused to acknowledge that partition and the continuing British presence were the root of the problem, and denounced those who questioned Britain's role as 'traitors'. (Curtis, 1984, p77)

The Republican movement expressed feelings of betrayal in that the RUC was part of the machinery of oppression. This had its origins in history as the RUC were primarily seen as being responsible for the maintenance of partition. Drawing on the work of Shackleford and Buss (1996), Lawther (2010) made the point that these historical feelings of betrayal not only shaped understandings of the past, but also shaped readings of the future. This manifested itself in the truth recovery debate. A key narrative is that because the police had been a force for repression to the Catholic, nationalist communities in the past, they would continue to hinder the search for truth in the future, particularly in relation to possible collusion between the RUC and paramilitary organisations.

The state and sectarianism

The RUC were, then, viewed as conduits of the British state by Republicans, but it is equally true that they have had a fractious relationship with the main Loyalist organisations, albeit not to the same degree. This is likely to be in part because of the way that paramilitaries are funded, which (as we saw in Chapter Three) bears many crossovers with organised criminality (Silke, 2000a, 2000b; Horgan and Taylor, 1999, 2003).

The RUC image of themselves as keepers of the peace, which came to light in the aftermath of the findings of the Pattern Review into Policing in the province, stands in contrast to what they see as Republican propaganda that they were, at best, bastions of discriminatory practice and at worst one and the same as paramilitary organisations. This was summarised by Les Rodgers, the former chairman of the Police Federation of Northern Ireland (PFNI), who stated at the Federation's annual conference in 1997 that since the Troubles began, it was the RUC that 'held this community together' when it could have 'disintegrated under the pressures of civil disorder' (cited in Lawther, 2010, p458).

The 1989 murder of catholic Laughlin Maginn was a key moment in understanding the complexities of Northern Ireland and the fractious relationship between Loyalist paramilitary organisations and the British state. In the aftermath to the murder of Maginn, it was revealed that security documents detailing information about suspected IRA members had gone missing from two security bases. Maginn had been murdered by the UDA (probably in the guise of the UFF) and they had justified this on the grounds that his killing was based on information taken from police files. This episode paved the way for the Stevens Inquiry (to be discussed later), as the Chief Constable of the RUC, Sir Hugh Annesley, appointed the high-ranking British police officer Sir John Stevens to look into allegations of collusion between Loyalist groups and members of the British security forces.

A footnote on page 14 of the Amnesty International report gives an indication of the nature of the allegations:

> In May 1989 two members of the security forces had been given 18-month suspended sentences for possessing documents containing information which was likely to be useful to [Loyalist] terrorists (including the photographs, names and addresses of suspects). One of them remained in the British Army. Because they pleaded guilty, their trial was brief – the Crown did not go into detail about what the two had said during interrogation (that is, that they passed on these documents knowing or suspecting that they could be used for murder). They were not charged with conspiracy to murder; nor were any of the named Loyalists who received documents. However, Terence McDaid, the brother of one of the persons on one of the photo-montages in question, was killed at the address provided. (Amnesty International, 1994)

The case of Maginn is indicative of the often complex relationship between Loyalist paramilitaries and the security forces for a long time thought to be one and the same by the Catholic/nationalist community. The report went on to stipulate that two members of the Ulster Defence Regiment (UDR), an infantry regiment of the British Army, were charged with the murder of Maginn. The UDR was created in the 1970s to relieve the RUC of some of its military functions. From the outset, the UDR was disliked by the nationalist community as many of its members were previously members of the Ulster Special Constabulary (known as the 'B-Specials'). These were a reservist police force whose membership was almost exclusively Protestant and Unionist. They were formed around 1920 – at the same time as the Northern Irish state – and were antagonistic to the original IRA in the war of independence. As Ruane and Todd (1996, p127) noted, 'many in the RUC, and virtually all the B Specials [USC] were defenders of the Protestant community first, defenders of the Protestant state second, and normal policemen third'.

From the outset, the UDR was accused of bias during the Troubles. The University of Ulster CAIN (Conflict Archive on the Internet) website has a section entitled 'Subversion in the UDR'. On this website is a link to a document thought to have been produced by British military intelligence in 1973.[3] The document was released by the Public Records Office in Kew, London, under the '30 year rule'. It showed how joint membership of the UDA and the UDR was widespread. Furthermore, it pointed out that this was subversive because even though the UDA was not outlawed as a terrorist organisation at the time, its 'aims were incompatible with the UDR'. Furthermore, attempts by UDR members to use their "knowledge, skills or equipment' to 'further the aims' of other organisations were acknowledged.

This interweaving of the UDR and Loyalist paramilitaries is brought into focus in the context of the Shankill Butchers gang. Over a period of a number of years throughout the 1970s, the Shankill Butchers engaged in shootings, throat cuttings and torture of mainly Catholics in Belfast. In his discussion of sectarian murder, Coogan (1995, p455) remonstrated how it is 'inconceivable' that a group not actively connected with paramilitary activity could have escaped justice for so long. Yet this is precisely what transpired with the Shankill Butchers, even though they met 'regularly and openly' in public. When finally brought to trial – in the aftermath of a botched murder – it became

---

[3]   http://cain.ulst.ac.uk/publicrecords/1973/subversion_in_the_udr.htm

apparent that members of the gang were members of both the UVF and the UDR (Coogan, 1995).

Collusion and the Stevens Inquiry

In the introduction to this book (Chapter One), we presented a cautionary tale concerning the difficulties of researching state criminality. Two examples relating to Northern Ireland were documented. These concerned research carried out during the 'Troubles' in the form of public inquiries, and those after the Good Friday Agreement in a discussion over the Boston College Tapes and research ethics.

Despite these warnings, we now consider one final point about inquiries in Ireland and the chances of uncovering the most damaging behaviours of a state, which for current purposes focus on collusion between security forces, state agencies and paramilitaries in the killing of numerous high-profile figures. This is not an easy task and we are again reminded by Rolston and Scraton (2005) about the limitations of the information at our disposal (that is data from independent inquiries). Indeed, Rolston and Scraton (2005, p561) emphasised that for the independent inquiries in Northern Ireland to 'establish and sustain credibility', it is vital for them to gain 'autonomy and independence from British State interests, while maintaining a commitment to the interests of the bereaved'; they acknowledged and underlined the difficulty of this task.

Patrick Finucane and Raymond McCord: Loyalist paramilitaries and the security forces

On 23 September 2004, the then Secretary of State for Northern Ireland, Paul Murphy, proclaimed: 'the Government is determined that where there are allegations of collusion the truth should emerge' (BBC, 2004). The murder of Loughlin Maginn, defined as a tipping point by Amnesty International (1994), created and confirmed widespread suspicion that there was collusion between the security forces and paramilitary organisations in Northern Ireland.

For Rolston and Scraton (2005, p561), however, it was the murder of Belfast lawyer Pat Finucane that 'goes to the heart of the dirty war operationalized by undercover police and army'. This was a war 'sanctioned by officials still in office, in the police, army and political life' (Rolston and Scraton, 2005, p561). This also included the Special Branch. What is key for our current purposes, is that obfuscation was paramount. Rolston and Scraton (2005) pointed out how the Force

Research Unit (FRU) – an undercover army unit answerable to the Ministry of Defence (MoD) – was involved in the murder of Finucane, but had 'actively resisted the Saville Inquiry':

> Just days before the [Stevens] inquiry sat, it [the FRU] destroyed 14 of the 19 army rifles fired on Bloody Sunday. The Saville team demanded the retention of the remaining five rifles, yet a further two were destroyed. All photographs taken on Bloody Sunday by ten military photographers were also destroyed ... Throughout the inquiry, the MoD has stalled proceedings by initiating judicial reviews. This represents a portent of the resistance future inquiries will face from powerful state interests. (Rolston and Scraton, 2005, p561)

In short, despite an increasing amalgamation of evidence, uncovering instances of collusion is not a trivial matter. If the case of Maginn gave impetus to the initial suspicions of collusion, then two further cases that have contributed to making this an enduring instance of state crime are those of Pat Finucane, as indicated, and Raymond McCord Jr. The murders of Finucane and McCord Jr sparked a number of inquiries into alleged collusion between Loyalist paramilitaries and British security forces. For Stevens (2003, p16), collusion was endemic between Loyalist paramilitaries, the RUC and the Army and was 'evidenced in many ways', ranging 'from the wilful failure to keep records, the absence of accountability, the withholding of intelligence and evidence, through to the extreme of agents being involved in murder'.

The second chapter of the Stevens Inquiry into collusion between the police and Loyalist paramilitaries revealed:

> Patrick Finucane was murdered in front of his wife and three children in his home on Sunday 12th February 1989. He was 39 years old and worked as a solicitor in Belfast. Mr Finucane was shot fourteen times by two masked gunmen who entered his house in the early evening. The gunmen escaped in a red Ford Sierra motor vehicle driven by an accomplice. The following day the Ulster Freedom Fighters (UFF) claimed responsibility for the murder. (Stevens, 2003, p7)

A report by the Police Ombudsman, Nuala O'Loan, in 2007 – also referred to as the 'Ballast report' – caused a significant amount of controversy. Here a police informer known as 'Informant 1' was linked to at least 10 murders from 1991 to 2000, including that of Raymond McCord Jr. The report found that because the accused in the murders was a police informant, there was evidence that the police failed to carry out a thorough investigation, which greatly increased the possibility that no-one would be arrested or sent to trial for Raymond McCord Jr's murder. The police ombudsman report took note of four allegations made by Raymond McCord Sr in relation to the murder of his son. These are presented in Table 7.1, alongside the conclusion reached by the ombudsman.

Table 7.1: Allegations made about police practice in relation to the death of Raymond McCord Jr and the associated findings of the Police Ombudsman

Allegation	Ombudsman finding
A senior UVF figure ordered the murder of Raymond McCord Jr and that he was a police informant	A police informant, known as Informant 1, is a suspect in the killing of Raymond McCord, but the identity cannot be divulged – **Allegation substantiated**
The police failed to carry out a thorough investigation of the murder and to keep Raymond McCord senior updated with progress	There were failings in the investigation of the murder which have significantly reduced the possibility of anyone being prosecuted for the murder. Although there was some contact between the police and Mr McCord in the days immediately following the murder, there was no single point of contact within the police for Mr McCord to receive progress reports – **Allegation substantiated**
No-one had been arrested or charged with the murder because the man who ordered it was a police informant and he, along with those working for him, had been protected from arrest for a number of years	Although a number of people were arrested for the murder, no-one has been charged, but there is no evidence that anyone has been protected from arrest. There is much evidence that significant amounts of intelligence were disregarded by the police and that they continued to use Informant 1 despite his criminal record and extensive intelligence of other serious criminality. This was because he had value to them as an informer – **Allegation partly substantiated on the grounds that suspects have been arrested in this case**
Unidentified police knew something was going to happen to Raymond McCord Jr, but that they did not warn him or his family about this danger to protect the police informant who was responsible for the murder	There is no evidence to support this – **Allegation not substantiated**

Source: adapted from O'Loan, 2007

As Table 7.1 details, many of the allegations made against the police in the case of Raymond McCord Jr's murder were substantiated. In relation to those that were not, the report went on to record some 'grave concerns' about the practices of some police officers in the RUC. These number 17 in total and relate to systematic malpractice and sometimes, but not always, involving the obstruction of police work so as to maintain the liberty of informants. One particular concern was the process of arresting informants suspected of murder and subjecting them to 'sham' interviews, where they were not questioned about the crime and where they were subsequently released without charge; a point which undermines the unsubstantiated allegation listed earlier. Some of the other concerns included (O'Loan, 2007):

- failure to arrest informants for crimes to which they had already confessed or treating informants as suspects for crime
- concealing intelligence indicating that on more than one occasion informants had been involved in murders and other serious crimes
- blocking searches of police informants' homes and other locations including a suspected UVF arms dump
- finding munitions in an informant's home and doing nothing about this
- withholding information about the location to which a group of murder suspects had allegedly fled after a murder
- not adopting or complying with the United Kingdom or Home Office Guidelines on matters relating to informant handling and not complying with the Regulation of Investigatory Powers Act once it came into force in 2000.

The conclusion reached was that in the absence of explanation as to why these events occurred, there was no other alternative but to suggest that this was collusion between certain police officers and identified UVF informants (O'Loan, 2007). It should be stressed at this stage that the case for collusion is compelling. Although this is so, it should also be stressed that this kind of state criminality was allegedly not restricted to the British state and the Loyalist paramilitaries.

Harry Breen, Bob Buchanan and An Garda Síochána/IRA collusion

On 20 March 1989, RUC Chief Superintendent Harry Breen and his colleague Superintendent Bob Buchanan were murdered near Jonesborough on the border between South Armagh and Louth. Breen was the most senior RUC officer to be killed in the Troubles. They had both travelled to Dundalk, County Louth, in the Republic of Ireland for a meeting with the Guardai scheduled for two o'clock. On their way back to the North and just after crossing the border into South Armagh, they were ambushed on the Edeneppa Road by a number of IRA volunteers and shot dead.

Harnden (1999, p216) described this incident as the most serious setback in the relations between the RUC and An Garda Síochána (hereafter Garda) – the police force of the Irish Republic. The PIRA claimed responsibility for the murder, but ever since the event there have been suggestions that they were tipped off by members of the Irish police force. This led to the establishment of the Smithwick tribunal by the Irish government in 2006. The tribunal's terms of reference were to look into 'suggestions that members of An Garda Síochána or other employees of the State colluded in the fatal shootings of RUC Chief Superintendent Harry Breen and RUC Superintendent Robert Buchanan on the 20th March 1989 ' (Smithwick, 2013, p2).

In addition, the tribunal's rules of procedure offered an interpretation of some of the key terms. For current purposes, His Honour Judge Peter Smithwick, the sole member of the tribunal panel, interpreted 'collusion' in the following manner:

> While (collusion) generally means the commission of an act, I am of the view that it should also be considered in terms of an omission or failure to act. In the active sense, collusion has amongst its meanings to conspire, connive or collaborate. In addition, I intend to examine whether anybody deliberately ignored a matter, or turned a blind eye to it, or to have pretended ignorance or unawareness of something one ought morally, legally or officially oppose. (Smithwick, 2013, p16)

Although the tribunal opened in 2006, it was not until June 2011 that public hearings began and that witnesses were called. In the aftermath of the murders there was much speculation that the Garda knew of an IRA mole working in the North Louth police force. As Harnden (1999, p237) noted, however, links between the IRA and the Garda 'had remained almost off limits'. Harnden elaborated the point by quoting one senior RUC detective who, on investigating such occurrences, labelled the level of infiltration by the IRA into the Garda as 'frightening', prompting Harden to conclude that this was one of the most 'important untold stories of the troubles'. As the Cory (2003) report – a report by Peter Cory, a retired Canadian judge – and the Smithwick tribunal showed, however, this is a story with much to be told but there are tremendous difficulties in doing so.

In the first and second editions of his book *Bandit Country* (1999), Harnden makes a number of accusations of collusion, not least describing with great clarity the sequence of events that led up to the murders of Buchanan and Breen. Summing up the situation, he was adamant that events indicated that the IRA must have been tipped off about the meeting earlier in the day and were able to put a plan in place at relatively short notice. In short, Buchanan and Breen drove into a hastily established IRA roadblock on the Edeneppa Road at around 3.30pm. They were shot several times on the spot. Buchanan almost certainly died with his foot still on the accelerator of his car as he tried to reverse away from the roadblock. Breen, meanwhile, tried to surrender by waving a white flag and was shot in the back of the head.

The question that remained was how did the IRA know where to set up the roadblock and to carry out the ambush? Harnden offered the following account:

> The 10 or 15 IRA men involved had almost certainly been placed on standby but it had not been known Buchanan was planning to travel that day ... Analysis of video footage from cameras outside Newry station and along the A1 all but ruled out the possibility that IRA dickers had monitored them on their way to Dundalk. There was also technical information which confirmed that the IRA had been contacted by someone within Dundalk station. RUC Special Branch received intelligence that a Garda officer had telephoned an IRA member to tip him off. (Harnden, 1999, p219-20)

It is the suggestion of a telephone tip-off that was – and is – central to this case. In his report into collusion, Cory investigated these claims, by conducting face-to-face interviews with Harnden as well as with another journalist who had made a similar allegation of collusion. The main conclusion Cory drew was that although Harnden seems unequivocal on the matter of collusion, his evidence was unconvincing. Harnden's case rested on his source inside the Garda, who he claims had tipped off the RUC Special Branch about an IRA mole serving as a Garda officer in Dundalk. Yet according to Cory (2003, para 2.76), the RUC 'denied that it had received intelligence information that a Garda officer had phoned an IRA man'. This claim was, in turn, backed up by enquiries carried out by both the RUC and the Garda at the time.

In short, Cory pressed Harnden on his sources and the journalist refused to divulge where he had obtained his information. In his summation of this part of the 'evidence' for collusion, Cory (2003, para 2.118) insisted: 'allegations that there was a mole or that a Garda member facilitated the murder of Officers Breen and Buchanan, appear to be based on hypothesis, speculation and a source or sources of information that the author[s] refused to disclose'. In addition, he continued, these stories were presented as if they were facts, before finally concluding he could not 'base any finding of collusion, or possible collusion on the contents of ... Harnden's book'.

This was not the end of the matter, though, as there were also various intelligence reports at the time worthy of consideration. In summarising these, Cory observed that various intelligence reports received around the time of the incident and sometime after were inconclusive. Some claim to provide evidence of an IRA mole, whereas others directly contradicted this. One key piece of evidence to come to light sometime after the event was, nonetheless, referred to by Cory as the 'Kevin Fulton statement'. Fulton was a British army agent who had infiltrated the IRA. In his statement to Cory, Fulton maintained:

> I was in Dundalk on the day of the ambush of Superintendent Buchanan and Chief Superintendent Breen. I am aware that, after the ambush took place, my senior IRA commander was told by a member of the PIRA that Garda B had telephoned to the Provisional IRA to tell them that officers Breen and Buchanan were at the Dundalk station. (Cited in Smithwick, 2013, p247)

It is worth mentioning at this point that 'Garda B' also crops up in Harnden's account and thus appeared to corroborate his take on events. This does not, however, alter significantly Cory's findings and one of his main beliefs that the PIRA probably 'did not need any assistance from the Garda to carry out the ambush and murders of the officers' (Cory, 2003, para 2.153), primarily due to their own intelligence capabilities. Even so, the Fulton statement did carry sufficient weight for Cory to recommend a public inquiry into the matter, which is where the Smethwick tribunal came in.

The history of the 'Troubles' tells us that inquiries can sometimes serve to further muddy the waters – not least because of a 'layering' effect that frequently takes place, whereby assessments are made on the back of previous findings, which are taken forward minus the initial warnings and caveats about the uncertainties surrounding the initial findings. In December 2013, Lord Justice Smithwick (2013) published his findings in a report over 430 pages long with over 1,000 appendices. Although the report does not name the Garda officers involved in collusion, Smithwick concluded that Harry Breen was the target of the ambush and:

> ... the IRA required positive identification that Harry Breen, in particular, had arrived at Dundalk Garda Station. Whilst his image was well known, and therefore he may well have been recognised by a member of the Provisional IRA observing the station, the optimum confirmation of his identity from the point of view of the Provisional IRA would likely be by a member of An Garda Síochána. Given that I am satisfied that the evidence points to the fact that there was someone within the Garda Station assisting the IRA, it also seems to me to be likely that the Provisional IRA would seek to exploit that resource by having that individual or individuals confirm the arrival of the two officers. (Smithwick, 2013, p429)

Conclusion

The case study of Northern Ireland is vital in understanding the complexity involved in unpacking state crime. The typology used by Kauzlarich et al (2001) (see Table 2.1 in Chapter Two) is found wanting as the definitions of 'international' and 'domestic' criminality become blurred. The bulk of this chapter has concentrated on the use of proxies for state criminality. Unlike in other areas where, under the conditions of neo-liberalism, various institutions or groupings have been created to oversee the functions of the state, in Northern Ireland the proxies in question have been paramilitary organisations.

We have argued here that collusion represents both criminal and terroristic activity, but it is an example of where state inaction has often been just as violent as state action. In Northern Ireland, collusion was part of a bigger picture known as 'dirty war', and although there is much about the Province that is unique, there is also a sense that in terms of state crime, it is part of a much broader mosaic.

EIGHT

Fighting 'the enemy within': internal state terrorism, Argentina's 'Dirty War' (1976-83) and the UK miners' strike (1984-85)

Continuing with the themes introduced in the previous chapter, Chapter Eight looks at Argentina's 'Dirty War', which commenced in 1976 and, in the UK, the miners' strike from 1984 to 1985. Both events were undertaken in the defence of neo-liberal policies, yet they were committed by different types of regimes: the former being a right-wing dictatorship, while the latter was a right-wing democratically elected government.

Initially, though, the chapter will attempt to show how Argentina's 'Dirty War' represented a blatant (in terms of severity) yet relatively hidden example of a state terrorising its own people through violent abduction and execution. The chapter charts how – following Isabel Peron's use of excessive force and power to combat right-wing opposition – a military coup headed by Lieutenant General Videla took control of Argentina in 1976. Neo-liberal economic policies became the order of the day, while the opposition to such policies were branded as 'subversives', thus allowing for the use of violence as a means to repress and control the supposedly unruly, if not dangerous, negative 'other' (Bietti, 2011). Moreover, the chapter also demonstrates how the Junta had learnt from the violent, public atrocities in Chile (during Pinochet's dictatorship) and attempted to keep hidden their attempts to eradicate any possible Peronist threat. State-ordered disappearances were viewed as the best means to both eliminate the 'enemy' and to remain undetected. In the absence of corpses or public arrest records, the government was able to deny all wrongdoing despite the estimated disappearance of over tens of thousands of people (Wright, 2007).

By contrast, the chapter moves on to show how Margaret Thatcher, in pursuit of a monetarist, free market agenda, utilised British police (and the armed forces) to break the resistance of one of the country's most powerful unions, the National Union of Mineworkers (NUM). In order to show the gravity of the repressive actions taken by the government, the chapter focuses on events surrounding the NUM picket in 1984 of the Orgreave coking plant – situated near Sheffield – where organised violent attacks were perpetrated against picketing miners. In response to the accusation that the government had not pre-planned the actions taken against the pickets, the chapter also broadens the debate to detail the aims and reasoning used by the Conservative government of the time to counter the effects of the NUM strike as a whole and thus justify and legitimise the tactics and measures deployed.

The chapter ends with the construction of a convincing argument that the Thatcher government used such violent, premeditated tactics to terrorise a section of its own community in pursuit of a specific ideological aim – whatever the cost. In other words, such actions not only constituted examples of state violence and even state terrorism (yet to a lesser scale to that conducted by the Argentinian Junta), but also sowed the seeds of long-lasting fissures that exerted ill-conceived examples of social harm. In a similar vein, the tactics of the Argentinian ruling Junta are deconstructed to demonstrate the extent to which state violence, state terrorism and social harm were inflicted on the citizens of Argentina. In sum, both examples in this chapter demonstrate the lengths to which a state can – and will – terrorise its own people, and the extent to which they will either legitimate or hide their actions in an attempt to pursue their own dogmas and ideologies (even if they are purportedly pursuing the same agenda).

Argentina's 'Dirty War' (1976-83) and political instability

As a starting point to these case studies, it is important to note that the events in Argentina (1976-83) represented the imposition of neo-liberal policies by a dictatorship as opposed to an elected government. If there was a mandate for change in the UK, this was certainly not the case in Argentina. Indeed, Argentina's 'Dirty War' was described as a period of state terrorism (Antonelli, 2009), whereby numerous acts of state violence were enacted to ensure that Argentinian citizens were compliant to military rule after the death of President Peron.

Prior to Argentina's 'Dirty War' (detailed later in this chapter), Juan Peron first came to power in 1946 and served two successive terms until 1955. Throughout his time in office he played a key role in the political turbulence of the country. Arguably, Peron threatened the stability of capitalism by favouring unionisation and the reduction of wage differences between skilled and unskilled workers (Robben, 2005). This apparent quest for social justice was, however, tempered, if not contradicted, by Peron's willingness to achieve his aims through physical oppression (Cox et al, 2008). Over the years, it was evident that Peron was not averse to deploying political violence as a means to silence his critics and those opposed to his political beliefs. Despite, and undoubtedly because of, this overt oppression, Peron was eventually deposed in 1955 after a *coup d'état*. Yet his political influence did not end with his deposition. When in (and subsequently when out of) office, Peron continued to encourage his followers to adopt and develop guerrilla tactics and groups to resist either military or civilian dictatorships opposed to his views (Robben, 2005, 2012; Wright, 2007), thus sowing the seeds for future conflicts.

After 18 years in exile and opposition, Peron was re-elected into office in 1973. He was faced with the onerous task of governing a politically divided country. Juan Peron did not serve his term of office, as he died in 1974 and his presidential responsibilities were passed on to his wife, Isabel. On coming to power, Isabel Peron declared a state of siege across Argentina. As Guest (1990) observed, this declaration of a state of siege empowered – if not legitimised – Isabel Peron to demand the use of excessive force and power to combat terrorism and terrorist groups. Particular attention was paid to those groups that held right-wing political views, as they tended to stand against her presidency. Violence escalated as a consequence, with the majority of acts being committed by those in power.

Change of regime and economy

Following two years of political unrest, Isabel Peron was deposed by a military coup headed by Jorge Rafael Videla, a senior commander of the Argentinian army. The military took charge of the country on 24 March 1976. Initially, many in Argentina believed that the end of violence was in sight and the country would be saved from chaos and civil unrest (Feitlowitz, 1998) once any signs of 'rebellion' had been quashed and reform fully established. This was not to be, as the military were planning to launch an assault on subversion under the pretext of waging war on Peronist guerrillas (Wright, 2007, p102) and the growth of an apparently immoral Argentinian culture (Arceneaux, 1997). With the intention of stamping out Argentina's culture of political mobilisation alongside a vow to thoroughly reform the country, the military constructed a strategy to protect its Christian culture against revolutionary onslaught (Robben, 2012) and fight 'the negative other: the subversive criminal, who, because of his role in the armed struggle and the ideological offensive, questioned the … Western values of the nation' (Bietti, 2011, p349).

As part of this war – which became known nationally and internationally as a 'Dirty War' – the military junta were determined to impose neo-liberal ideals through the installation of a free market capitalist economy (Marchak with Marchak, 1999; Klein, 2007): an economy that was completely at odds with the Peronist stance of old, but one which, in the minds of the military at least, held all the answers. Neo-liberalism, it was argued, located the source of 'subversion' – and by implication the immoral culture – since it focused on the perceived problems surrounding the growth of a populist state and the economic benefits and privileges accrued by specific businesses and labour groups from their monopolistic access to a non-competitive socioeconomic base. Waging war on the collectivist groups was, therefore, essential in that these groups had to be prevented from:

> … controlling political choice, restricting labor markets, bidding up wage rates beyond levels of productivity, and protecting jobs in poorly run, subsidized firms … [which ran] counter to principles of individual freedom since they reduced profits and abridged the rights of 'independent ' workers. (Pion-Berlin, 1988, p396)

As a consequence, the military accepted neo-liberalism as both 'a means to stabilise governability in Argentine society and as an attempt to redefine power relations', while still 'valuing neo-liberalism as a goal in and of itself commensurate with economic growth and prosperity' (Arceneaux, 1997, p339).

Violence, disappearances and social engineering

As with any form of social upheaval, this transition towards a free market capitalist economy was not – and would not be – a benign process. The Junta were well aware of this. They believed, for example, that the citizens of Argentina had to be terrorised into acceptance of the new socioeconomic relations. To achieve this, violence was used to repress and control. Such violence came from the top and was systematically aimed at the so-called 'subversives' (Wright, 2007; Cox et al, 2008), who were deemed to be any individual against the military regime and their political objectives (Taylor, 2005).

To make matters worse, the aforementioned term 'subversive' was never truly defined (Wright, 2007). It was deliberately vague and easily applicable. Between 1976 and 1983, tens of thousands of people were:

... direct victims of repression ... The characteristic technique was disappearance, in which unarmed citizens were kidnapped by gangs of armed men, often in the middle of the night from their family homes. Disappearance was followed by forced removal to clandestine detention centers, extensive torture, and, almost always, murder. (Brysk, 1994, p679)

During this period there were also numerous accounts of, but extremely traumatic, temporary incidences (in terms of survival and release but not necessarily recovery) relating to kidnapping, torture, rape and extortion conducted by the police and other state-sponsored forces. More insidiously – if that were possible – there was the kidnapping of children and the detention of pregnant women, who were tortured or mistreated until they gave birth. They were then killed, whereas their children were subsequently taken and illegally adopted by friends, relatives of the torturers and, in the respect of this case study, supporters of the Junta. All of this reflects the barbaric acts of social engineering undertaken by the military Junta (Brysk, 1994). A further indication of the barbaric nature of the onslaught against the 'subversives' came in 1995, when former Naval Lieutenant Commander Adolfo Francisco Scilingo admitted that '1,500 to 2,000 live and drugged bodies of victims had been jettisoned into the Atlantic from planes' (Knudson, 1997, p93).

In many ways, the Argentine situation reflected a broader pattern on the continent as free market ideas, stemming from the University of Chicago's Economics Department, were imposed on Chile, Uruguay and Brazil at the same time and with brutal consequences:

The Argentine junta excelled at striking the right balance between public and private horror, carrying out enough of its terror in the open so that everyone knew what was going on, but simultaneously keeping enough secret that it could always be denied. In its first days in power, the junta made a single dramatic demonstration of its willingness to use lethal force: a man was pushed out of a Ford Falcon (a vehicle notorious for its use by the secret police), tied to Buenos Aires's most prominent monument, the 67.5 meter high white Obelisk, and machine gunned in plain view. After that, the junta's killings went underground, but they were always present. (Klein, 2007)

All told, few were left immune. The military's 'Dirty War' culminated with the denial of personal and collective freedoms, with torture, death and the disappearance of more than 15,000 individuals (Pion-Berlin, 1988). The true extent of the atrocities and the exact figures are still being contested (Brysk, 1994).

Legitimising violent oppression

As intimated earlier, the 'Dirty War' that ensued was fought against the regime's own people. To legitimise such actions, the military Junta had to qualify why it was doing so. In this respect, it was partly 'in reprisal against terrorist attacks by urban guerrillas of preceding years, … [that] the ruling military itself coined the phrase "dirty war", making clear that they deemed any means justified in combating threats – real or perceived – to Argentina's oligarchical social structure' (Knudson, 1997, p93).

By way of further justification of their atrocities, the political speeches that followed the military coup resembled those given in Nazi Germany. Like how Jews were placed as outsiders in Nazi Germany, anyone against the regime of the Junta was not considered to be an Argentinian citizen (Feitlowitz, 1998) and, because of such, the military argued it was justifiable to wage war on them. War was also justified by a variety of military spokesmen – including Videla in 1977 – on the grounds that the Junta was responding to the violent tactics of the aforementioned terrorists and guerrillas. As General Camps (head of the Buenos Aires Provincial Police) explained, the 'subversives made it [the war] dirty. They chose the forms of combat and determined our actions' (Robben, 2012, p307-8). Furthermore, the 'subversive' collectivists were deemed to be 'antinationalist, nihilistic, economically delinquent, antireligious, anti-government, social democrats, human rights groups, and solidarity organizations' (Pion-Berlin, 1988, p401). In short, the term 'subversive' was used to describe and condemn anyone perceived to be an enemy of the state and, because of such allegations, was used to justify the acts of violence undertaken by the military regime in the name of the state.

Yet in spite of this supposed justification of their actions, the Junta were well aware of the fact that they were violating international law. Why else would they have resorted to hiding the victims of their oppression? Indeed:

> The number of disappeared rose in 1977 and, while
> levelling off somewhat in 1978, remained quite high.

> Though rational calculation of adversarial strength may have accounted for state repression from 1974 till 1976, during the peak of guerrilla activity, it could not do so thereafter, when many noncombatants and innocent civilians were victimized by the regime. (Pion-Berlin, 1988, p385)

Why else would they state that 'there were mistakes that, as it happens in all war conflict, could ... surpass the limits of respect for fundamental human rights' (*La Nación*, 1983, p14; Pion Berlin, 1988, p385). Disappearance, therefore, represented one of the best ways to avoid being accountable for their acts of violence and terror.

Another way to avoid accountability was the significant veil of silence thrown across the media. Without doubt: 'The Argentine press during the dirty war was so effective in a mass cover-up that it took 13 years for any commanding officer to admit – even after trials and pardons – that abduction, torture had indeed been carried out on a wide scale' (Knudson, 1997, p109).

Thatcherism in the UK

By taking events chronologically, it is possible to trace similar socioeconomic ambitions in the UK that overlapped with those in Argentina. After the 1979 election, for instance, the incoming Thatcher government followed – over successive governments – a two-pronged fusion of a hitherto incompatible policy agenda (Gamble, 2002). One strand was that of traditional, authoritarian Conservatism, while the other was free market neo-liberalism. In relation to the events relating to the defeat of National Union of Mineworkers (NUM), it is the second strand that was the most poignant and, as intimated in Chapter Two, the ideological pursuit of neo-liberal dogmas provided the platform for state criminality/immorality.

Primarily, the position and strength of trade unions and the monopolistic power of nationalised industries was an anathema to Margaret Thatcher and the neo-liberal cause. From the outset, plans had been laid to tackle the perceived problems of an unproductive public sector. Key words and phrases such as 'market forces', 'sound money', 'financial discipline' and 'profit' abounded in government and media rhetoric alike (Towers, 1985). The trade unions represented a threat to such economic ambitions. Not only did the unions artificially raise wage levels above their 'natural' market level, but they also challenged the inalienable 'right' of management to make crucial decisions (that is, pit closures) on the grounds of economics (Towers, 1985). That said:

The extraordinary nature of the covert operations against the miners' leaders only makes sense when seen in the context of the long-run determination of the Tory Party – and of Margaret Thatcher above all – to avenge absolutely and unequivocally their double humiliation at the hands of the miners in the strikes of 1972 and 1974. (Milne, 2004, p6)

The coalfield and the community

Traditionally, when a pit is sunk, a village is built around the colliery. As a consequence, it is dependent on that colliery, since the community within the village was created precisely because of the existence of coal (Richards, 1996). In sum, the pit 'loomed large over every activity' (Bulmer, 1978, p28, cited in Richards, 1996, p20), in that the income of the village relied on the pit paying wages which, in turn, enabled spending in local shops, clubs and bars. A thriving pit, therefore, contributes to a communal, locally based economy unlike any other industrial equivalent. Conversely:

> ... the loss of coal mining jobs and colliery closures removes the material basis around which the social relations of coal mining communities have been constructed and to which the culture and way of life in these villages crucially relate. Thus colliery closures ... represent ... most fundamentally a threat to a way of life in coal mining communities that was highly valued by many living in them. (Hudson et al, 1984, p216-28, cited in Winterton and Winterton, 1989, p250)

This downward spiral does not end there, though. Without alternative employment for all the redundant workers surrounding the colliery, then consumption nationally also decreases, whereas social security expenditure increases with rising unemployment figures. As we shall see later in this chapter, both trends affect the viability of arguments declaring collieries to be uneconomic based purely on production costs and market demand. Indeed, unemployment figures did rise significantly as pit closures took place up to 1984.

In the Barnsley travel-to-work area, for instance, unemployment rose from a higher national average of 13.9% in March 1982 to 15.9% by March 1984, which was again above the national average. Similarly, the figures for Doncaster went from 15.9% to 16.7% respectively (Adeney and Lloyd, 1986, p25). Both areas were important mining areas and (as the earlier quotation from Hudson *et al* (1984) partially recognises) both the miners and the NUM were well aware of the predicament facing the unemployed individual and economic decline locally and, by implication, nationally as closures increased and spread. All of which, it can be argued, created an environment of genuine concern on the build-up to the 1984–85 strike: concern that was exacerbated by the drastic treatment of Cortonwood Colliery in South Yorkshire by the government/National Coal Board (NCB).

The miners' strike 1984-85

Arguably, the miners' strike of 1984–85, alongside the ensuing conflicts, 'provided a vivid case study of the rationales and processes of capitalism and liberal democracy' (Towers, 1985, p8). The strike began in March 1984 and by the end of that year some 150,000 mineworkers had been on strike for nearly 10 months (Glyn, 1985, p23). It had been the longest mass strike in UK history (Winterton, 1993). Central to the dispute was the economic case for pit closures put forward by both the government and NCB officials. In this respect, the NCB planned to reduce coal production by 4 million tonnes which, in turn, implied the closure of approximately twenty collieries with the loss of 20,000 jobs (Glyn, 1985, p23; Ram, 1985, p1553; Winterton, 1993, p9).

Since many men and communities were reliant on the mining industry, the NUM was naturally opposed to such closures, especially when they were told there was no alternative (Towers, 1985). The assertion that these pits were uneconomic was premised upon government plans to cut capacity on the basis that there was no market for the high-quality coal being excavated (Towers, 1985; Adeney and Lloyd, 1986; Winterton and Winterton, 1989; Richards, 1996). To make matters worse, energy demand in the 1980s was lower than the projections forecast in 1973 with the onset of the oil crisis (Winterton, 1993). New coal reserves opened up by transnational oil companies did not help either. Consequently, the efforts of the government and the NCB in 1984 concentrated on a strategy to reduce costs and improving competitiveness, whereby the planned:

> ... new capacity of 25 million tonnes to be introduced by 1990 ... [would come from] 12.5 million tonnes from the new Selby colliery complex and 12.5 million tonnes from the reorganisation of existing collieries and the use of new production technologies. This new capacity would replace not only 9 million tonnes of exhausted capacity, but also 16

million tonnes of capacity from high-cost collieries, which were to be closed before their reserves were exhausted. (Winterton, 1993, p6)

The threat of closure was particularly true of Cortonwood Colliery, where output matched the required reduction demanded in Yorkshire for the 1984-85 financial year (Winterton and Winterton, 1989; Richards, 1996). On 1 March 1984, it was announced by the NCB that Cortonwood was to be closed despite the recent investment of over £1 million to guarantee the pit a further five years' working life (Richards, 1996). The announcement acted as a trigger for strike action (Church et al, 1991). Such an announcement breached accepted protocol. The meeting in which the closure was announced was a regularly scheduled colliery review meeting, where pits with 'problems' were discussed. Announcing or demanding closure was not part of accepted procedure. Cortonwood should have been made 'the subject of a reconvened review meeting thereby enabling the NUM to investigate the pit and to organise the attendance of Cortonwood's Branch officials' (Richards, 1996, p99). Instead, the Yorkshire area NUM were given four weeks' notice when it was announced that the pit had to close by mid-April (Winterton and Winterton, 1989; Richards, 1996): hence the calls for strike action.

Fighting the strike: government tactics and the pro-government role of the media

Margaret Thatcher protested that she:

> repeatedly made it clear ... prime responsibility for dealing with the ... [1984-85] strike lay with the managements of the NCB and those other nationalised industries involved (the CEGB [Central Electricity Generation Board] ..., BSC [British Steel Corporation] ... and British Rail (BR)). (Thatcher, 1993, p347)

However, there was plenty of evidence to suggest otherwise.

When the strike did occur, premeditation on the part of the government was clearly apparent. Arguably, the strike was anticipated and the government wanted not only to confront – but also to defeat – the miners and destroy the powers of their union. A prime example of this premeditation was encapsulated in the Ridley Report of 1978 (Towers, 1985). On coming to power, the Thatcher government used the recommendations of the report to confront the perceived political threat posed by the NUM. The proposed steps to take were (Towers, 1985, p14) to:

- build up maximum coal stocks, particularly at the power stations
- make contingency plans for the import of coal
- encourage the recruitment of non-union lorry drivers by haulage companies to help move coal where necessary
- introduce dual coal/oil firing in all power stations as quickly as possible.

All in all, coal stocks were amassed, additional supplies were brought in from abroad and – outside the nuclear sector – the introduction of oil firing reduced the dependence of power stations on coal (Ram, 1985). Such steps could not have been taken by the NCB alone. Nor could they be implemented by a union of the managers of all the nationalised industries involved. Yet all were implemented.

Tellingly, however, the most damning recommendation and eventual policy pursued was to starve the strikers of their money supply, by cutting benefits available to strikers and their families (Ram, 1985; Towers, 1985) and, as a consequence, make the NUM finance them. Just as tellingly, this was precisely what the government did as the strike progressed. Furthermore, the recommendations of 1978 were supported by legislation hastily introduced from 1980 to 1984, which was designed to undermine and restrict the power of the unions as well as severing – or at least weakening – the financial links that he unions had with the Labour Party (Towers, 1985). Of key importance here, though, was the rendering of picketing as a criminal act which, as a consequence, legitimised the government's act of raising a fully trained, anti-picket, '20,000-strong special police task force, equipped with … state of the art anti-riot gadgetry' (Ram, 1985).

In a more sinister twist, the Thatcher government equated, in 1984, the war against the Argentinian Junta over the Falklands/Malvinas two years earlier with a war against the enemy without. The dispute with the miners, however, was equated by Thatcher with a war against 'the enemy within' (Milne, 2004). In accordance with most warlike situations, intelligence agencies had a prominent role to play. In leaked papers to *The Guardian* (29 November 1993, cited in Milne, 2004, p4) in the winter of 1990-91 it was revealed by the Government Communications Headquarters (GCHQ) disaffected staff that Margaret Thatcher had personally authorised a 'Get Scargill' campaign during and after the 1984-85 strike. MI5 coordinated and ran operations to

prison sentence of up to 10 years (Vanson, 1985; Mansfield, 2014). The 'rioters' were never convicted in the ensuing trials on the basis that the arrests were: 'entirely unjustified and derived from systemic abuse. Arrests were false, allegations were fabricated, statements were orchestrated. All of ... which never required a jury verdict because they ... [the police cases for prosecution] collapsed when subjected to the scrutiny of cross-examination' (Mansfield, 2014, unpaginated).

Even to this day, not one police officer has been prosecuted or disciplined. Clearly, there is evidence of some form of cover-up. Moreover, it is evidence which cannot be blamed solely on the misconduct of individual police officers. Given the collapse of the prosecution cases, the alleged violent acts of the strikers cannot be deemed to be at the root of police aggression either. Planning, training, organisation (of 10 different forces) had to come from higher up, most likely from the government itself. At the very least, the government had to have authorised the gathering of the disparate police forces.

In the aftermath of the strike

Six years after the Thatcher government came to power in 1979, the UK public were feeling the devastating effects of both the pit closures and a 'short sharp shock' neo-liberal agenda of unemployment, 'intended to tone up an economy deemed to have grown flaccid through excessive wage settlements' (Ram, 1985, p1552). Some 3.2 million workers in the UK (13.1% of the labour force when seasonally adjusted) found themselves in enforced unemployment. This was compared to 1.3 million who were jobless (or a national average of 5.3%) when Margaret Thatcher came to power (Ram, 1985, p1552). The young, those in South Wales, Scotland, the north of England and Northern Ireland were the most affected due to the 'redundancy of entire communities' (Ram, 1985, p1552). Most were prominent mining areas. Nevertheless, the redundancies and projected redundancies have continued to the present day. In the 1990s, for instance, it was recorded that the 'deep-mined coal industry faces closure of 31 of the existing pits as a result both of further increases in coal imports and, more particularly, the construction of gas-fired power stations' (Glyn, 1992, p2638).

All of this meant that the economic argument for the past and future cuts simply did not make economic sense and, arguably, reflected the ideological dogmatism of the Thatcher-led government:

- The coal output lost through the closures of the pits concerned had to be made up from other energy sources. Imports of coal and gas (especially coal) had an adverse effect on the balance of payments, and many of the UK fields were worked by overseas-owned oil companies who remit their profits abroad (Glyn, 1992).
- There was an assumption that the redundant miners would find alternative employment, but that assumption was flawed at a time that was characterised by high unemployment. Even if the miners did find employment, jobs were finite during this period and their employment would result in someone else not being employed. Thus unemployment levels and social security costs rose either way.

Neo-liberal immorality or legitimate action? Raising questions about state action in Argentina and the UK

Out of this discussion arise a number of key questions over the morality of the implementation of neo-liberal economies within Argentina and the UK. Of the two case studies given in this chapter, the case of Argentina is the most obviously criminal, and we would argue, immoral.

The disappearances and the social engineering tactic of giving new-born children to families supportive of the regime epitomise this immorality. The fact that such activities remained hidden is also indicative of the fact that, by keeping such actions hidden, the regime recognised the immorality surrounding the preservation and expansion of its neo-liberal agenda. Yet the regime also tried to legitimise its agenda through the assertion that, in geopolitical terms, – 'the occidental world is at a disadvantage since its democratic way of life and respect for individual freedoms leaves it exposed to the insidious forms of foreign aggression and influence' (Pion-Berlin, 1988, p389). The attempts to implement a neo-liberal regime were threatened by a left-wing, insurgent influence which not only undermined the economy but also the essential way of life and standards of the Argentinian people.

Given the oppression and terror exerted by the Junta, this was hardly a legitimising tactic of any credence. Rather the opposite was the case. Even though the geopolitical debate says little about the defence of neo-liberalism and Western, Christian way of life domestically in Argentina, there are limits to providing security for the state. As Pion-Berlin (1988) succinctly put it:

> ... it would only make sense to speak of cause and
> effect were we to assume that the geopolitical doctrine
> unambiguously provided a license for unbridled state power
> and militarization of society. Neither seems to be the case,
> suggesting that military regimes (and the Argentina regime
> in particular) may have misinterpreted the geopolitical
> doctrine entirely. (Pion–Berlin, 1988, p390)

Some would argue that this misinterpretation was slightly benign,
as the interpretation and implementation of the Junta's actions were
undertaken with full understanding and deliberately.

Although actions undertaken against the miners' strike in the
UK were less horrific, they were, nonetheless, deliberate and the
Thatcherite government was fully aware of what it was doing. Likewise,
there are related questions to those posed in Argentina that also have
to be asked. In the face of government hostility, how legitimate, for
example, were the claims of the miners to keep their jobs in order to
secure the stability of their communities against market force demands
for profit marketisation, cost–cutting and the investment in new
technology to reduce the workforce? This was despite the fact that:
'In 1984 NCB figures put subsidies in France at £19.19 per tonne;
in West Germany at £12.06 and in Britain at £4.11. Figures from
Eastern Europe, and particularly Poland which was a major factor in
1984, were impossible to come by' (Adeney and Lloyd, 1986, p24).

With these figures in mind, it was hardly legitimate for the NCB
and the government to question the economic viability of the pits,
let alone demand closures and capacity reductions. Moreover, claims
that many pits were uneconomic omitted to include the devastating
socioeconomic costs of destroying whole communities reliant on the
nearby pit. Given the particular association of the community with the
pit, it can hardly be said that the interests and way of life were being
protected by the enforcement of a neo–liberal agenda.

Even on purely neo–liberal terms, however, the pro–government
actions can be shot down. Besides the previously mentioned costs of
increased unemployment and the associated benefit costs, there was
yet another cost to the free market economy whether it was obvious
or not. With the destruction of the pit communities, coupled with
the lack of alternative employment, tens of thousands of miners had
to rely on benefits. Because of this, tax revenue – from earnings from
mining – declined (Glyn, 1985). Reliance on benefits resulted in less
disposable income. In turn, this reliance meant less of an ability of
the miners and their families to be consumers in a consumer–based

economy. Therefore, less consumption in the immediate mining communities around the village initially had an impact on the local economy, and then, as low ability to consume spread elsewhere, the national economy was also affected. In neo-liberal terms, little of this epitomised the productive, booming, free-market, consumerist, neo-liberal economy of prosperity and investment.

When taking this argument a step further, the effects on associated industries need to be considered. For instance, eight years after the strike and the privatisation of many of the remaining pits to British Coal, Glyn (1992, p2638) developed his argument against the further closure of 31 pits (discussed earlier), when he stipulated that these closures go beyond the 25,000 miners directly affected. In his analysis, Glyn stated:

> Firstly other industrial workers and staff employed by BCC (British Coal Corporation) would inevitably lose their jobs as the industry contracted. At present there are around 33 non-miners employed by BCC for every 100 miners. Assuming their numbers fall nearly in line with the number of miners, as has happened over the last decade, implies a further 7,600 job losses at BCC. But many other workers also depend for their jobs on work for the coal industry. About 7,000 private contractors' employees work in British Coal's deep mines; in total some 73,000 workers provide inputs for BC collieries. Closure of 31 pits and reduction of output by some 31 million tonnes a year would imply around 31,500 more workers would lose their jobs. (Glyn, 1992, p2638)

The mention of 'the last decade' suggests a spiral of decline since the announcement of pit closures and productivity reductions before the 1984–85 strike. Thus the economic costs to the government and the economy declined even more. Greater reliance on benefits, less disposable income and consumption, and lesser tax payments were all symptoms of a destructive imposition of neo-liberal policies at a time of heightened unemployment. The neo-liberal case simply did not hold, so who did benefit and who should have been held to account? These questions are not, and were not, easily answered in terms of incontrovertible proof. But even now, they are questions that survivors of the past government of the UK need to answer and should still be accountable for.

In the final analysis, both the Argentinian Junta and the Thatcher government in the UK attempted to legitimise their actions with repeated claims that they were responding to, or pre-empting, existing or future threats to their tenure. In Argentina, the threat came from the Junta-designated 'subversives', while in the UK the actions taken by Thatcher and the state apparatus were justified on the grounds of fighting 'the enemy within'. Ironically, both the 'subversives' and the 'enemy within' were juxtaposed with notions of 'freedom' and 'autonomy' as the state attempted to establish and preserve the ideal of a truly 'free' market economy in a legitimate way.

State violence, terrorism and genocide?

Despite the attempts to legitimise – and even deny – their actions, the Argentinian Junta can be accused of committing criminal acts against its own people. As this chapter has described, there is plenty of evidence to substantiate the claim that the people of Argentina were victims of state violence and were terrorised by the military Junta and its associates, thus constituting acts of state terrorism. To cement such an accusation, Judge Rozanski went a step further. When trying retired Police Commissioner-General Miguel Osvaldo Etchecolatz in 2006, Rozanski ruled that 'these crimes had been committed in the framework of genocide when the military ruled over Argentina through torture, assassinations and massive disappearances (Robben, 2012, p305).

Almost in a linear way, the accusation of 'genocide' can be traced over the years following the decline of Argentina's military dictatorship. As this chapter has outlined, the military Junta and state officials justified their violent tactics to suppress and control the subversive threat to the Argentinian state. As also pointed out, they went as far as attempting to deny that such acts took place. However, 'state terrorism' was the preferred term among Argentinians living in exile (Robben, 2012). The hitherto mentioned denials of torture and disappearance acted as a catalyst for the survivors to 'substantiate the repression, and accumulate proof in support of the charge of state terrorism' (Robben, 2012, p309). Numerous testimonies in magazines, books and the media combined with the 1985 trial of Lieutenant-General Videla, Admiral Massera and three other Junta commanders led to: 'painful testimonies by survivors of clandestine detention centers, mothers searching for their disappeared children and grandmothers trying to recover their grandchildren … [which] contrasted with the curt answers and lapses of memory on the part of military officers' (Robben, 2012, p309).

In 1998, the use of the heinous act of 'genocide' was set firmly on the agenda, when Spanish judge Baltasar Garzón stated that genocide had taken place in Argentina when the Junta attempted to establish a new social order and specifically target the Argentinian Jewish community, who were perceived to represent a threat to the Christian culture of Argentina (Roht-Arriaza, 2005; Robben, 2012). By the mid-2000s, the human rights movement also started to replace the term 'state terrorism' with 'genocide'. Human rights lawyer Emilio Mignone began the process in earnest. He declared that the term 'genocide' applied to Argentina in the respect that the military had been guilty of true genocide as it committed assassinations *en masse* without any recognisable trial (Frontalini and Caiati, 1984; Robben, 2012). Given all of this, a convincing case can be made against Videla's Junta: that it was not only guilty of state violence and state terrorism but also of the ultimate atrocity of genocide.

By contrast, the case against Margaret Thatcher's government is not as clear-cut. Granted, the spectre of riot police and charges by baton-carrying policemen on horseback instilled a sense of intimidation and terror at Orgreave, yet this can hardly fit the definition of terrorism given in Chapters Four, Six and Seven, where terrorism is equated with more lethal activities. Certainly, there were no incidences of 'genocide' during the miners' strike, but there was evidence of state violence: even if it was on a smaller scale to that exerted by the Argentinian military. There was also ample evidence of the government justifying its actions by 'othering' a section of the community. In this case, though, it was specifically the British coal miners – and by implication all other trade unions – who were seen as 'the enemy within'. Nevertheless, the brutality at Orgreave and the excessive use of force by the police and allegedly the army did resonate with the atrocities committed in Argentina. It is little wonder that Arthur Scargill invoked scenes of Latin America. It is in relation to this aspect of Margaret Thatcher's governmental plans and tactics that a case of state violence can be built against the Conservative government of the time.

Moreover, elements of state intimidation – designed to instil a sense of terror – can be levelled at the government during the strike of 1984–85. Besides the cavalry charges, lines of riot-shield-carrying police officers beating their shields to create a barrage of noise was a direct attempt to orchestrate a sense of fear among the striking miners. Add to this the numerous false arrests, beatings in captivity and false charges, and there is little doubt that a significant number of those picketing at Orgreave felt terrorised (Vanson, 1985). This was also substantiated by the accusation that police lapel numbers were missing and the overriding suspicion that not all of those wearing a police uniform were actual police constables. Rather, the prevalent belief of those individuals present was that many were army soldiers or some other military personnel trained to disable the pickets (Vanson, 1985).

So far, a number of crimes can be levelled at both Argentina and the UK over these specific case studies. That said, the crimes defined so far only relate to the actions of the time. They are static, and such criminal definitions do not account for the passage of time and the after-effects of the crimes committed. As a consequence, a more longitudinal, holistic approach needs to be taken, and it is here where viewing criminal acts through the lens of 'social harm' can and should be taken. Only then, can the full devastating effects of such governmental/state actions be accounted for and, more importantly, held to account both publicly and in the eyes of a truly independent judiciary and the law (whether it be national and/or international).

Going beyond definitions of state violence and state terrorism – social harm as an expansive analytical tool

Although the terms 'state terrorism' and 'state violence' (taking aside the accusations of 'genocide' in the case of Argentina) have been used to describe state actions intended to enforce conformity, control and adherence to a neo-liberal agenda in both Argentina and the UK, the case against these two regimes is still incomplete. They are incomplete in that the full devastating effects of the actions of each regime cannot be traced within the confines of any narrow definition of 'state violence' or 'state terrorism'. Likewise, a combination of the two definitions would not be sufficient either. In this respect, the concept of 'social harm' needs to be incorporated into the analysis, thus providing a more comprehensive picture.

As we have seen in Chapter Two, the definition given involves individuals or groups and, as such, can include ideological discrimination against social groupings or can allow for definitions of crime that tackle needs-based social harms inflicted by the powerful on the less powerful. Social harm, therefore, may relate to enduring adverse consequences to health or career advancement. Put simply, the concept of social harm goes beyond conventional or marginal definitions of crime in the dominant legal policy, enforcement and academic agendas, since it encompasses crimes of commission and omission to overcome or expose cover-ups, corruption, disinformation, unaccountability and violations of domestic and/or international laws (Ross, 2003).

Certainly in Argentina during the 'Dirty War', Videla's regime was guilty of commissioning a large-scale cover-up of its atrocious actions. The very fact that numerous individuals were hidden from the international and public gaze paid testament to that. In relation to crimes of commission, this chapter has amply demonstrated that the Junta commissioned itself, other parts of the armed forces and the police to instigate kidnappings, torture and the killing of thousands of individuals. In addition, there was evidence of social engineering with the illicit placement of newborn children into the 'care' of prominent supporters of the military regime. As a result, communities, mothers, wives, sisters and broken families were left scarred and filled with grief. They were also left in fear of their own lives even after the 'Dirty War' had long since ended. As late as July 2010:

> a military solidarity organisation published hundreds of names and addresses of trial witnesses and alleged former guerrillas on the internet, accompanied with the threatening message: 'Know the names of the terrorists and their addresses: They could be your neighbors and teachers and approach you as friends ... They live among us.' (Robben, 2012, p313)

As had happened during the 'Dirty War' witnesses failed to turn up to trials. Notably, in the trial of Etchecolatz the key witness, Julio Lopéz, failed to turn up on the final day. The fear was that retired policemen had made him disappear (Robben, 2012). Under these circumstances, justice was definitely not served. As intimated earlier, numerous trials and pardons, not convictions, have occurred. Again, it amounts to a travesty: especially for those still wanting to know what happened to their loved ones and those hoping to be reunited with their kidnapped children.

On a smaller scale in the UK, however, the infliction of social harm was less obvious, but does, nonetheless, follow similar characteristics. There was evidence in state cover-up of the events at Orgreave, exemplified by the fact that those arrested were found not guilty and the police reports were all too similar, as if each officer had been dictated to (Vanson, 1985). In relation to the media, there was not a veil of silence, but, as shown earlier, a rather aggressive support for the government. As for the future, the destruction of one of the most powerful unions in the country and the subsequent denigration of union powers nationwide, meant that there was a resultant denial of the right to withdraw labour and to protect wage levels, full-time hours and employment (Glyn, 1985). One could even make the connection with the introduction of 'flexible working', fixed-term and part-time contracts and, ultimately, the introduction of zero-hour contracts and the rise of a precariat (those in precarious employment) (Standing, 2011). All fit with the Thatcherite fight to preserve the inalienable 'right' of management to manage; all have led to a lack of wage security and the associated problem of poverty and unemployment.

Returning to the coal miners, the actions of the UK government resulted in the destruction of communities and pit villages and a subsequent increase in unemployment. Families and local communities were left scarred, both emotionally and financially. With echoes of Durkheim, E.F. Schumacher (1960) – the economic adviser to the Coal Board at the time – set out 25 years earlier a convincing case against the premature closure of pits and why it constitutes social harm:

> It is a policy of doubtful wisdom and questionable morality for this generation to take all the resources and leave for its children only the worst. But it is surely a criminal policy if, in addition, we wilfully sterilise, abandon and thereby ruin, such relatively inferior resources as we ourselves have opened up, but do not care to utilise. This is like the spiteful burglar who does not merely pinch the valuables but in addition destroys everything he cannot take. (E.F. Schumacher, cited in Glyn, 1985, p30)

Glyn (1985) went on to point out that during a time of mass unemployment such a scenario is doubly criminal: in that it is not just mineral resources but also human resources that are wasted. They are wasted because 'most of the apparent benefit from grabbing the best resources is swallowed up by ensuring that those wasted human resources can be kept alive' (Glyn, 1985, p30).

By ending this chapter with the concept of social harm, it has been made clear that a fuller picture of the crimes and harms that have been inflicted on both the Argentinian and UK citizenry have been gleaned. Social harm goes beyond the confines of state violence and state terrorism. It looks beyond the actual commission of the act to reveal the longer-lasting devastation that such acts inflict: thus uncovering the bigger picture and building a more formidable case for the perpetrators to be held accountable.

NINE

Conclusion: the role, nature and control of state crime

The impossibility of uncovering unconventional criminality

We have been at pains throughout this book to show that uncovering the nature and extent of unconventional criminality is an almost impossible task. State crime is no different. While there is undoubtedly much known about it, the gaps in the knowledge base can still be described as 'substantial'. That which is known of state crime usually involves high-profile cases with far-reaching consequences, yet the more workaday practices of state administration can also foster elements of criminality that are almost impossible to detect and, therefore, to know about.

Doig (2011, p97–8) sums this up, by quoting at length the work of Huberts and colleagues. It is worth repeating the key issues here:

> Most researchers are more interested in the cases that attract a lot of attention such as large scale corruption, political murder, prison torture, et cetera. Even though that focus is understandable because of the seriousness of the cases, it clearly hinders the developments of a body of knowledge on the amount and character of rule and law breaking by government bodies. As a consequence, there is little or no contemporary empirical research available on rule breaking in a broader sense. (Huberts et al, 2006, p16 cited in Doig, 2011, p97–8)

Huberts and colleagues list a series of 'unknown knowns':

> We do not know ... how often government organisations and officials break environmental and safety laws, nor do we know how their quality or rate of compliance compares to private citizens and companies ... This lack of knowledge is problematic for theories of political and administrative crime, as well as for the body of knowledge of political and

administrative ethics and integrity … This also illustrates the practical importance of the phenomenon. Governmental rule and law breaking is potentially very damaging for the integrity and credibility of the state in general and law and rule enforcement by the state in particular. (Huberts et al, 2006, p16 cited in Doig, 2011, p97-8)

Fundamentally, it is unclear how often states do not adhere to the laws that they make. As indicated, in Western democratic states we only get an inkling that this happens at all as we have a relatively free press. Even so, it is those cases with a sufficiently high profile that actually make the news – reinforcing the point that the media tend to take episodic happenstances but present them as if they are endemic.

Definitional and legislative limitations

To add to the confusion, Chapter Two forcibly pointed out that state crimes could not be easily defined. To reiterate, the state defines what constitutes a crime and what does not. Logically, this means that a state can legitimise its own actions by not legislating against them. Moreover, the transformation from government to governance in most Western societies has meant that there has been a simultaneous concentration of power in the centre of government (serving to regulate but not govern the neo-liberal, laissez-faire state) alongside a dispersal of the decision-making process among various 'institutions and actors that are drawn from but also beyond government' (Stoker, 1998, p18).

Key stakeholders and a variety of actors thus perform what was hitherto considered to be functions of the state. From our perspective, this diffusion of decision-making adds to the confusion in defining state crime and, as we pointed out, legislating against – and the prosecution of – such crimes: not least because the question of accountability becomes more obscure in that it is difficult to distinguish crimes committed for personal gain from crimes committed by the state.

Furthermore, when Chapter Two outlined some of the more prominent definitions of state crime, it became apparent that the picture is even more obscure and, in turn, this highlighted the gaps in criminological knowledge of state crime and its nature. Primarily, we noted that working definitions of state crime ranged from the narrow to the all-encompassing, which spanned the constructivist-realist scale.

It was also clear that there was considerable overlap with other forms of crime. In support, Chapter Three highlighted these overlaps by introducing the way in which states can and do collude with organised crime syndicates in the pursuit of capitalistic interests. Alongside the case of HSBC money laundering and Mexican drug trafficking (Monaghan, 2014) discussed in the introduction, the complexity of criminal collusion, immorality and control/detection was again brought to the fore.

Chapter Four continued with the trends followed in Chapter Three. The chapter considered the nature of the international drugs trade in some detail. In particular, the chapter delved into the relationship between the 'war on drugs' and the lucrative spoils that states (the US in this case) were accruing from the Iran–Contra affair, to name but one example.

Chapter Seven also introduced examples of state collusion and criminality. This time, however, the focus was on terrorism and how the British (Royal Ulster Constabulary) and Irish (Guardai) police worked with and encouraged oppositional paramilitary organisations in Northern Ireland.

Nevertheless, despite the emergence of a clearer visualisation of criminal activity from our numerous case examples, we still felt there was a somewhat incomplete comprehension of state crime and the immorality of the powerful.

From neo-liberalism to social harm

To counter the acknowledged gaps in our understanding – and to counter influential media bias, the definitional and legislative problems that affect prosecution – our overarching stance was, therefore, to take a more holistic approach that synthesised the nature of the new global hegemony of neo-liberalism (and its drive towards making more and more profit), governmental alliances (with other nation states, organisations and powerful individuals), contraventions of international law, political violence/terrorism and the devastating consequences of inflicting social harm. More importantly, our contention was – and is – that individually each of these areas of focus cannot reveal the full extent of immoral behaviour or criminality on their own. There needs, we argued, to be a consideration of all of these aspects, so that a detailed account of how each aspect interacts with the others can emerge. By doing so, a less myopic and a more comprehensive picture can be pieced together. It is precisely this panoramic view that can be forcibly used to hold the perpetrators to account.

To illustrate this interaction, the book's examination of political violence pulled all the strands together as the chapters began to unfold. Crucially, violence was not depicted as being unidimensional; on the contrary, a number of dimensions were brought out in the various case studies introduced. Nevertheless, these dimensions stemmed from two fundamental interpretations (see Žižek, 2008) before they became interwoven with the other strands:

- On the one hand, violence – and indeed political violence – was acknowledged to relate to physical harm in terms of killing (Chapters Six, Seven and Eight when discussing Iraq, Northern Ireland and Argentina respectively), injury (Chapter Eight in the examination of the events during the miners' strike) and even torture (Chapter Six and Abu Ghraib).
- On the other hand, violence can be objective, in that it is systemic: systemic in terms of the socioeconomic system. From our perspective, Žižek's (2008) notion of such violence is exemplified by the relentless pursuit to implement a neo-liberal system in Argentina, Iraq and the UK and the suppression of opposition.

Moreover, Box's (1983) assertion that capitalism – and by implication neo-liberalism – is inherently criminal also tallies with the stance that this book has taken.

Throughout the book, neo-liberalism constantly emerges as a source of immorality, corruption and criminality. Although in different guises and manifestations, it has been made clear that neo-liberalism fails to live up to the promise of being a liberating, democratising and civilising force that neo-conservative and New Right thinkers hold the system to be. Part of the reason for this, we contend, has been the emphasis placed upon the making of profit by the capitalist interests concerned. In Chapter Two, this was discussed in depth. Not only did the book emphasise that capitalist ventures under a neo-liberal regime serve individual interests at the expense of more collective interests (generally the poorer, less powerful sections of society), but it also pointed out how powerful business corporations tended to influence and capture the general policy agenda of government. This was a two-way process (described as a 'revolving door'), whereby the government gain powerful, influential allies in creating and maintaining their power base. Nowhere was this made more apparent than in Chapter Five with the discussion of Rupert Murdoch and his media empire; nowhere was it more obvious that such liaisons were highly immoral if not criminal given Murdoch's anti trade union stance (Chapter Eight), support for the invasion of Iraq (Chapter Six) and the demonisation of the so-called 'scrounging', irresponsible 'underclass' (Chapter One).

Profit and gain, however, add more corrupting influences. Big business does not court such alliances without a return for its investment in time and money. With this in mind, we revealed a number of immoral/corrupt practices perpetrated by organisations and corporations to procure a mutually beneficial cooperation with relevant government officials and politicians. Chapter Five, for instance, charted the nefarious activities of Rupert Murdoch's 'empire' to obtain power and secure the expansion of his media empire. In particular, donations to the US campaigns of political candidates were listed, while in the UK the offer of lucrative book contracts to leading politicians was noted, despite the knowledge that sales would not recoup the advances made.

Our position over these issues was that power begets power – and it was this power (in terms of political influence) that significantly eased the passage for expansive acquisitions to the Murdoch empire (especially in the UK). With expansion, of course, come more power and more wealth and influence as greater advertising and promotional space/opportunities become available with the increase in monopolistic media platforms that run contrary to the 'free trade', 'liberating' ideals of neo-liberalism.

In a similar vein, we also charted the monopolistic capture of reconstruction contracts in Iraq (Chapter Six) and how corporate America profited from lucrative acquisitions at the expense of the Iraqi people, who were subject to mass unemployment, long-term loss of livelihoods and the enforcement of neo-liberal aims and ideology completely at odds with their previous way of life. The resentment, social harm and destabilisation of the region were also charted, to demonstrate the long-term consequences of what was, essentially, an illegal invasion. Crucially, it was pointed out that social harm, violence and destitution still persist in Iraq, and it is this bigger picture that needs to be accounted for, as opposed to just the initial act of violence, which only tells part of the story.

Lasting observations and future optimism

The most prevalent observation that we have made in this book relates to the limitations of existing criminal laws (whether international or national) and the questions surrounding accountability and who polices these individual pieces of legislation. It is our belief that each of the definitions cited earlier in this chapter and in Chapter Two is insufficient in isolation and, because of this, can be avoided through subterfuge, obfuscation and definitional vagueness. It is our stance that an amalgamation of these definitions needs to be undertaken, so that the full extent of criminal/immoral behaviour by states and the powerful can be brought out.

In this respect, the lens of social harm brings together all the elements of such behaviour. Furthermore, social harm has a longitudinal dimension that keeps criminal and moral behaviour under scrutiny well beyond the initial, more obvious violations of morality and/or criminal law. As already commented on here and in earlier chapters, the socioeconomic, ecological and psychological after-effects of war, invasion, torture, genocide and unnecessary unemployment can be measured as they affect communities, families, the ecosystem, social infrastructure and communal health and livelihood issues (see Chapters Six, Seven and Eight in particular).

In sum, an examination of the dubious actions by the state and the powerful can spark a prolonged sense of moral outrage in the eyes of the public well beyond the initial atrocity. Indeed, it is our belief that a protracted public moral outrage will act as a catalyst for holding rogue state actions and the corrupt acts of the powerful accountable: hence the original desire and motivation for us to write this book.

Inevitably, however, this book becomes incomplete with the passage of time. When compiling this conclusion in August 2015, for instance, there are reports emerging about Islamic State using mustard gas against Kurdish forces in Iraq, which relates back to the effects of social harm depicted earlier and the consequences of the Iraq invasion by the 'willing coalition'. Reports are also coming out of China, where a chemical factory has exploded, killing at least a hundred and injuring well over five hundred citizens living in the area. In a reminder of the Bhopal disaster, one has to ask why the factory was built in such a populated area and who sanctioned its construction. Other issues that need to be discussed concern the Guantanamo Bay detention camp and the question of illegal rendition and torture of suspected terrorists. Elsewhere, there needs to be an examination of President Assad's suppression and killing of his own population in Syria. Biased media reporting, racially motivated police killings of ethnic minorities in the US, state collusion and the influence of capitalist interests also require further scrutiny.

Hopefully, another edition of this book will follow as events unfold. Criminology, sociology and social policy need to keep abreast of such developments, to prevent further travesties from going undetected – if not prevented in the first place.

References

Adeney, M. and Lloyd, J. (1986) *The Miners' Strike 1984-5: Loss Without Limit*, London: Routledge & Kegan Paul

Advisory Council on the Misuse of Drugs (2002) *The Classification of Cannabis under the Misuse of Drugs Act (1971)*, London: Home Office

Advisory Council on the Misuse of Drugs (2005) *Further Consideration of the Classification of Cannabis Under the Misuse of Drugs Act (1971)*, London: Home Office

Advisory Council on the Misuse of Drugs (2008) *Cannabis: Classification and Public Health*, London: Home Office

Albanese, J. (2004) North American organised crime, *Global Crime*, 6 (1) 8–18

Alcock, P. (1996) *Social Policy in Britain: Themes and Issues*, Basingstoke: Macmillan Press

Aldridge, M. and Evetts, J. (2003) Rethinking the concept of professionalism: The Case of Journalism, *British Journal of Sociology*, 54 (4) 547–64

Altheide, D. and Grimes, J. (2005) War Programming: The Propaganda Project and the Iraq War, *The Sociological Quarterly*, 46 (4) 617–43

Althusser, L. (1971) Ideology and ideological state apparatuses, in Althusser, L. (ed.) *Lenin and Philosophy and other Essays*, NY: Monthly Review Press

Alvarez, A. (2001) *Governments, Citizens, and Genocide: A Comparative and Interdisciplinary Approach*, Bloomington: Indiana University Press

Amann, D. (2005) Abu Ghraib, *University of Pennsylvania Law Review*, 153 (6) 2085–141

Amnesty International (1994) *Political Killings in Northern Ireland*, London: Amnesty International

Anand, B. and Attea, K. (2003) 'News Corporation', Harvard Business School Case Study 9-702-425

Andreas, P. and Nadelman, E. (2006) *Policing the Globe: Criminalization and Crime Control in International Relations*, Oxford: Oxford University Press

Antonellli, M.A. (2009) State terrorism, clandestine language: notes on the Argentine Military Dictatorship, *PMLA*, 124 (5) 1794–1799

Arceneaux, C.L. (1997) Institutional design, military rule, and regime transition in Argentina (1976-1983): an extension of the Remmer Thesis, *Society for Latin American Studies*, 16 (3) 327–50

Arsenault, A. and Castells, M. (2008) Switching power: Rupert Murdoch and the global business of media politics: A Sociological Analysis, *International Sociology*, 23 (4) 488-513

Atkinson, R. (2013) London: where only the wealth of a global elite can find a home, *The Guardian*, www.theguardian.com/commentisfree/2013/jul/22/london-wealth-global-elite-home

Barak, G. (1991) *Crimes by the Capitalist State: An Introduction to State Criminality*, Albany: State University of New York Press

Barker, R. (2012) *Political Legitimacy and the State*, Oxford: Oxford University Press

Barton, A. (2003) *Illicit Drugs: Use and Control*, London: Routledge

Baudrillard, J. (2003) *The Spirit of Terrorism*, London: Verso

BBC (2004) Full statement of Finucane inquiry, BBC News, http://news.bbc.co.uk/1/hi/northern_ireland/3684302.stm

BBC (2010) Bloody Sunday: PM David Cameron's Full Statement, BBC News, www.bbc.co.uk/news/10322295

BBC (2011) Drug submarine seized by Colombian navy, BBC News, www.bbc.co.uk/news/world-latin-america-12461089

BBC (2012) HSBC to pay $1.9bn in US money laundering penalties, BBC News, www.bbc.co.uk/news/business-20673466

BBC (2014) Iraq Crisis: What is a Caliphate? In 90 Seconds, BBC News, www.bbc.co.uk/news/world-middle-east-28849919

Beck, U. (2002) The silence of words and political dynamics in the world risk society, *Logos*, 1 (4) 1-18

Becker, H. (1963) *Outsiders*, NY: Free Press

Bell, D. (1953) Crime as an American way of life, *The Antioch Review*, 13 (2) 131-54

Bellamy, A. (2004) Ethics and Intervention: The "Humanitarian Exception" and the Problem of Abuse in the Case of Iraq, *Journal of Peace Research*, 41 (2) 131-47

Benson, M.L. and Simpson, S.S. (2009) *White Collar Crime: An Opportunity Perspective*, London: Routledge

Bewley-Taylor, D. (1999) *The United States and International Drug Control, 1909-97*, London: Pinter

Bietti, L. (2011) The commemoration of March 24th, 1976: understanding the exceptionality of the present political discourse about the "dirty war" in Argentina, *Journal of Language and Politics*, 10 (3) 347-371

Birrell, D. (1994) Social Policy Responses to Urban Violence in Northern Ireland, in Dunn, S. (ed.) *Managing Divided Cities*, Staffordshire: Keele University Press, http://cain.ulst.ac.uk/issues/policy/birrell.htm

Björnehed, E. (2004) Narco-terrorism: The merger of the war on drugs and the war on terror, *Global Crime*, 6 (3-4) 305-24

Blackman, S. (2004) *Chilling Out: The Cultural Politics of Substance Consumption, Youth and Drug Policy*, Buckingham: Open University Press

Bottoms, A. (1995) The philosophy and politics of punishment and sentencing, in C. Clarkson and R. Morgan (eds) *The politics of sentencing reform*, Oxford: Clarendon Press, 17-50

Box, S. (1983) *Power, Crime and Mystification*, London: Tavistock

Box, S. (2001) Crime, power and ideological mystification, in Muncie, J., McLaughlin, E. and Langan, M. (eds) *Criminological Perspectives: A Reader*, London: Sage

Braithwaite, J. (1989) *Crime, Shame and Reintegration*, Cambridge: Cambridge University Press

Brown, R. (2005) Reconstruction of Infrastructure in Iraq: End to a Means or Means to an End?, *Third World Quarterly*, 26 (4/5) 759-75

Bruce, S. (2004) Turf war and peace: Loyalist paramilitaries since 1994, Terrorism and Political Violence, 16 (4) 501-21

Brysk, A. (1994) The politics of measurement: the contested count of the disappeared in Argentina, *Human Rights Quarterly*, 16 (4) 676-92

Bulmer, M. (1978) Social structure and social change in the twentieth century, in Bulmer, M. (ed.) *Mining and Social Change*, London: Croom Helm

Burke, J. (2004) *Al Qaeda: The True Story of Radical Islam*, London: IB Taurus

Burnham, J. and Pyper, R. (2008) *Britain's Modernised Civil Service*, London: Palgrave Macmillan

Butler, E. (1995) Markets and the future of welfare, in Gladstone, D. (ed.) *British Social Welfare: Past, Present and Future*, London: UCL Press, 241-64

Calabrese, A. (2005) Profits and patriots: US media coverage of the Iraq war, in *World Association for Christian Communication*, http://north-america.waccglobal.org/index.php/en/15-Profits-and-patriots-US-media-coverage-of-the-Iraq-war

Callaghan, J. (1973) *A House Divided: The Northern Ireland Dilemma*, London: Harper Collins

Callinicos, A. (2005) Iraq: Fulcrum of World Politics, *Third World Quarterly*, 26 (4/5) 593-608

Cameron Commission (1969) *Disturbances in Northern Ireland*, Belfast: HMSO

Carlson, M. and Berkowitz, D. (2014) 'The emperor lost his clothes': Rupert Murdoch, News of the World and journalistic boundary work in the UK and USA, *Journalism*, 15 (4) 389-406

Carrabine, E., Cox, P., Lee, M., Plummer, K. and South, N. (eds) (2009) *Criminology: A Sociological Introduction*, London: Routledge

Casciani, D. (2014) Hacking probes: what happens next?, www.bbc.co.uk/news/uk-28027911

Caulkins, J., Kilmer, B., Reuter, P. and Midgette, G. (2014) Cocaine's fall and marijuana's rise: questions and insights based on new estimates of consumption and expenditures in US drug markets, *Addiction*, 110, 728-36

Chambliss, W. (1989) State organized crime: The 1988 American Society of Criminology Presidential Address, *Criminology*, 27 (2) 183-208

Chatwin, C. (2003) Drug policy developments within the European Union: the destabilizing effects of Dutch and Swedish drug policies, *British Journal of Criminology*, 43 (3) 567-82

Chenoweth, N. (2001) *Virtual Murdoch: Reality Wars on the Information Highway*, London: Secker and Warburg

Chibnall, S. (2004) *Law and Order News: An Analysis of Crime Reporting in the British Press* (2nd edn), London: Routledge

Chouvy, P.-A. (2011) (2011) Southeast Asia's thriving drug trade, *World Politics Review*, 25 October 2011

Christensen, J. (2015) On Her Majesty's secrecy service, in Whyte, D. (ed.) *How Corrupt is Britain?*, London: Pluto Press Kindle Edition

Christie, N. (1986) Suitable enemy, in Bianchi, H. and von Swaaningen, R. (eds) *Abolitionism: Toward a Non-Repressive Approach to Crime*, Amsterdam: Free University Press

Church, R., Outram, Q. and Smith, D. (1991) The militancy of British miners, 1893-1986: interdisciplinary problems and perspectives, *The Journal of Interdisciplinary History*, 22 (1) 49-66

Cicourel, A.V. (1964) *Method and Measurement in Sociology*, NY: Free Press

Clark, G.L. and Dear, M.J. (1984) *State Apparatus: Structures and Language of Legitimacy*, Boston: Allen and Unwin

Clarke, J., Cochrane, A. and Smart, C. (1987) *Ideologies of Welfare: From Dreams to Disillusion*, London: Hutchinson

Clarke, M. (1990) *Business Crime: It's Nature and Control*, Cambridge: Polity Press

Cochrane, A. and Talbot, D. (2008) The search for security, in Cochrane, A. and Talbot, D. (eds) *Security: Welfare, Crime and Society*, Maidenhead: Open University Press

Cockburn, A. and St Clair, J. (1998) *Whiteout: The CIA, Drugs and the Press*, London: Verso

Coleman, C. and Moynihan, J. (1996) *Understanding Crime Data*, Buckingham: Open University Press

Conde, C.H. (2010) Philippines expects record highs in extortion, *New York Times*, March, 7 2010 available online at http://www.nytimes.com/2010/03/08/world/asia/08phils.html?_r=0

Coogan, T.P. (1995) *The IRA*, London: Harper Collins

Coomber, R. (2010) Reconceptualising drug markets and drug dealers – the need for change, *Drugs and Alcohol Today*, 10 (1) 10-13

Cory, P. (2003) *Cory Collusion Inquiry Report: Chief Superintendent Breen and Superintendent Buchanan*, www.patfinucanecentre.org/**cory**/breenbuchanan.pdf

Cox, D., Levine, M. and Newman, S. (2008) *Politics Most Unusual: Violence, Sovereignty and Democracy in the 'War on Terror'*, Basingstoke: Palgrave Macmillan

Craib, I. (1984) *Modern Social Theory*, London: Harvester Wheatsheaf

Crainer, S. (2002) *Big Shots: Business the Rupert Murdoch Way: 10 Secrets of the World's Greatest Deal Maker*, London: John Wiley & Sons

Cressey, D. (1969) *Theft of the Nation: The Structure and Operations of Organized Crime in America*, NY: Harper Row

Croall, H. (1998) *Crime and Society in Britain*, London: Longman

Croall, H. (2001) *Understanding White Collar Crime*, Buckingham: Open University Press

Croall, H. (2009) Community safety and economic crime, *Criminology and Criminal Justice*, 9 (2) 165-85

Curtis, L. (1984) *Nothing But the Same Old Story: The Roots of Anti-Irish RacismI*, London: Information on Ireland

Daly, M. and Sampson, S. (2013) *Narcomania: How Britain Got Hooked on Drugs*, London: Windmill Books Kindle Edition

Davies, N. and Hill, A. (2011) Missing Milly Dowler's voicemail was hacked by the News of the World, *The Guardian*, July, 5 2011 available online at http://www.theguardian.com/uk/2011/jul/04/milly-dowler-voicemail-hacked-news-of-world

Deacon, A. and Patrick, R. (2011) A new welfare settlement? The coalition government and welfare to work, in Bochel, H. (ed.) *The Conservative Party and Social Policy*, Bristol: Policy Press

Deacon, D. (2004) Politicians, privacy and media intrusion in Britain, *Parliamentary Affairs*, 57 (1) 9-23

De Keseredy, W. (2011) *Contemporary Critical Criminology*, London: Routledge

Department of the Taoiseach (1997) *Bloody Sunday and the Report of the Widgery Tribunal*, http://www.taoiseach.gov.ie/attached_files/Pdf%20files/BloodySunday.pdf

Dishman, C. (2005) The leaderless nexus: when crime and terror converge, *Studies in Conflict & Terrorism*, 28 (4) 237-52

Ditton, J. and Duffy, J. (1983) Bias in Newspaper Reporting of Crime News, *British Journal of Criminology*, 23 (2) 159-65

Dodge, T. (2006) Iraq: The Contradictions of Exogenous State-Building in Historical Perspective, *Third World Quarterly*, 27 (1) 187-200

Doig, A. (2011) *State Crime*, Cullompton: Willan

Dorling, D. (2014) *Inequality and the 1%*, London: Verso

Doward, J. (2009) Colombia's endangered species at the mercy of jungle drug cartels, *The Observer*, Sunday, 25 October 2009, www.guardian.co.uk/environment/2009/oct/25/colombia-endangered-species-cocaine

Dudai, R. (2012) Informers and the transition in Northern Ireland, *British Journal of Criminology*, 52 (1) 32-54

Durkheim, E. (1964) *The Division of Labour in Society*, NY: Free Press

Eastwood, N., Shiner, M. and Bear, D. (2014) *The Numbers in Black and White: Racial Disparities in Policing and Prosecution of Drug Offences in England and Wales*, London: Release, www.release.org.uk/sites/default/files/pdf/publications/Release%20-%20Race%20Disparity%20Report%20final%20version.pdf

Edwards, A. (2011) *The Northern Ireland Troubles: Operation Banner 1969-2007*, London: Osprey

Edwards, R. (2014) US Fired Depleted Uranium at Civilian Areas in 2003, Iraq War Report Finds, *The Guardian*, 19 June 2014

Elias, N. (2000) *The Civilizing Process* (revised edn), Oxford: Blackwell

Etzioni, A. (1995) *The Spirit of Community: Rights, Responsibilities and the Communitarian Agenda*, London: Fontana Press

Etzioni, A. (1997) *The new golden rule: Community and morality in a democratic society*, London: Profile Books Ltd

Etzioni, A. (1998) A Matter of Balance, Rights and Responsibilities, in Etzioni, A. (ed.) *The Essential Communitarian Reader*, Oxford: Rowman & Butterfield Publishers Inc.

European Commission (2001) Joint Report from Commission Services and Europol - Towards a European Strategy to Prevent Organised Crime, Commission Staff Working Paper, SEC (2001) 433 (Brussels, 13 March)

Farrall, S. and Hay, C. (2010) Not so tough on crime? Why weren't the Thatcher Governments More Radical in Reforming the Criminal Justice System?, *British Journal of Criminology*, 50 (4) 550-69

Farrell, G. (2013) Five tests for a theory of the crime drop, Crime Science, 2 (1) 1-8, www.crimesciencejournal.com/content/2/1/5

Feeley, M. and Simon, J. (2003) The new penology, in McLaughlin, E., Muncie, J. and Hughes, G. (eds) *Criminological Perspectives: Essential Readings*, London: Sage

Feitlowitz, M. (1998) *A Lexicon of Terror: Argentina and the Legacies of Torture, Revised Version*, Oxford: Oxford University Press

Felbab-Brown, V. (2010) *Shooting Up: Counter-Insurgency and the War on Drugs*, NY: Brookings Institution Press

Felbab-Brown, V. (2011) War and drugs in Afghanistan, *World Politics Review*, 25 October 2011

Fleetwood, J. (2011) Five kilos: Penalties and practice in the international Cocaine Trade, *British Journal of Criminology*, 51 (2) 375-93

Fortson, R. (2005) *Misuse of Drugs: Offences, Confiscation and Money Laundering* (5th edn), London: Sweet and Maxwell.

Foucault, M. (1977) *Discipline and Punish*, NY: Random House

Friedman, M. (1962) *Capitalism and Freedom*, Chicago: University of Chicago Press

Friedrichs, D.O. (1996) *Trusted Criminals: White-Collar Criminals in Contemporary Society*, Belmont: Wadsworth

Friedrichs, D.O. (1998) Introduction, in Friedrichs, D.O. (ed.) *State Crime, Vol. 1: Defining, Delineating and Explaining State Crime*, Aldershot: Ashgate

Friedrichs, D.O. (2000) State crime or governmental crime: making sense of the conceptual confusion, in Ross, J.I. (ed.) *Controlling State Crime*, New Brunswick: Transaction Publishers

Friedrichs, D.O. (2003) 'State crime or governmental crime: making sense of the conceptual confusion', in Ross, J.I. (ed.) *Controlling state crime*, New Brunswick: Transaction Publishers

Friesendorf, C. (2007) *US Foreign Policy and the War on Drugs: Displacing the Cocaine and Heroin Industries*, London: Routledge

Frontalini, D. and Caiati, M. (1984) *El Mitto de la "Guerra Sucia"*, Buenos Aires: Centro de Estudios Legales y Sociales

Furedi, F. (2002) *Culture of Fear: Risk Taking and the Morality of Low Expectation*, London: Continuum

Gamble, A. (1988) *The Free Economy and the Strong State*, London: Palgrave Macmillan

Gamble, A. (2002) Political memoirs, *The British Journal of Politics and International Relations*, 4 (1) 141-51

Garland, D. (1994) Of crimes and criminals: the development of criminology in Britain, in Maguire, M., Morgan, R. and Reiner, R. (eds) *The Oxford Handbook of Criminology*, Oxford: Oxford University Press

Garland, D. (1996) The limits of sovereign states: strategies of crime control in contemporary society, *British Journal of Criminology*, 36 (4) 445-71

Garland, D. (2000) The culture of high crime societies: some preconditions of recent law and order policies, *British Journal of Criminology*, 40 (3) 347-75

Garland, D. (2001) *The Culture of Control, Crime and Social Order in Contemporary Society*, Oxford: Oxford University Press

George, V. and Wilding, P. (1994) *Welfare and Ideology*, Hemel Hempstead: Harvester Wheatsheaf

Glyn, A. (1985) Economy and the UK miners' strike, *Social Scientist*, 23-31

Glyn, A. (1992) Economic costs of coal pit closure programme in UK, *Economic and Political Weekly*, 27 (49/50) 2638-641

Gomery, D. (1986) Vertical integration, horizontal regulation: The Growth of Rupert Murdoch's US Media Empire, *Screen* (3-4) 78-86

Goodman, G. (1985) *The Miners' Strike*, London: Pluto Press Kindle Edition

Gordon, D. (2003) Iraq, War and Morality, *Economic and Political Weekly*, 38 (12/13) 1117-20

Grabosky, P. and Stohl, M. (2010) *Crime and Terrorism*, London: Sage

Graham, P. and Luke, A. (2005) The Language of Neofeudal Corporatism and the War on Iraq, *Journal of Language and Politics*, 4 (1) 11-39

Green, P. and Ward, T. (2004) *State Crime: Government's Violence and Corruption*, London: Pluto Press Kindle Edition

Greenslade, R. (2003) Their master's voice, London: *The Guardian*, 17 February 2003, www.theguardian.com/media/2003/feb/17/mondaymediasection.iraq

Guest, I. (1990) *Behind the Disappearances: Argentina's Dirty War Against Human Rights and the United Nations*, Pennsylvania University of Pennsylvania Press

Gupta, D.K. (2008) *Understanding Terrorism and Political Violence: The Life Cycle of Birth, Growth, Transformation and Demise*, Abingdon: Routledge

Habermas, J. (1971) *Toward a Rational Society*, London: Heinemann Education

Habermas, J. (1976) *Legitimation Crisis*, London: Heinemann Education

Habermas, J. (1979) *Communication and the Evolution of Society*, London: Heinemann

Habermas, J. (1987) *The Theory of Communicative Action*, Cambridge: Polity Press

Habermas, J. (1990) *Moral Consciousness and Communicative Action*, Cambridge: Polity Press

Habermas, J (1996) *Between Facts and Norms: Contributions to a Discourse Theory of Law and Democracy*, Cambridge: Polity Press

Hall, J.A. and Ilkenberry, G.J. (1989) *The State*, Milton Keynes: Open University Press

Hall, S. (1984) The State in question, in McLennan, G., Held, D. and Hall, S. (eds) *The Idea of the Modern State*, Milton Keynes: Open University Press

Hallin, D.C. and Mancini, P. (2004) *Comparing Media Systems: Three Models of Media and Politics*, Cambridge: Cambridge University Press

Halper, S. and Clark, J. (2004) *America Alone: The Neo-Conservatives and the Global Order*, NY: Cambridge University Press

Hari, J. (2015) *Chasing the Scream: The First and Last Days of the War on Drugs*, London: Bloomsbury Press

Harnden, T. (1999) *'Bandit Country': The IRA and South Armagh*, London: Hodder and Stoughton

Harvey, D. (2003) *The New Imperialism*, Oxford: Oxford University Press

Hayek, F. (1944) *The Road to Serfdom*, Chicago: University of Chicago Press

Hayek, F. (1988) *The Fatal Conceit: The Errors of Socialism: The Collected Works of Friedrich August Hayek*, in Bartley III, W.W. (ed.), London: Routledge

Held, D. (1989) *Political Theory and the Modern State*, Cambridge: Polity Press

Held, D. (1995) *Democracy and the Global Order*, Cambridge: Polity Press

Herman, E.S. and Chomsky, N. (1988) *Manufacturing Consent: The Political Economy of the Mass-Media*, NY: Pantheon Books

Hesmondhalgh, D. (2006) Bourdieu, the media and cultural production, *Media, Culture & Society*, 28 (2), 211-31

Hewitt, C. (1981) Catholic Grievances, Catholic Nationalism and Violence in Northern Ireland during the Civil Rights Period: A Reconsideration, *British Journal of Sociology*, 32 (3) 362-80

Kovalcheck, K.A. (1987) Catholic grievances in Northern Ireland: appraisal and judgement, *British Journal of Sociology*, 38 (1) 77-87

Kovessy, P. (2014) Qatar Supports Syria Aerial Bombing, but urges Non-military Solution, *Doha News*, 25 September 2014

Lawther, C. (2010) Securing the past: policing and the contest over truth in Northern Ireland, *British Journal of Criminology*, 50 (4) 455-73

Leigh, D. and Evans, R. (2005) Files show the extent of Murdoch lobbying, *The Guardian*, 3 January 2005, www.theguardian.com/politics/2005/jan/03/uk.freedomofinformation

Levi, M. (1987) *Regulating Fraud: White Collar Crime and the Criminal Process*, London: Tavistock

Levi, M. (2007) Organized Crime and terrorism, in Maguire, M., Morgan, R. and Reiner, R. (eds) *The Oxford Handbook of Criminology* (4th edn), Oxford: Oxford University Press

Lin, S. (2007) US Lying about Halabja: Justifying the Invasion of Iraq, *Economic and Political Weekly*, 42 (36) 3625-32

Lister, R. (2010) *Understanding Theories and Concepts in Social Policy*, Bristol: Policy Press

Lowe, V. (2003) The Iraq Crisis: What Now?, *The International and Comparative Law Quarterly*, 52 (4) 859-71

Lund, B. (2002) *Understanding State Welfare: Social Justice or Social Exclusion?*, London: Sage

MacGregor, I. with Tyler, R. (1986) *The Enemies Within: The Story of the Miners' Strike, 1984-5*, London: Collins

Maguire, M. (2007) Crime data and statistics, in Maguire, M., Morgan, R. and Reiner, R. (eds) *The Oxford Handbook of Criminology* (4th edn), Oxford: Oxford University Press

Mair, M. and Jones, P. (2015) Politics, government and corruption: the case of the Private Finance Initiative, in Whyte, D. (ed.) *How Corrupt is Britain?*, London: Pluto Press Kindle Edition

Makarenko, T. (2004) 'The crime-terror continuum': Tracing the interplay between transnational organised crime and terrorism, *Global Crime*, 6 (1) 129-45

Mannheim, H. (1965) *A Comparative Criminology: A Text Book Vol. 2*, London: Routledge and Kegan Paul

Mansfield, M. (2014) Orgreave was a massive injustice. And so is 30 years without a proper inquiry, *The Guardian*, 18 June 2014, www.theguardian.com/commentisfree/2014/jun/18/orgreave-injustice-miners-ipcc-investigation-start-now

Marchak, P. with Marchak, W. (1999) *God's Assassins: State Terrorism in Argentina in the 1970s*, London: McGill-Queen's University Press

Marsh, I. and Melville, G. (2009) *Crime, Justice and the Media*, Abingdon: Routledge

Matthews, R. and Kauzlarich, D. (2007) State crime and state harms: a tale of two definitional frameworks, *Crime, Law & Social Change*, 48 (1–2) 43-55

McAuley, J.W. (2003) *An Introduction to Politics, State and Society*, London: Sage

McCabe, S. and Wellington P. with Alderson, J., Gostin, L. and Mason, C. (1988) *The Police, Public Order and Civil Liberties: Legacies of the Miners' Strike*, London: Routledge

McCoy, A. (1991[1972]) *The Politics of Heroin: CIA Complicity and the Global Drugs Trade*, NY: Lawrence Hill

McEvoy, K. (2001) *Paramilitary Imprisonment in Northern Ireland: Resistance, Management and Release*, Oxford: Clarendon Press

McKnight, D. and Hobbs, M. (2011) 'You're all a bunch of pinkos': Rupert Murdoch and the Politics of Harper Collins, *Media, Culture and Society*, 33 (6) 835-50

McWilliams, J.C. (1991) Through the past darkly: The Politics and Policies of America's Drug War, *Journal of Policy History* 3 (4) 356-92

Medani, K. (2004) State Building in Reverse: The Neo-Liberal "Reconstruction" of Iraq, *Middle East Report*, 232, 28-35

Metcalf, M., Jenkinson, M. and Harvey, M. (2014) *Images of the Past: The Miners' Strike*, Barnsley: Pen and Sword

Michalowski, R. (2010) In search of "state" and "crime" in State Crime Studies, in Chambliss, W., Michalowski, R. and Kramer, R.C. (eds) *State Crime in a Global Age*, Cullompton: Willan

Miliband, R. (1969) *The State in Capitalist Society*, London: Weidenfeld & Nicholson

Miller, D. (2015) Neoliberalism, politics and institutional corruption: against the 'institutional malaise hypothesis', in Whyte, D. (ed.) *How Corrupt is Britain*, London: Pluto Press Kindle Edition

Mills, C.W. (1956) *The Power Elite*, NY: Oxford University Press

Mills, C.W. (1959) *The Sociological Imagination* (5th edn), London: Oxford University Press

Mills, J.H. (2003) *Cannabis Britannica: Empire, Trade and Prohibition*, Oxford: Oxford University Press

Milne, S. (2004) *The Enemy Within: The Secret War Against the Miners*, London: Verso

Milner Jr, M. (2015) *Elites: A General Model*, Cambridge: Polity Press

Mirrlees-Black, C. and Ross, A. (1995) *Crime Against Retail and Manufacturing Premises: Findings from the 1994 Commercial Victimisation Survey*, London Home Office (Research Study no. 146)

Mishra, R. (1984) *The Welfare State in Crisis*, Brighton: Wheatsheaf

Mishra, R. (1990) *The Welfare State in Capitalist Society*, London: Harvester Wheatsheaf

Moloney, E. (2002) *A Secret History of the IRA*, London: Penguin

Monaghan, M. (2011) *Evidence Versus Politics: Exploiting Research in UK Drug Policy Making?*, Bristol: Policy Press

Monaghan, M. (2014) Corporate crime, in Atkinson, R. (ed.) *Shades of Deviance*, London: Routledge

Mowlam, M. (2002) *Momentum: The Struggle for Peace, Politics and the People*, London: Hodder and Stoughton

Mulcahy, A. (2006) *Policing Northern Ireland: Conflict: Legitimacy and Reform*, Cullompton: Willan

Murray, C. (1984) *Losing Ground*, NY: Harper Collins

Murray, C. (1996a) The emerging British underclass, in Lister, R. (ed.) *Charles Murray and the Underclass: The Developing Debate*, London: IEA Health and Welfare Debate, 23-53

Murray, C. (1996b) Underclass: the crisis deepens in Lister, R. (ed.) *Charles Murray and the Underclass: The Developing Debate*, London: IEA Health and Welfare Debate, 99-135

Murray, C. (2001) *Underclass + 10: Charles Murray and the British Underclass 1990-2000*, London: CIVITAS

Mythen, G. (2014) *Understanding the Risk Society: Crime, Security and Justice*, Basingstoke: Palgrave

Mythen, G. and Walklate, S. (2008) Terrorism, risk and international security: the perils of asking 'what if?', *Security Dialogue*, 39 (2-3) 221-42

National Fraud Authority (2014) *Annual Report and Accounts 2013-14: Annual Report Presented to the House of Commons*, www.gov.uk/government/publications/national-fraud-authority-annual-report-2013-to-2014

Nelken, D. (1994) White collar crime, in Maguire, M., Morgan, R. and Reiner, R. (eds) *The Oxford Handbook of Criminology* (1st edn), Oxford: Oxford University Press

Nelken, D. (2007) White collar and corporate crime, in Maguire, M., Morgan, R. and Reiner, R. (eds) *The Oxford Handbook of Criminology* (4th edn), Oxford: Oxford University Press

Newburn, T. (2007) *Criminology*, Cullompton: Willan

Nocera, J. (2011) The tables are turned on Murdoch, *New York Times*, http://www.nytimes.com/2011/07/19/opinion/19nocera.html

OECD (2009) *Revolving Doors, Accountability and Transparency – Emerging Regulatory Concerns and Policy Solutions in the Financial Crisis: Report for the Expert Group on Conflict of Interest*, 5 May 2009, OECD Conference Centre Paris, www.oecd.org/officialdocuments/publicdisplaydocum entpdf/?cote=GOV/PGC/ETH(2009)2&doclanguage=En

O'Hearn, D. (1983) Catholic grievances, catholic nationalism: a comment, *British Journal of Sociology*, 34 (3) 438-45

O'Hearn, D. (1985) Again on the discrimination in the North of Ireland: a reply to the rejoinder, *British Journal of Sociology*, 36 (1) 94-101

O'Loan, N. (2007) *Statement by the Police Ombudsman for Northern Ireland on her Investigation into the Circumstances Surrounding the Death of Raymond McCord Junior and Related Matters*, www.policeombudsman. org/PONI/files/9a/9a366c60-1d8d-41b9-8684-12d33560e8f9.pdf

Oldham, J. and Massey, R. (2001) Chemical war: herbicides drug crops and collateral damage in Colombia, *After the Fact: A Publication of the Institute of Science and Interdisciplinary Studies*, Winter, http://isis. hampshire.edu/download/atfw01.pdf

Office for National Statistics (2015) *Improving crime statistics in England Wales*, available online at http://www.ons.gov.uk/ons/rel/crime-stats/crime-statistics/year-ending-june-2015/sty-fraud.html

Page, R. (2007) *Revisiting the Welfare State*, Maidenhead: Open University Press

Paoli, L., Spapens, T. and Fijnaut, C. (2010) Drug trafficking, in Brookman, F., Maguire, M., Pierpoint, H. and Bennett, T. (eds) *Handbook on Crime*, Cullompton: Willan

Parsons, T. (1967) *The Social System*, London: Routledge & Kegan Paul

Patman, R.G. (2006) Globalisation, the new US exceptionalism and the war on terror, *Third World Quarterly*, 27 (6) 963-86

Pearson, G. (2007) Drug markets and dealing: from street dealers to Mr Big, in Simpson, M., Shildrick, T. and MacDonald, R. (eds) *Drugs in Britain: Supply, Consumption and Control*, London: Palgrave

Pennink, E. (2015) Operation Elveden: Sun journalist found guilty of paying a police officer for stories, *The Independent*, May 22, 2015 available online at http://www.independent.co.uk/news/uk/crime/ operation-elveden-sun-journalist-found-guilty-of-paying-a-police-officer-for-stories-10271443.html

Pfeffer, J. and Salancik, G. (1978) *The External Control of Organisations: A Resource Dependence Perspective*, NY: Harper Row

Pierre, J. and Stoker, G. (2000) Towards multi-level governance, in Dunleavy, P., Gamble, A., Holliday, I. and Peele, G. (eds) *Developments in British Politics 6*, Basingstoke: Macmillan

Scott, A. (1995) *Ideology and the New Social Movements*, London: Routledge

Scott, A.R. (2013) Tales of the unexpected: reflections on the application of the Bribery Act to chequebook journalism, *Journal of Media Law*, 5 (2) 276-96

Scott, W.R. (1992) *Organizations: Rational, Natural and Open Systems*, Engelwood Cliffs, NJ: Prentice-Hall

Scraton, P. (2004) From deceit to disclosure: the politics of official inquiries in the United Kingdom, in Smyth, M. and Williamson, E. (eds) *Ethics, Power, Knowledge and Consent*, Cullompton: Willan

Sear, C. (2005) *Electoral franchise: who can vote?*, London: House of Commons Library

Seddon, T., Ralphs, R. and Williams, L. (2008) Risk, security and the 'criminalization' of British drug policy, *British Journal of Criminology*, 48 (4) 818-34

Shackleford, T. and Buss, D. (1996) Betrayal in mateships, friendships and coalitions, *Personality and Social Psychology Bulletin*, 22, 1151-64

Shapiro, H. (1999) *Waiting for the Man: The Story of Drugs and Popular Music*, London: Helter Skelter

Shawcross, W. (1993) *Rupert Murdoch: Ringmaster of the Information Circus*, London: Pan

Sikka, P. (2015) Accounting for corruption in the 'big four' accountancy firms, in Whyte, D. (ed.) *How Corrupt is Britain*, London: Pluto Press Kindle Edition

Silke, A. (2000a) In defence of the realm: financing Loyalist terrorism in Northern Ireland – part one: extortion and blackmail, *Studies in Conflict and Terrorism*, 21 (4) 331-61

Silke, A. (2000b) Drink, drugs and rock 'n' roll: financing Loyalist terrorism in Northern Ireland – part two, *Studies in Conflict and Terrorism*, 23 (2) 107-27

Singer, M. (1971) The vitality of mythical numbers, *Public Interest*, 23, Spring

Slapper, G. and Tombs, S. (1999) *Corporate Crime*, Harlow: Longman

Slapper, G. and Tombs, S. (2002) Corporate crime, official statistics and the mass media, in Jewkes, Y. and Letherby, G. (eds) *Criminology: A Reader*, London: Sage

Smith, P. and Harvey, P. (2010) *Business Crime Scoping Exercise*, London: Ipsos Mori, https://www.gov.uk/government/uploads/system/uploads/attachment_data/file/116598/horr33-report.pdf

Smith, S.J. (1984) Crime in the News, *British Journal of Criminology*, 24 (3) 289-95

Smithwick, P. (2013) *Report of the Tribunal of Inquiry into Suggestions that Members of An Garda Síochána or Other Employees of the State Colluded in the Fatal Shootings of RUC Chief Superintendent Harry Breen and RUC Superintendent Robert Buchanan on the 20th March 1989*, http://opac.oireachtas.ie/AWData/Library3/smithwickFinal03122013_171046.pdf

SOCA (2006/7) Serious Organised Crime Agency (2006/7) *The United Kingdom threat assessment of serious organised crime*, London: SOCA, available online at http://news.bbc.co.uk/1/shared/bsp/hi/pdfs/31_07_06_socareport.pdf

Standing, G. (2011) *The Precariat: the dangerous class*, London: Bloomsbury

Stevens, A. (2011) *Drugs, Crime and Public Health: The Political Economy of Drug Policy*, London: Routledge

Stevens, J. (2003) *Stevens Inquiry: Overview and Recommendations*, London: Metropolitan Police Service

Stoker, G. (1998) Governance as theory: five propositions, *International Social Science Journal*, 50 (155) 17-28

Strange, S. (1996) *The Retreat of the State*, Cambridge: Cambridge University Press

Summers, A. (2012) The secret life of J Edgar Hoover, London: *The Guardian*, Sunday 1 January 2012, www.theguardian.com/film/2012/jan/01/j-edgar-hoover-secret-fbi

Sundar, N. (2004) Toward an Anthropology of Culpability, *American Ethnologist*, 31 (2) 145-63

Sutherland, E. (1937) *The Professional Thief*, Chicago: University of Chicago Press

Sutherland, E. (1949) *White Collar Crime*, NY: Holt, Reinhart and Winston

Tappan, P.W. (1947) Who is the criminal?, *American Sociological Review*, 12 (1) 96-102

Taylor, A. (2005) *The NUM and British Politics*, vol. 2, Aldershot: Ashgate

Taylor, P. (1998) *Provos, The IRA and Sinn Fein*, London: Bloomsbury

Taylor, P. (2000) *Loyalists*, London: Bloomsbury

Taylor, P. (2002) *Brits: The War Against the IRA*, London: Bloomsbury

Tharoor, I. (2013) Viewpoint: why was the biggest protest in world history ignored?, *World Time*, http://world.time.com/2013/02/15/viewpoint-why-was-the-biggest-protest-in-world-history-ignored/

Thatcher, M. (1993) *The Downing Street Years*, London: Harper Collins

Tilly, C. (1985) State formation as organised crime, in Evans, P., Rueschemeyer, D. and Skocpol, T. (eds) Bringing the State Back In, Cambridge: Cambridge University Press

Tombs, S. (2015) Corporate theft and impunity in financial services, in Whyte, D. (ed.) *How Corrupt is Britain?*, London: Pluto Press Kindle Edition

Tombs, S. and Whyte, D. (2001) Media Reporting of Crime: Defining Corporate Crime Out of Existence?, *Criminal Justice Matters*, 43 (1) 22-23

Tombs, S. and Whyte, D. (2002) Unmasking Crimes of the Powerful, *Critical Criminology*, 11 (3) 217-36

Tombs, S. and Whyte, D. (2007) *Safety Crimes*, Cullompton: Willan

Tombs, S. and Whyte, D. (2010) A deadly consensus: worker safety and regulatory degradation under New Labour, *British Journal of Criminology*, 50 (1) 46-65

Tonry, M. (1995) *Malign Neglect: Race, Crime and Punishment in America*, NY: Oxford University Press

Tonry, M. (2010) The costly consequences of populist posturing: ASBOs, victims, 'rebalancing' and diminution of in support for civil liberties, *Punishment and Society*, 12 (4) 387-413

Towers, B. (1985) Posing larger questions: the British miners' strike of 1984-85, *Industrial Relations Journal*, 16 (2) 8-25

Toynbee, P. (2012) Cameron's big cut 'idea' will only backfire on the Tories, *The Guardian*, Monday 25 June, www.guardian.co.uk/commentisfree/2012/jun/25/cameron-benefit-cut-will-backfire

Turvill, W. (2013) 'Incredible' £19.5m so far spent on operations Weeting, Elveden and Tuleta, 8 April, 2013 available online at http://www.pressgazette.co.uk/incredible-%C2%A3195m-so-far-spent-operations-weeting-elveden-and-tuleta

United Nations (2000) *Convention against Transnational Organised Crime*, Palermo, Sicily: United Nations

United Nations Office on Drugs and Crime (UNODC) (2005) *World Drug Report*, Vienna: United Nations Office on Drugs and Crime

UNODC (2007) *World Drug Report*, Vienna: United Nations Office on Drugs and Crime

UNODC (2014) *World Drug Report*, Vienna: United Nations Office on Drugs and Crime

United States Government (1987) *Report of the Congressional Committees Investigating the Iran Contra Affair With Supplemental Minority, and Additional Views*, Washington, DC: United States Congressional Serial Set, available at https://archive.org/details/reportofcongress87unit

Vanson, Y. (Director, 1985) *The Battle for Orgreave*, YouTube https://www.youtube.com/watch?v=dn7DZSagDI4

von Lampe, K. (2008) Organised crime in Europe: conceptions and realities, *Policing*, 2 (1) 7-17

Wacquant, L. (2001) The penalisation of poverty and the rise of neo-liberalism' *European Journal on Criminal Policy and Research*, 9 (4) 401-12

Wacquant, L. (2009) *Punishing the Poor: The Neoliberal Government of Social Insecurity*, London: Duke University Press

Walgrave, S. and Verhulst, J. (2009) Government Stance and Internal Diversity of Protest: A Comparative Study of Protest against the War in Iraq in Eight Countries, *Social Forces*, 87 (3) 1355-87

Watson, T. and Hickman, M. (2012) *Dial M for Murdoch: News Corporation and the Corruption of Britain*, London: Allen Lane

Weber, M. (1948) Politics as Vocation, in Gerth, H.H. and Mills, C.W. (eds) *From Max Weber: Essays in sociology*, London: Routledge & Kegan Paul

Weigratz, J. (2015) The New Normal: Moral Economies in the 'Age of Fraud', in Whyte, D. (ed.) *How Corrupt is Britain*, London: Pluto Press Kindle Edition

Whyte, D. (2014) Regimes of permission and State-Corporate Crime, *State Crime Journal*, 3 (2) 237-46

Whyte, D. (ed.) (2015a) *How Corrupt is Britain?*, London: Pluto Press Kindle Edition

Whyte, D. (2015b) Introduction: a very British corruption, in Whyte, D. (ed.) *How Corrupt is Britain*, London: Pluto Press Kindle Edition

Whyte, J. (1983) How much discrimination was there under the Unionist regime, 1921-1968?, in Gallagher, T. and O'Connell, J. (eds) *Contemporary Irish Studies*, Manchester: Manchester University Press

Widgery, J. (1972) *Report of the Tribunal appointed to inquire into the events on Sunday, 30 January 1972, which led to loss of life in connection with the procession in Londonderry on that day by The Rt. Hon. Lord Widgery, O.B.E., T.D.*, London: HMSO

Wiggershaus, R. (1986) *The Frankfurt School: Its History, Theories and Political Significance*, Cambridge: Polity Press

Wilks-Heeg, S. (2015) Revolving-Door Politics and Corruption, in Whyte, D. (ed.) *How Corrupt is Britain*, London: Pluto Press Kindle Edition

Wilks-Heeg, S., Blick, A. and Crone, S. (2012) *How Democratic is the UK? The 2012 Audit*, Liverpool: Democratic Audit, www.democraticaudit.com/wp-content/uploads/2013/07/auditing-the-uk-democracy-the-framework.pdf

Williams, K. (2010) State crime, in Brookman, F., Maguire, M., Pierpoint, H. and Bennett, T. (eds) *Handbook on Crime*, Cullompton: Willan

Wilson, J.Q. and Herrnstein R. (1985) *Crime and Human Nature*, NY: Simon and Schuster

Windle, J. (2013) How the East influenced drug prohibition, *The International History Review*, 35 (5) 1185-99

Windle, J. and Farrell, G. (2012) Popping the balloon effect: assessing drug law enforcement in terms of displacement, diffusion and the containment hypothesis, *Substance Use and Misuse*, 47 (8/9) 868-76

Winterton, J. (1993) The 1984-85 miners' strike and technological change, *The British Journal for the History of Science*, 26 (1) 5-14

Winterton, J. and Winterton, R. (1989) *Coal, Crisis and Conflict: The 1984-85 Miners' Strike in Yorkshire*, Manchester: Manchester University Press

Woodiwiss, M. (2003) *Organized Crime and American Power*, Toronto: University of Toronto Press

Woodiwiss, M. (2005) *Gangster Capitalism: The United States and the Global Rise of Organized Crime*, London: Constable and Robinson

Woodiwiss, M. and Hobbs, D. (2009) Organized crime and the Atlantic alliance: moral panics and the rhetoric of organized crime policing in America and Britain, *British Journal of Criminology*, 49 (1) 106-28

Wright, T.C. (2007) *State Terrorism in Latin America: Chile, Argentina and International Human Rights*, MD: Roman & Littlefield

Wright, A. (2011) *Organised crime*, London: Routledge

Young, J. (1974) *The New Criminology*, NY: Harper Row

Young, J. (1999) *The Exclusive Society: Social Exclusion, Crime and Difference in Late Modernity*, London: Sage

Young, J. (2003) The exclusive society: social exclusion, crime and difference in late modernity, in McLaughlin, E., Muncie, J. and Hughes, G. (eds) *Criminological Perspectives: Essential Readings*, London: Sage

Zaitch, D. (2001) *Trafficking Cocaine: Colombian Drug Entrepreneurs in the Netherlands*, The Hague: Kluwer International

Zedner, L. (2007) Pre-crime and post-criminology?, *Theoretical Criminology*, 11 (2) 261-81

Žižek, S. (2008) *Violence: Six Sideways Reflections*, London: Profile

Index